THE CONFEDERATE CULTURE AND ITS WEAKNESSES

HOW CULTURE CONTRIBUTED TO THE CONFEDERATE DEFEAT

JON P. ALSTON

THE CONFEDERATE CULTURE AND ITS WEAKNESSES
HOW CULTURE CONTRIBUTED TO THE CONFEDERATE DEFEAT

iUniverse books may be ordered through booksellers or by contacting:

iUniverse
1663 Liberty Drive
Bloomington, IN 47403
www.iuniverse.com
844-349-9409

ISBN: 978-1-6632-5151-0 (sc)
ISBN: 978-1-6632-5150-3 (e)

Library of Congress Control Number: 2023904557

Print information available on the last page.

iUniverse rev. date: 05/25/2023

CONTENTS

Acknowledgments vii
Introduction ix

Chapter 1 The Culture of the Confederacy 1
Chapter 2 The Slave-Based Culture of the Confederacy 33
Chapter 3 The Alpha Complex 62
Chapter 4 The Cavalier Mindset 85
Chapter 5 Honor 127
Chapter 6 Five Blows to Southern Honor 158
Chapter 7 Individualism 184
Chapter 8 Localism 225
Chapter 9 The Culture of Violence and Aggression 260

Afterword 291
Bibliography 293
Index 313

ACKNOWLEDGMENTS

I am indebted to many persons. My early career benefited from the friendship and advice of Arnie Vedlitz, Jane Sell, Charlie Peek, and George Lowe. I only wished I had made them my models for teaching and scholarship. These friends amazed me with their willingness to work hard and still find time to help students and colleagues. My good friend Thanh le showed me to persevere. My coauthor, Takei Isao, remains a respected author and friend. Other good friends, including Bruce Dickson, Wayne McCormack, Richard Startzman, and Dwight Bronnum, were always supportive. My wife endured years of Civil War talk and remains a valuable critic and editor. Both she and our daughter, Margaret, remain the loves of my life.

INTRODUCTION

To understand today, you have to search yesterday.
—Pearl S. Buck

A significant portion of Civil War literature focuses on the question of whether the South might have avoided the Civil War or ultimately won it. While the Union won the Civil War by winning battles and destroying Confederate military and civilian resources, Northern victory was facilitated by the dysfunctional cultural aspects of the Confederacy. Southern culture(s) resulted in white Southerners making military, financial, economic, ideological, personal, and political mistakes that led to war and eventual defeat. The culture of the Confederacy was indeed a culture of defeat.

By 1861, the South and North had developed fundamental cultural differences, in large part derived from the South's near-total economic and social reliance on the institution of slavery. The South's relative lack of industrial capacity, for example, was due to the Southern elite's preference for investments in agricultural land and in enslaved persons rather than in factories and commerce. More prestige was given in the Southern culture to plantation owners than to factory owners and merchants.

The result was a more static agricultural society led by slaveholders who grew cotton and other crops by enslaved labor. Nor did the South contain a large enough number of those whose business organizational skills could be transferred to a military context. The South also lacked an adequate number of skilled craftsmen to maintain the machinery to support millions of soldiers. Corps and army commanders could not requisition enough shoes for their command throughout the war or adequately feed their rank-and-file soldiers.

James M. McPherson (Boritt 1992, 18–19) divided historians', generals', apologists', and autobiographers' Civil War analyses, explanations, and personal defenses of their positions into two types. The first explanation, defined as *external*, deals with the Union's ability to win battles based on such elements as better railroad networks, larger armies, better financial policies, better generals after 1862, and better military material and logistics (see also Donald 1996). This orientation focuses on how the North won the Civil War.

The second general category of explanation proposed by McPherson is defined as *internal*. This perspective focuses on Confederate weaknesses, such as weak leadership, inadequate food distribution, interpersonal and ideological conflicts, lack of dedication to the Confederacy, and political decentralization (see also Beringer et al. 1986). This position focuses on how the Confederacy lost the war.

The cultural approach of the present book reflects an *internal* orientation that maintains that the culture of Southern society contained characteristics unfitted to successfully fight a prolonged semimodern war. This perspective is similar to that of David Hackett Fischer (1989) who urged historians to adopt a more comprehensive cultural approach in their studies.

Note on Monetary Values

I follow Paul Starobin's (Starobin 2017) computation of multiplying 1860 prices by twenty-eight to compare with current prices. A bale of cotton weighing 450–500 pounds was worth $49–55 in 1860 or $1,272–$1,540 in today's currency. The original amount may seem small by modern standards, but in 1860 a loaf of bread cost one penny. An unskilled worker earned up to thirty-five dollars a month.

A Confederate private was first paid $11 a month or $308 in current dollars. A Confederate general's monthly basic pay was $301 ($8,418 in current dollars). Robert E. Lee's monthly pay in 1864 was $604, which included bonuses for fuel, extra rations, horse feed, being commander of an army, being in the field, and years in the Old Army with a current value of $16,912 (Nofi 1995, 382). Ulysses S. Grant, during 1862, received $220 per month plus a $52 bonus for servants. Confederate General Braxton Bragg earned $401 per month because he was both commander of the Department of Tennessee and the commander of the Army of Tennessee. All officers received bonuses, including extra food rations, a clothing allowance, and hay for their horses.

Presidents Abraham Lincoln's and Jefferson Davis's annual base salaries were $25,000, or $700,000 in current dollars, but both received extra bonuses.

Officers on both sides were paid the same basic amount, but Union officers did not suffer as large a decrease in the value of their pay through inflation during the war. Confederate officers received special bonuses for years served in the antebellum "Old" US Army. At first, Confederate cavalry troopers brought their own horses and were paid rental fees of fifty cents a day in addition to bonuses based on their horses' war-related wounds or death.

CHAPTER 1

THE CULTURE OF THE CONFEDERACY

The past is never dead; in fact, it's not even past.
—William Faulkner

Definition of Culture

The term *culture* as defined by social scientists is socially transmitted information or models on how to behave from one generation to the next (Cronk 1999, 12). The fact that culture is absorbed by the young, taught to new members of groups, and defended against other models of behavior contributes to the stability of societies.

Members learn how to conform and are also taught to want to conform, though the latter is seldom completely achieved. This process of socialization results in cultural patterns that are maintained without much change for generations because they become ritualized. Language, standards of morality, religious beliefs, and political ideologies are stable cultural items from one generation to the next.

Culture changes slowly and is a process in which one or more parts change more quickly than others. External events, including war, force cultures to change to one degree or another. Generational changes are also influenced by both internal and external events.

A position in society is called a *status* and includes a person's gender, age, and occupation. Sociologists do not use this term to denote social rank. Instead, they use the phrases "high status" or "low status" to denote the relative prestige and hierarchical positions in a society. Of major importance is the fact an individual always holds many statuses at the same time and throughout a lifetime (or even beyond death, such as saints, ancestors, founding fathers, or heroic figures). Some statuses will be more relevant than others for an individual, and some may conflict with one another.

Statuses are attached to specific types of behavior, called *status roles*, which describe how norms or rituals are to be performed. These roles offer social stability and standards of behavior. While not all members consistently conform to cultural expectations, norms are standards of behavior, and roles are the specific ways norms are to be followed. Norms tell us *to be* honest, but roles tell us *how* to be honest.

Norms and Cultural Standards

Norms define specific standards of behavior, such as those found in a legal system, a military code, or the Ten Commandments. Norms also include less precise descriptions of a variety of protocols and social rituals. Weddings tend to follow general normative protocols that witnesses would recognize in spite of wide role variations in the specifics of music, dress, location, et cetera.

Norms can also change or be redefined, especially in times of war. A major normative conflict during the Civil War was how the military should treat civilians (Foote 2021). Antebellum military officers during the Civil War were trained to avoid harming civilians when they posed no military threats. However, the definition of "no military threats" was ambiguous. The mayor and two members of the city council of Atlanta, Georgia, complained that Major General William T. Sherman's order for civilians to evacuate the city was unnecessarily cruel and against the accepted normative rules of war. The city leaders noted (Sherman 2021, 390):

> We … thought it might be that you had not considered this subject in all of its awful consequences, and that on more reflection you, we hope, would not make this people an exception to all mankind, for we know of no such instance ever having occurred—surely never in the United States—and what has this helpless people done, that they should be driven from their homes, to wander strangers and outcasts, and exiles, and to subsist on charity?

The authors of this letter noted that the norms of war did not include the evacuation of civilians as well as inflicting unnecessary cruelty. Sherman was not adhering to the normative standards of how civilians were to be treated.

Sherman answered that he was changing the roles (rituals) of war by punishing citizens of the Confederacy for the coming and continuation of the war (Sherman 2021, 392):

> You cannot qualify war in harsher terms than I will. War is cruelty, and you cannot refine it; and those who brought war into our country deserve all the curses and maledictions a people can pour out … You might as well appeal against the thunder-storm as against these terrible hardships of war. They are inevitable.

Sherman noted that Atlanta and its citizens provided arms and munitions to Confederate armies and were as involved in the war as were the members of its armies.

A cultural view of the dysfunctional nature of Southern values is presented by Steven Hardesty. He supports the argument that Southern values dealing with how to conduct the Civil War led to Confederate defeat, though the South also had many advantages in its culture that Confederates did not utilize (Hardesty 2016, 207–8):

> The Confederate war went wrong because major elements of southern culture at the mid-point of the nineteenth century would not let it go right … *The South lost its war because its military and political leaders could not transcend the limits of the space-based culture that helped bring on the Civil War.* (emphasis added)

The above quote supports this book's thesis that the culture of the Confederacy—no matter how brave and dedicated its citizens—contained elements that made it more likely it would fail to achieve independence. We accept Grady McWhiney's thesis (McWhiney 2002, 1):

> Southerners are not like other Americans, and they never have been … the population of the United States is more culturally divided along regional rather than racial lines.

We show how viewing the Civil War from a cultural perspective of Southern culture explains many of the errors that influenced the Confederate society's collapse and caused its citizens to lose the Civil War.

Situational Factors and Cultural Change

Changes in culturally derived behavior are often the result of changing conditions defined as *situational factors.* A drought will force residents to move from a farm to a distant city and result in changes in occupations and lifestyles. Civil War casualties and inflation forced many women to change their former statuses as housewives and mothers and work outside the home in the war industries and government agencies. The war also forced the enlistment of so many male teachers that women were allowed for the first time to teach higher grade levels. Other women for the first time became involved in organizations supporting the troops. Many women gained the status of "refugees." This change of status position turned women's worlds upside down from being housewives and hostesses to being dependent upon others.

Situational Factors and Status Change

Situational changes result in changes in a person's statuses and their related roles. A number of Confederate soldiers were *conditional Confederates.* They would support the Confederacy until their loyalty to themselves or their families became more demanding when situations changed.

Conditional Confederates included those who served in the military for personal rather than for patriotic reasons. To many, the opportunity to take part in a war promised excitement and the possibility of gaining military honors or the opportunity to leave home. For these men, the respect given to enlistees by the community (including young ladies) and the excitement of "seeing the elephant" (experiencing battle) were major reasons for enlistment during the first year of the war. Many of these excitement seekers deserted when the excitement faded and when they realized the dangerous and arduous nature of war (Glatthaar 2008, 410).

An enlistment to avoid a loss of honor rather than for patriotic reasons is illustrated by the experience of Arkansan Henry Stanley. Stanley refused to enlist at the same time as other young men in his community. One day, he received a package from an anonymous source containing "a chemise and petticoat," indicating that he was a coward and unmanly and therefore should dress as a woman rather than as a man. Henry enlisted soon after (Neal and Kremm 1997, 87). Stanley had violated the role demands of his male status to be brave and aggressive and willing to enlist and be respected as a Confederate soldier.

The Confederate Congress passed a conscription bill during April 1862. Part of the bill included the promise that those who reenlisted could continue to reelect their company and regimental officers. Most of those officers who lost their rank by not being reelected resigned their commissions (Glatthaar 2008, 86). In essence, these socially privileged men (most were from the upper and middle classes) did not want to be part of an army unless they could maintain their officer-related ranks. Doing otherwise would result in a loss of prestige as well as the comforts and privileges of officer rank. These previous officers were in the habit of giving orders rather than obeying them.

Rebel officers enjoyed a number of perks not available to men in the ranks, in addition to higher pay, better food, and riding horses instead of marching on foot along with their command. Officers were allowed one or more body servants (i.e., enslaved men). Many officers and some enlistees brought with them enslaved men to perform duties such as cleaning, washing, and cooking. Conditional officers were those who did not want to lose the perks attached to their officer ranks. When they lost their ranks, these officers resigned from the military rather than serve in the noncommissioned ranks.

Conditional Confederates also included those who used the war for personal reasons, such as selling cotton and sugar to Union merchants or ignoring the needs of the Confederacy by continuing to grow cotton instead of food crops for the Confederate military and civilians.

Conditional Confederates were represented in the manufacture of arms and other supplies for the Confederacy. When the war began, a number of entrepreneurs prepared to receive military contracts by establishing corporations to support the war effort. These men may have done so partly for patriotic reasons, but they primarily expected to gain profits for their efforts (DeCredico 1990, 31–32). Most of these newly formed members of the military-industrial complex failed after the war ended.

Politicians and community leaders raised military units in part to enhance their own political careers rather than from feelings of patriotism. These officers were needed during the war since they were able to convince large members of the community, county, or state to enlist. Many of these "political" generals proved to be inept military leaders and worse, largely because they were often more concerned with their own image over the concerns of the Confederacy.

Galvanized Yankees

Conditional Confederates included *galvanized Yankees* or *whitewashed Rebels*. These were Confederate soldiers who had been captured, swore an allegiance to the United States, and joined the Union military rather than remaining in a prison camp. An estimated six thousand Confederate prisoners joined Union military units to fight in the West against Indians, man forts as Outpost Guardians, escort supply wagons, and guard and reconnect telegraph lines (Brown 2012, 3–9). The 1,600 or more Union prisoners who enlisted in the

Confederate armies were called *galvanized Confederates* (National Park Service 1992, 1–4; Brown 2012, 210).

Many galvanized Yankees originated from the northern counties of Alabama. Their populations were primarily Unionist and anti-secessionist. These hill country residents owned few enslaved persons and were hostile toward the slaveholding Southern elite. Refusing to volunteer for military service, these anti-secessionists were treated harshly as traitors by Confederate partisans.

Enough southern Appalachian Alabamians volunteered to form the First Alabama Cavalry. These Southern Unionists became infamous for their hostility toward Confederates as they sought revenge for the damage they had experienced from loyal Confederate neighbors and guerrillas. An Alabama newspaper's editorial denounced them as traitors (Butler 2021, 42):

> No punishment is too great for such wretches and if justice has her own they will specdily grace the gallows.

William Tecumseh Sherman appointed the unit as his personal guard.

The most famous galvanized Yankee was Henry Morton Stanley who became a celebrity when he located the explorer David Livingston at Lake Tanganyika, Africa. Stanley was born in Wales and emigrated to America. He was befriended and later adopted by a New Orleans merchant. Although not loyal to the Confederacy and considering himself an Englishman rather than an American, Stanley became caught up in the war enthusiasm and enlisted on July 1, 1861.

Stanley was captured during the Battle of Shiloh. Sent to an overcrowded Union prison pen with horrible conditions, Stanley pledged allegiance to the Union and was recruited into the US artillery in 1862 (Brown 2012, 54). He soon became ill with dysentery, caught while in prison, and was mustered out as no longer fit for service. He later enlisted in the US Navy, but he became bored and soon deserted. Stanley was a member of both the Union and Rebel infantries and the US Navy!

North-South Cultural Differences

We disagree with Kenneth Milton Stampp (1980, 256–59) and others that the South never developed a distinct culture. Northerners, Southerners, and foreign visitors reported that the two regions developed very different cultures during the colonial period through the 1860s and beyond. It is clear that Southerners themselves believed their region was culturally different from the North.

In 1785, Thomas Jefferson noted the two regions had developed distinctive cultural differences during the eighteenth century based on, he thought, both climate and the presence of slavery in the South.

Jefferson described these cultural differences in 1785 in a letter to the Marquis de Chastellux. Jefferson states that a self-aware Southern culture was established during the colonial era (Cobb 2005, 10):

> In the North, they are cool, sober, laborious, independent, jealous of their own liberties, and just to those of others, interested, chicaning, superstitious and hypocritical in their religion. In the South they are fiery, voluptuary, indolent, unsteady, jealous of their own liberties, but tramping on those of others, generous, candid, without attachment or pretensions to any religion but that of the heart.

The image of Southerners as described by Virginian elite and owner of enslaved persons, Thomas Jefferson, is similar to that of a Bostonian made seventy years later (and by South Carolinian J. W. Cash one hundred years later). Henry Adams, great-grandson and grandson of US presidents, was a member of the Harvard University class of 1858. Adams was a critical person who spared only relatives. Adams modestly declared in his autobiography that he knew very little and was ignorant. However, he also insisted everyone he encountered knew even less than he did while few were able to teach him anything of value.

Adams was critical of his Southern collegiate classmates. He was especially critical of William Henry "Rooney" Fitzhugh Lee, the son of Robert E. Lee. Adams found Rooney Lee to be representative of a rigid and traditional culture (Adams also considered himself to be more comfortable in the eighteenth century within a Bostonian context). Henry Adams found Southern Harvard students were representatives of a simplistic American subculture (Adams 1999, 57–58):

> Lee, known through life as "Roony," was a Virginian of the eighteenth century, much as Henry Adams was a Bostonian of the same age. Roony Lee had changed little from the type of his grandfather, Light Horse Harry. Tall, largely built, handsome, genial, with liberal Virginian openness towards all he liked, he had also the Virginian habit of command and took leadership as his natural habit … The habit of command was not enough, and the Virginian had little else. He was simple beyond analysis; so simple that even the simple New England student could not realize him. No one knew enough to know how ignorant he was;

> how childlike; how helpless before the relative complexity of a school.

Adams refers to the Southern elite's anti-intellectualism and local and insular mindset: Southerners rejected information threatening their traditional values and lifestyle. This ethnocentrism leads to ignorance of outsiders' values and interests (Hardesty 2016, 9). Though many were well educated in the humanities, few Southerners could be called cosmopolitan.

This anti-intellectualism was noted by Robert E. Lee when he found that many officers in the Army of Northern Virginia believed practical knowledge of military tactics and logistics was less important than inbred Southern courage and a warlike temperament. In this context, the West Point culture conflicted with the general Southern culture. The former stressed discipline and training. The latter valued individualism and tactics of attack. Lee was a superb tactician whose plans were complex and demanded exact timing of troop maneuvers. His plans would fail, and did, when subordinates did not follow Lee's orders.

A similar but slightly more positive view of the Southern culture among the wealthy was reported on May 1, 1861, by antislavery British journalist William Howard Russell (Russell, n.d., letter 6):

> These [i.e., Southern planters] gentlemen are well-bred, courteous, and hospitable ... They travel and read, love field sports, racing, shooting, hunting, and fishing, are bold horsemen, and good shots. But, after all, their State is a modern Sparta—an aristocracy resting on a helotry, and with nothing else to rest upon.

Henry Adams continued his negative evaluations of Southern culture after his graduation from Harvard University. A fervent abolitionist, Adams's characterization of the Confederate elite was negative (Adams 1999, 100):

> The Southern secessionists [i.e., the Southern elite] were certainly unbalanced in mind—fit for medical treatment, like other victims of hallucination—haunted by suspicion, by *idees fixes*, by violent morbid excitement; but this was not all. They were stupendously ignorant of the world. As a class, the cotton-planters were mentally one-sided, ill-balanced, and provincial [i.e., local] to a degree rarely known. They were a close society on whom the new fountains of power had poured a stream of wealth and slaves that acted like oil on flame. They showed a young student [i.e., Adams] his first object-lesson of the way in which excess power worked when held by inadequate hands.

Mark Twain (1835–1910) remains one of the most insightful critics of antebellum Southern culture. Twain (a.k.a. Samuel Langhorne Clements) is unique in that he blames a British author for the Southern dysfunctional culture. Twain believed that antebellum culture was based on the novels of Sir Walter Scott who invented a "sham" medieval culture accepted as their own by Southerners (Twain 1883, 348):

> [T]he duel, the inflated speech, and the jejune romanticism of an absurd past that is dead, and out of charity ought to be buried. But for the Sir Walter disease, the character of the Southerner ... would be wholly modern, in place of modern and medieval mixed, and the South would be fully a

> generation further advanced than it is ... It was Sir Walter that [sic] made every gentleman in the South or a Colonel, or a General or a Judge, before the war ... For it was he that [sic] created rank and caste down there, and also reverence for rank and caste, and pride and pleasure in them ... Sir Walter had so large a hand in making southern character, as it existed before the war, that he is in great measure responsible for the war.

A twentieth-century critic of Southern culture, W. J. Cash (Cash 1991, 428–29) presents similar views made by Thomas Jefferson and Henry Adams of the Southern subculture:

> Proud, brave, honorable by its lights, courteous, personally generous, loyal, swift to act, often too swift, but signally effective, sometimes terrible, in its action—such was the South at its best ... Violence, intolerance aversion and suspicion toward new ideas, an incapacity for analysis, an inclination to act from feeling rather than from thought, an exaggerated individualism and a too narrow concept of social responsibility, attachment to fictions and false values, above and a tendency to justify cruelty and injustice in the name of those values, sentimentality and a lack of realism—these have been its [i.e., Southern culture] characteristic vices in the past.

Many in the South believed they were members of a different, more regal race than Northerners. Typical among those who held such views, agricultural scientist Edmund Ruffin, was an extreme Southern nationalist and secessionist. Ruffin could not imagine living in a country dominated by Yankees and their culture after the Confederacy lost the war. He entered the last entry in his diary on June 18, 1865 (two months after the surrender of Robert E. Lee), including the statement below, and then committed suicide (Ethier 2008):

> And now with my latest writing and utterance, and with what will be near my latest breath, I here repeat and would willingly proclaim my unmitigated hatred to Yankee rule—to all political, social and business connections with Yankees, and the perfidious, malignant and vile Yankee race.

William R. J. Pegram, an artillery commander in the Army of Northern Virginia, believed Northerners were members of an immoral, money-oriented, and cowardly subspecies. Pegram wrote to his brother (Carmichael 1995, 35):

> I pray God that it [i.e., his brother's release from a Yankee prison] may be soon, that you may again be enabled to take up arms in defense of our beloved country, against this ungodly, fanatical, depraved Yankee race ... Oh! I do pray that we may be established as an independent people, a people known and recognized as God's Peculiar People.

White Southerners by the late 1850s believed they were members of a different race from Yankees. The differences between the two cultures were seen as genetic and no longer the result of only economic, political, and cultural factors. The absolute differences between South and North was expressed in historical terms (Gildersleeve 1915, 11):

> The hate of Celt to Saxon, and the contempt of Saxon for Celt, simply paled and grew expressionless

> when compared with the contempt and hate felt by the Southron towards the Yankee anterior to our Civil War and while it was in progress. No Houyhnms ever looked on Yahoo with greater aversion; better, far better, death than further contamination through political association.

Southern Belief of Their Superiority

Southerners believed they were maintaining traditional values and behavior when seceding. It was the North, Southerners held, which had strayed from the traditional American culture and the original interpretation of the Constitution. There was no contradiction in the mind of Southerners with supporting secession and maintaining a patriotic reverence for George Washington and other founding fathers. It was the Northerners who were unwilling to maintain the work of the founding fathers. The result was that Confederates thought themselves as patriotically superior because they were following the Constitution while Northerners were no longer doing so.

A supporter of the typical belief in Southern cultural superiority, Congressman Lamar declared that Northerners were rejecting the Constitution in their antislavery behavior—as well as a common sense of victimization. Northern behavior *forced* the slave states to consider secession. Most of Southerners' discussions with Northerners contained implied threats, bullying statements, and braggadocios of their presumed power and superiority. The quote below is a typical example of Southern boasts, demands, and threats. Lamar threatened secession if his (and Southerners') views were not accepted (*Harper's Weekly*, volume 5; February 2, 1861, 66):

> Never have I desired a dissolution of this Union; but should the Republican party obtain the control of

> the Government, I shall be for disunion ... For the future, I would demand that all the compromises and guarantees of the Constitution shall be rigidly enforced, and I would stake the Union upon the issue ... I shall have no fears for the South. With a territory larger than all of Europe; with our cotton now swelling up in value to more than two hundred million dollars; with our rice, and sugar, and tobacco; with a people united in feeling and sentiment, she has within her own borders all the elements of a splendid republic ... the South, with the strong arms and brave hearts of her gallant sons, will build up her own eternal destiny.

Culture and War

T. Harry Williams (Donald 1996, 57) suggests that while the personality and talents of generals are important factors in the winning (and losing) of battles, how a war is fought is partly the result of cultural factors. Historian Frank E. Vandiver (1984, 3 and 21) also stressed the importance of culture on the thinking and behavior of leaders during a war. On a more general level, strategist Karl von Clausewitz (Clausewitz 1997, 41, 109, and 311) wrote in 1830 that nations fought in ways that resembled the cultures and social structures of their societies.

Historian David J. Eicher wrote (Eicher 2006, 10), "The Confederacy was born sick," meaning that the Confederate culture contained dysfunctional elements making a successful independence less likely. Leon Trotsky claimed, "The army is a copy of society and suffers from all its diseases, usually at a higher temperature." Trotsky also wrote that the cultures of societies also contain strengths that are augmented during a war. These views support the proposition that a nation's likelihood of winning a war is more difficult if its culture is dysfunctional.

A cultural difference dealing with how war should be fought is related to the cultural definition of the purpose of individual battles. The traditional view among American military professionals was that a war could be ended by one decisive battle in the Napoleonic manner. That was why both most Northerners and Confederates expected that the Civil War would be short: only one or a few battles were needed to decide the conflict.

This traditional view of "battles as decisive events" encouraged West Pointers, as trained military professionals, to view battles as discrete events. Lee expected the battle of Antietam or Gettysburg would lead to the end of the war. If an army was not destroyed after a battle was fought, the traditional pattern was for each opponent to return to its respective camp to recuperate, rearm, and replace casualties (Hess 2008, 206). The Japanese attack of Pearl Harbor (battle as a decisive event) on December 7, 1941, was expected to cripple the US Navy and American will so that the United States would no longer be a threat to Japan and, hopefully, sue for peace.

The contrary view is that battles should not be considered as discrete events but rather as "battles as processes" in which battles form a series toward a goal. The sequential capture of Japanese-occupied islands in the Pacific by US forces was a process leading to the defeat of Japan.

West Point cadets were taught that battles were discrete events. Though graduates of West Point, Grant and Sherman visualized campaigns as processes in which long-term goals (capturing Vicksburg, defeating Lee, and capturing Atlanta) are achieved. Sherman aggressively fought Joseph E. Johnston for one hundred miles before they reached the outskirts of Atlanta. Sherman's goal was to reach Atlanta. He did not expect to fight a major battle to destroy the Army of Tennessee. Sherman was also unwilling to chance a major battle with Johnston, but he was willing to force him to retreat. Sherman's goal was not to destroy the Army of Tennessee but to reach and capture Atlanta.

Meanwhile, Grant kept attacking Lee as the Army of Northern Virginia experienced a large number of casualties until Lee retreated to be penned up in the fortifications of Petersburg.

Grant decided that, with the North's larger population, the Confederacy could not afford to lose a greater proportion of casualties even when the Confederates achieved often symbolic military victories. Instead of attempting to destroy a Rebel army in one coup, Grant learned to be satisfied by achieving a gradual attrition of enemy manpower. This was a lesson Lee would never learn.

Subcultures

The concept of culture includes smaller groups than a society defined as *subcultures*. The South itself was a subculture of the society of the United States. The North included a number of regional subcultures, such as the German and Quaker settlements, the New England states, and the more frontier Northwest. The South similarly contained its own distinct subcultures, including the Appalachian areas, the Texas and Arkansas frontiers, the antislavery Piedmont area of North Carolina, the western Virginian area of Thomas "Stonewall" Jackson, and the more aristocratic Tidewater region of Virginia of Robert Edward Lee.

Subcultures include more than cultural divisions based on geography. Social classes can also become subcultures. It is obvious that poor farmers form a different subculture than members of the upper class. Often, a social class develops from being a cultural category to a self-aware distinct subculture. During the antebellum era, Southern planters—those who owned twenty or more enslaved persons—defined themselves as a subculture whose members were destined to control the South's power centers. They expected to be leaders of the Southern institutions and the Southern populations.

The separation of West Virginia from the state of Virginia was influenced by the existence of very different social and political subcultures in the state. These differences were formalized by the statehood of West Virginia into the Union in June 1863. An indication of the political fracture in Virginia was the antislavery and pro-Union attitudes found in the western counties. A majority (64 percent) of voters from these counties voted against secession. It's been estimated that an equal number of West Virginians fought for the Union and the Confederacy, indicating strong subcultural divisions even in the newly formed state of West Virginia.

An Appalachian Subculture

Many families living in the Appalachian areas were against or indifferent to the Confederacy. The members of the Union's First Alabama Cavalry Regiment were recruited from ten upper counties in Appalachia, Alabama (Butler 2021, 41). There were few slaves and large plantations in the area because cotton couldn't be grown at that altitude or in that soil. The majority of the population had been against secession and believed the down-country cotton-planting elites promoted secession for their own advantages and interests.

Friends and relatives were often loyal to the Union or the Confederacy together. Families were pitted against families (often also neighbors) based on their position on either the need to secede or remain in the Union. Male friends and relatives also enlisted together.

In one instance, four brothers and three brothers-in-law from one extended family joined the Union First Alabama (Butler 2021, 42). Most (2,066) of the 2,678 Alabamans serving in Union armies enlisted in the First Alabama Cavalry Regiment, and 345 troopers

(17 percent) from the First Alabama Cavalry Regiment and five officers died in action.

The First Alabama proved to be reliable and effective. William T. Sherman selected the regiment as part of his March to the Sea and appointed a number as his personal escort. The regiment was also given the honored position at the head of one of the wings during the march. The company gained the reputation of being extremely destructive and avid property thieves even when compared to Sherman's northern "bummers" as they foraged for food. They also destroyed what they didn't need and what wasn't useful to the Confederacy. The commander and unit were officially sanctioned for their extremely destructive behavior. The Union First Alabama was an example of the different subcultures in the Confederacy.

The First Alabama Company became part of history for another reason. Marching at the head of one of Sherman's columns, members of a squad of the company as well as their horses, were killed or wounded when they set off buried land mines (called "torpedoes"), an event using land mines for the first time. A group of Confederate prisoners was then ordered to locate and disarm any remaining mines. One prisoner was sent to the rebel line to report that any more mines would be disabled by prisoners (Davis 1980, 94). Sherman was outraged by the use of land mines and called the practice an "assassination." He believed the practice was beyond the (cultural) acceptable rituals of war behavior. The Rebels had violated a norm of war.

Two Confederate Armies and Rates of Venereal Disease

A situation illustrating both situational and subcultural differences in behavior is found in the contrasts of the relative rates of venereal disease reported in the two most important Confederate armies. The behavior of members of the Army of Northern Virginia and the Army of Tennessee in this instance indicates a minor existence of subcultures.

An indication of the importance of situational factors in behavior is the fact that venereal disease rates decreased during the last part of the war for both armies because of increased discipline, a series of religious revivals, and troops that were busier campaigning than staying in more isolated camps. Troops enjoying longer campaign pauses or those stationed near cities, such as Richmond, Virginia, or Dalton, Georgia, had more opportunities to consort with "debased" women (Daniel 1991, 98–99).

The soldiers of the Army of Tennessee consistently experienced a higher rate of venereal disease than did Robert E. Lee's Army of Northern Virginia even though its longest-serving commander, Braxton Bragg, was a strict disciplinarian. During the first five months of 1863, the rate of new cases among John Pemberton's Army of Vicksburg (though stationed in a large city) reported a venereal disease rate of one man for each 330. The corresponding rate for the Army of Tennessee was one case per 183 (Daniel 1991, 99) or roughly twice that of the Army of Vicksburg. Union treatment of venereal disease was one case per 273 men, or 182,000 total cases during the war.

Even when campaigning, the members of the Army of Tennessee continued to exhibit both a relative lack of discipline and a corresponding higher rate of venereal disease than the Army of Northern Virginia. The western and frontier backgrounds of the troops of the Army of Tennessee were influential cultural reasons for their unique rate of sexual disease. Lower morale due to interpersonal conflicts among officers and battle losses might also have been causes. The west contained a number of well-known bordellos. Memphis, Tennessee, and New Orleans, Louisiana, were famous throughout the South for their large number of brothels.

Sexual activities would be expected of young men (average age twenty-four) away from home for the first time and free of parental and community supervision. The common practice of placing "pure and unsoiled" women on symbolic pedestals had its darker side, allowing sexual exploitation of white women from the lower classes as well as Black American women. As the war continued, increasing numbers of white Confederate women were forced to become prostitutes because they had become widows or refugees and were too poor to feed their families.

A member of the Union's Sanitary Commission reported during 1864 on the rampant sexual behavior of the soldiers in an Army of the Potomac military camp in Virginia. The rank-and-file men had built near the camp a small village of sixty houses to shelter prostitutes. The busiest time for the prostitutes was on payday, when long lines of troopers paid three dollars each for a "turn." Prostitutes were estimated to be earning as much as three hundred dollars on these days (Commanger 2000, 359).

The women were also available to read (for pay) the men's letters from home and to write replies. Their literacy indicates a number of these prostitutes had experienced a cultural change of downward social mobility because of the war. A woman who was literate during the 1860s was likely to have been a member of the middle or upper class before the war.

The Southern Culture of Violence

Many Southern subcultural elements have remained relatively constant, though the South also experienced extensive cultural changes over two hundred years. An example of the stability of specific cultural items is the "culture of violence" found in Southern society. Historically, Southern colonies and later states exhibited higher levels of acceptance of and rates of personal violence—including homicide—than similar rates found in Northern states (Nisbett and Cohen 1996). This tendency toward violence is maintained when contemporary southerners emigrate north. States outside the South containing larger percentages of southern-born residents exhibit higher-than-average rates of violent acts.

Violence was common in the South, especially when men drank alcohol. Ted Ownby describes two men drinking in a saloon (Ownby 1990, 53):

> One word brought on others, and Will was being heartily cursed by Don when he seized a china dish and beer mug and hurled them at Don, causing the blood to flow. Will ran out doors and Don after him. Don fired his pistol twice, hitting Will twice, who fell dead.

The tendency to use violence to solve personal and social problems has been a consistent cultural Southern trait (Fischer 1989, 892):

> Violence simply *is* done in Texas and the southern highlands, and always has been done in this culture—since before the Civil War and slavery and even the frontier—just as it had been done in the borderlands of North Britain before emigration [*i.e.*, from Great Britain].

Horace V. Redfield reported on intranational and international comparisons of homicide rates during the postwar period (Redfield 1880, 15):

> It is in the late slave States that the number of homicides in proportion to population is far in excess of the rate ever known in the Northern States, or in England for the past four hundred years … the number of homicides in the Southern States is proportionally greater than in any country

> on earth the population of which is rated as civilized.

Redfield is careful to eliminate possible spurious social conditions influencing rates of homicide. Redfield compares homicide rates in Northern and Southern counties in terms of proportion of foreigners, presence or absence of large urban centers, and state-level statistics, including the summary that, "murder and manslaughter is about *fifteen hundred percent* [italics in the original], more frequent in Louisiana than in Maine" (Redfield 1880, 95). Redfield recommends that the number of homicides in the South would decrease if the common practice of carrying concealed weapons were criminalized (Redfield 1880, 123). He believed that fighting would continue since violence was ingrained in Southern culture, but that brawling and roughhousing would be less lethal than when lethal weapons are used.

Redfield finds that homicide is seldom punished or seen as criminal behavior in the South as contrasted to the North. These acts are part of Southern culture of violence that are often defined as justifiable. A senior prelate of the Episcopal Church was quoted in 1879 (Redfield 1880, 42):

> It is a fact that my adopted state [i.e., Kentucky] has a fearful history of unpunished murder [by whites]. Every portion of her soil and every year of her history have been tarnished by these acts of mistaken chivalry but real brutality. For many years before the war, I was forced to become familiar with events which in this section [i.e., the state of New York] would have raised a cry of righteous indignation, while there they were put down as justifiable homicide.

Ideal and Real Cultures

Ideal culture defines *how* a person should act. Whether or not an individual chooses (or knows how) to follow cultural expectations is another matter. Elements of culture include behavioral standards, though people may pay lip service to these ideal norms. Ideal cultural standards in this context provides a worldview, mindset, or *Weltanschauung*. Real culture describes how people actually behave.

A central cultural identification of white men in both the North and South during the 1800s was being considered a gentleman. The Northern ideal models of behavior derived from middle- and upper-class residents in Northern cities such as Boston, Philadelphia, and New York, while standards of gentlemanly characteristics in the South were derived primarily from the elite plantation owners of Virginia and South Carolina. The concept of "gentleman" determined a man's (the equivalent for women was being a lady or ladylike) place in the middle and upper levels of society. Abraham Lincoln was criticized while president by both Northerners and Southerners for not having the speech, posture, dress, or manners of a gentleman. A Confederate children's song illustrates the significance of being a gentleman (Ayers 2017, 164):

> Jeff Davis rides a white horse,
> Abe Lincoln rides a mule,
> Jeff Davis is a gentleman,
> Abe Lincoln is a fool.

Enslaved persons rode mules and were seldom allowed to ride horses. Lincoln is triply insulted because he rides a mule similar to an enslaved man and is a fool. The message is that, as a mule rider and a fool, Lincoln could not be a respected gentleman and is therefore unworthy of his office. By contrast, Davis rides a white horse because he is a gentleman, emphasizing his knightlike and "noble" character. Robert E. Lee also rode a white horse before the war, was always impeccably dressed, and behaved as a gentleman. The implicit meaning of the above poem is that a nongentleman like Lincoln could easily be defeated by a nation led by white elite Southern gentlemen riding horses similar to medieval knights.

Daniel R. Hundley (1860, 72) described the ideal Southern gentleman:

> Remarkably easy and natural, never haughty in appearance, or loud of speech—even when angry rarely raising his voice above the ordinary tone of gentlemanly conversation. … He is ever well-educated, and draws his language from the "well of pure English undefiled."

Hundley recognized that few Southerners conformed to this ideal because the term referred only to those with aristocratic family backgrounds, higher education, "faultless" physiques, and active owners of plantations or younger and single members of plantation-owning families.

Hundley admits there are those who pretended to be gentlemen. He includes as a false gentleman anyone who is a "cotton snob" (i.e., someone who owns a cotton-growing plantation and is wealthy but doesn't behave as a gentleman) or a "Southern bully." Some of these "false" gentlemen did not know how to adequately behave as true gentlemen, and others refused to do so. Others were self-involved "coxcombs." Hundley devotes almost the same amount of his book describing these false gentlemen as he does describing those worthy of being called true gentlemen. The former was a major problem since they contradicted the ideal Southern self-image as partly inherited (Hundley 1860, 43):

> A certain class of underbred snobs, whose money enables them for a time to pretend to the character and standing of gentlemen, but whose natural

> inborn coarseness and vulgarity invariably lead them to disgrace the honorable title they assume to wear.

Wade Hampton and Nathan Forrest

Major General Nathan Bedford Forrest, a skilled cavalry leader and former slave dealer from Tennessee, was culturally different from cavalry Lieutenant General Wade Hampton from South Carolina. Both were among the owners of the largest numbers of enslaved persons and among the wealthiest members of the Southern population, but they also originated from very different subcultures.

Forrest was considered to be an uncouth, socially unpolished and no gentleman. His first occupation and the basis of his wealth was the low-prestige occupation of dealing in slaves. Hampton was respected as the model of a Southern cavalier: well-spoken, dignified, and gracious. Hampton and his family were on the same respected and elite social level as the families of Robert E. Lee (Virginia) and Pierre G. T. Beauregard (Louisiana).

At nineteen, Forrest shot a neighbor's ox that had repeatedly entered the Forrest cornfield. When the owner came with his own musket and threatened to shoot him, Forrest aimed his own weapon at the neighbor and threatened to do the same. The neighbor gave in and left (Wyeth 1989, 15–16). Forrest continued this aggressive behavior throughout his life. By contrast, Hampton was known for his generosity, public service, and courtesy toward all.

Forrest was self-educated and semiliterate ("I never see a pen but what I think of a snake") while Hampton grew up in a house that was full of books, was first tutored at home, studied at a military-style boarding school, and graduated from South Carolina College. He received a classical education expected of cultured gentlemen of the era. Hampton, as would be expected of a student with his high social status, joined a literary and debating club while attending college (Cisco 2006, 23). His diploma was signed by his father, a member of the college's board. Wade Hampton III later also became a member of the board. His and his father's board memberships are indications of the high social rank enjoyed by the Hampton family.

Hampton was a respected leader of the Southern aristocracy. Forrest was born in the more frontier state of Tennessee and raised in semipoverty. Forrest enlisted as a private, and, although he was rapidly promoted, his command was never enlarged commensurate to his responsibilities and successes. Hampton raised and financially supported and led the "Hampton Legion."

In spite of their social class differences, Hampton and Forrest were culturally similar in a number of ways. Both were fervent patriots of the Confederacy. They each acquired reputations of bravely leading their troops into battle and personally killing a number of the enemy.

Both remained anti-Black American after the war ended and used violence to limit the political and social equality of non-whites. Hampton was supported by the Red Shirts during his successful 1871 gubernatorial candidacy. The "Red Shirts" was a paramilitary terrorist organization whose members killed and intimidated their political opponents (i.e., Republicans and Black Americans wishing to vote). Forrest was the first leader of the Ku Klux Klan.

Contrasting Subcultural Values in Boston and Charleston

The differences in cultural values between the South and the North are illustrated in a study contrasting Boston, Massachusetts, and Charleston, South Carolina, during 1828–1843 (Pease and Pease 1991). During the 1830s, Charleston's elite decided an additional railroad line was needed for the city's future economic development. Investors organized the South Carolina Canal and Railroad Company and chose Elias Horry as the second president of the company. Horry had been a merchant and had studied law. He had also been active in politics, including serving twelve years in the South Carolina House of Representatives and as mayor of Charleston. Horry was representative of successful politicians in antebellum America by developing extensive social contacts needed in a culture largely based on familial and local ties.

In spite of his merchant background, socially upwardly mobile Horry owned eleven plantations, making him member of the local elite (Pease and Pease 1991, 16). Ignored were Horry's large debts and complete lack of corporate managerial experience (the venture did not complete its goals). More important than possible construction and administrative skills were Horry's high-elite status and his extensive social networks among the elite members of Charlestown.

Horry's selection as railroad president is contrasted with a similar situation in Boston, Massachusetts. Boston's elite chose Patrick Tracy Jackson for a position similar to Horry's. Jackson was a leading industrialist in the development of Massachusetts's textile industry. His selection was based in large part on his business experience and acumen for his appointment to lead the commission to build a railroad. As would be expected, Jackson's other qualities were his social networks and his membership in the business elite class.

Northerners chose a manager with practical managerial experience and industrial-related skills as well as his social qualifications. By contrast, Southerners chose someone whose qualifications were political and elite membership.

In defense of the Southern character, there were railroads in the South as modern as any in the nation. The Charleston-Hamburg rail line in South Carolina began as a six-mile track in 1828. Typical of Southern railroads, the purpose of the Charleston-Hamburg line was to transport cotton to the Charleston seaport. Reorganized, the line was extended, and by 1833, the rail line was 136 miles long. Its equipment was modernized, making it the longest steam-powered railroad line in the United States for a time. By 1860, the future Union states enjoyed twenty-one thousand miles of railroad tracks, and the future Confederacy had nine thousand miles of track. Southern culture was not completely anti-technology, but it consistently lagged behind the Union.

The Cultural Diversity of the Southern Farming Population

Whites working the land formed the majority of the white Southern population and were subdivided into a number of subcultural groups that reflected regional, ethnic, and wealth differences. The South during the nineteenth century was primarily rural, and 82 percent of the 1860 white labor force worked in agriculture (North: 40 percent). The common stereotypes of Southerners were largely based on stereotypes of either the poorest ("crackers") or the wealthiest farmers (the owners of enslaved persons plantation planters as portrayed in the "Moonlight and Magnolia" myth).

General William T. Sherman divided the white population of Georgia into two types based on both wealth and political attitudes. Sherman ordered his command to differentiate "between the rich, who are usually hostile [to the Union], and the poor and industrious, usually neutral or friendly." The term "industrious" refers to those who did not own slaves and performed their own labor. These poorer nonslaveholders were to be, in theory, allowed to keep a portion of their livestock and commodities when soldiers foraged during Sherman's Savannah Campaign.

Those working/owning the South's farms can be ranked into eight cultural groups (adapted from Wagner, Gallagher, and Finkelman 2002, 674, and Hundley 1860):

> *Large-scale planters*: producing primarily monocrops based on enslaved labor for sale to Northern and foreign markets. They dominated the political,

social, and economic institutions of the South. Members of this group owned at least twenty enslaved persons.

Commercial farmers: those owning or leasing five slaves or less and often hiring temporary free laborers. They produced grain crops—primarily corn and wheat—as well as hay and livestock for personal consumption and for sale in neighboring towns and cities. These were the Jeffersonian "yeomen" idealized in the antebellum era.

Smaller-acreage farming families: often located in more isolated or frontier areas. These farmers, their families, and the category below were characterized as the "mudsills" of society by planter James Henry Hammond and the more fortunate were called "clodhoppers." The more prosperous of these farmers were derogatorily called "one-horse farmers." Some owned one or two enslaved persons and worked alongside them in the fields. Members of this group resisted secession, and many held weak loyalties to the Confederacy.

Landless farmers: hired for often a season or for specific tasks. Males from this rank and the previous rank formed the bulk of the Confederate and Union armies. Many leased lands from wealthy planters. Roughly 25 percent of the South's farmers in 1860 were tenants.

Migratory laborers: hired for specific tasks, such as harvesting crops, chopping wood, and clearing land. These laborers were often hired by planters to perform work that was too dangerous for slaves, such as draining swamps, building levees, or dredging rivers.

Women and children: important parts of the farming population. Members of low-acreage farming families were not allowed to be idle, and a man could not maintain a farm without a spouse and male children.

Enslaved Black Americans: Four million Black Americans were enslaved in 1861 and provided the labor for most of the nation's exports. An estimated 90 percent of the slaves were agricultural workers. Many members of this group resisted the Confederacy in a number of ways, including work slowdowns, becoming spies and guides for the Union military, and enlisting in the Union armies.

CHAPTER 2

THE SLAVE-BASED CULTURE OF THE CONFEDERACY

The sin of racial pride still represents the most basic challenge to the American conscience. We cannot dodge this challenge without renouncing our highest moral pretensions.
—Arthur M. Schlesinger

The increasing cultural divergence between the North and the South during the first half of the nineteenth century was multidimensional. It is difficult to determine which factor among many was the major cultural item causing the North-South split. David M. Potter argues that the institution of slavery in the Southern states was the root of the increasing cultural, economic, and ideological differences between the two American subcultures (Potter 1976, 41–42):

> Slavery presented an inescapable ethical question which precipitated a sharp conflict of values [i.e., cultural conflict]. It constituted a vast economic interest, and indeed the Emancipation Proclamation was the largest confiscation of property in American history … *Also, slavery was*

> *basic to the cultural divergence of North and South* [emphasis added]—because it was inextricably fused into the key elements of southern life—the staple crop and plantation system, the social and political ascendancy of the planter class, the authoritarian system of social control ... The southern commitment to the use of slave labor inhibited economic diversification and industrialization and strengthened the tyranny of King Cotton.

Southerners themselves recognized the central part slavery played for their well-being and separate subculture. The Southern "civilization" existed only because the existence of slavery. That is why their political and other institutions protected slavery so vehemently. Slavery was too important to be attacked and possibly weakened or destroyed.

In 1832, Thomas R. Dew published a very popular defense of slavery. Dew blamed Northerners for bringing Black Americans to the American soil and believed slave owners had the responsibility of maintaining slavery irrespective of whether or not slavery was wrong. Dew also assumed slavery was a benign system of labor (Faust 1981, 61):

> We cannot get rid of slavery without producing a greater injury to both masters and slaves, there is no rule of conscience or revealed law of God which *can* condemn us.

Ann Snyder was typical in defending slavery as the basis for a superior Southern civilization (Snyder 1893, 19):

> The natural and necessary product of a noble civilization is a noble and a princely manhood.

> Consequently the slave-holding States, by sheer force of a superior intellectuality, dominated the National Government and affected the character of all legislation by the impress of their masterly minds. The inevitable effect of this upon the North was to create and to foster that feeling of jealousy that naturally existed, to add fuel to the fires of slavery agitation, and to widen sectional lines.

Ann Snyder adds a novel reason in the above quote for the coming of the Civil War: Northerners wanted to destroy Southern culture because they were envious of Southern superiority.

James P. Holcombe was a leading secessionist and delegate at Virginia's Secession Convention. He stated (Thomas 2021, 98) that the institution of slavery was "indissolubly [*sic*] interwoven with the whole framework of [our] society." He then characterized the cultural differences between the North and South as being as wide as those between Great Britain and France because slavery disappeared in the Northern states as free labor became dominant while the system of enslaved labor in the Southern states prospered and achieved central social and cultural importance.

The number of slaves a family owned became an indication of high social status and prestige. Aside from the wealth and the leisure resulting from owning enslaved workers, slave owners became the social as well as the economic leaders of the South. The members of well-established eastern slave-owning families did not accept as equals the "new" enslaved Deep South owners if their high social standing had been less than three generations or more. On the local level, however, large size of plantations was an indication of prestige and social leadership.

The members of families owning the largest number of enslaved persons in Virginia and the Carolinas were considered the true aristocrats of Southern society, in large part because many of their families had been economic, social, and political leaders for at least eighty years. These families, including the Lees, claimed family members who had fought in the War for Independence, the War of 1812, and the Mexican War. They formed both a military and elite subculture and became role models for others.

The owners of the largest number of enslaved persons in the Deep South, though socially newcomers, were politically active and tended to be as radical—or more—and wealthier than their counterparts in the east. North Carolinian Mary Chesnut condescendingly dismissed the western elite as having (Woodard 1981, 69) "wealth—without civilization." Many of these Deep South newcomers were surprised when they arrived in Richmond, Virginia, and discovered they were not completely accepted by the local elites.

The centrality of slavery to the Confederates is indicated by the extensive legal elements protecting slavery in the Confederate Constitution. When the constitution for the Confederacy was being written, the delegates copied most of the original US Constitution but added stronger provisions to support the institution of slavery. They were also willing to openly use the word "slave." Below are listed some of the Confederate Constitution's items protecting slavery:

Article 1, Section 9.4 states:

> No bill of attainder, ex post facto law, or law denying or impairing *the right of property in negro slaves shall be passed* [emphasis added].

Article 4, Section 2.1 concludes:

> And the right of property [i.e., slaves] in said states shall not be thereby impaired.

Article 4, Section 3.3 says:

> In all such [future acquired] territory the institution of negro slavery … shall be recognized and protected … and the inhabitants of the several Confederate states and Territories shall have the right to take to such Territories any slaves lawfully held by them in any of the States or Territories of the Confederate states.

The Economics of Slavery

In today's dollars, a healthy enslaved male in his twenties cost up to $28,000 or more in 1861. The high cost of slaves explains in part why half the owners of enslaved persons owned five or fewer enslaved persons (Wagner et al. 2002, 80). However, the major avenue for social mobility of whites in the South remained owning more land and more enslaved laborers. In spite of cycles of bad weather, economic downturns, and high costs, the rising prices for cotton during most of the 1850s made the purchase of field slaves and cotton-producing land very good investments.

Robert Collins offered advice on the amount of work field-hands were expected to perform (Collins 1862, 156):

> Hours of work—In the winter time, and in the sickly season of the year, all hands should take breakfast before leaving their houses. This they can do and get to work by sunrise, and stop no more until twelve o'clock, then rest for one hour for dinner, then work until night. In the spring and Summer, they should go to work at light and stop at eight o'clock for breakfast, then work until

> twelve o'clock and stop for two hours for dinner, and work from two o'clock till night.

The above advice can be considered to be more ideal than factual. Enslaved workers resisted orders as much as they could though field hands had little liberty and were often closely supervised in the western states. Robert E. Lee's father-in law, Virginian George Washington Parke Curtis, did not personally manage his three plantations and 197 enslaved workers. The enslaved workers were loosely supervised with the result that his plantations were not very productive. Curtis left large debts when he died in 1857.

Owners of enslaved persons enjoyed the belief that the enslaved were both grateful to their owners and willing to work as expected. Many owners liked to think they had complete control though they seldom did so. A planter advised (Levine 1992, 30):

> That the slave should know that his master is to govern absolutely, that he is to obey implicitly. That he is never for a moment to exercise his will or judgement in opposition to a positive order.

Owners had complete legal rights to enforce their demands, but the enslaved managed to gain some independence as long as they never openly challenged or disobeyed their owners.

The division of labor in the South's enslaving-based culture was unconsciously noted by teenage diarist Kate Stone. A series of storms in Mississippi resulted in the levees protecting the local plantations in danger of leaking and collapsing. Kate recorded (Anderson 1995, 15):

> There are great fears of tremendous overflow. Men [i.e., white] are watching and the Negroes are working on the levees day and night.

Levees were often as high as fifteen feet and thirty feet thick at the base. Neighboring plantation owners and overseers would gather enslaved laborers to work on weakened levees since one failed levee could flood neighboring plantations and fields. As Kate Stone recorded, the whites watched while the enslaved persons worked. While cotton was considered "king," the real "kings" were the white owners of numerous enslaved persons.

Enslaved labor cost roughly thirty-five dollars a year to maintain and could be made to work harder and longer hours than free labor (Hummel 1996, 40). Enslaved labor could also be put to work on nonagricultural projects, such as building railroads, at a cost half the amount per mile than it did in the North employing free labor. With the use of enslaved labor, railroads in the South cost $15,000 per mile to build and between $30,000 and $35,000 in the North (Thomas 2021, 42).

Slavery included the ownership of an enslaved female person's offspring. Thomas Jefferson estimated that the births of his enslaved women augmented their value by 4–10 percent per year (Rosenthal 2018, 130). Jefferson's plantation included numerous mulattos.

Though slave breeding was seldom openly discussed, the practice was significant in planters' economic considerations. A healthy female was often valued equally to a young male field hand because she could both work in the cotton fields or elsewhere and periodically give birth.

Thomas Jefferson realized the cultural importance of slavery in the South. Jefferson recognized that slavery would be difficult if not impossible to eliminate in the South because of its economic importance. Emancipation would cripple the Southern states' economies and would also threaten the social status quo. While Northern abolitionists—including Abraham Lincoln—did not at first understand the centrality of slavery, Jefferson understood the issue when he remarked, "We have the wolf by the ears, and we can neither hold him, nor safely let him go. Justice is on one scale, and self-preservation in the other."

The "Cornerstone" Defense of Slavery

The South was a slave-based society, and the presence of slavery dominated its politics, economy, religion, intellectual efforts, and all institutions in general (Berlin 2003, 8–10). The presence of slavery was so important to Southerners that they were willing to secede from the Union and initiate a war because they believed that the complete control of "their" enslaved persons was threatened. Some believed that they would rather lose their independence than allow enslaved men to be given arms and their liberty if they fought for the Confederacy.

One of the clearest rationales for secession is illustrated by the March 21, 1861, "Cornerstone Speech" delivered by Alexander Stephens, vice president of the Confederacy and one of the most respected politicians of the South.

Stephens had earlier opposed secession, but he announced he would accept secession if his state, Georgia, joined the Confederacy. He proved to be exceptionally unfit in his position as vice president. He early quarreled with Jefferson Davis on a point of honor and spent most of the war at his plantation criticizing Davis and his administration. In addition to personal antagonisms, Stephens was a strict states' rights advocate, especially on the issues of the military draft, the centralization and control of resources, and the existence of tariffs. Davis was forced to centralize much of the Confederacy's economy and other resources in order to conduct the war, and to Stephens's dismay, these actions conflicted with the dogma of the states' rights (Hébert 2021, 62).

Stephens's "Cornerstone" speech is a clear political statement declaring that the major reason for secession was the perceived threat to the institution of slavery and to white supremacy (Commager 2000, 600–601):

> The new Constitution has put at rest forever the agitating questions relating to our peculiar

> institutions—African slavery as it exists among us—the proper status of the negro in our form of civilization. This *was the immediate cause of the late rupture and present revolution* … Its [the Confederate government] … foundations are laid, its cornerstone rests, upon the great truth that the negro is not equal to the white man; that slavery, subordination to the superior race, is his natural condition and moral condition … The substratum of our society is made of the material fitted by nature for it, and by experience we know that it is the best, not only for the superior but for the inferior race … It is, indeed, in conformity with the Creator [emphasis added].

Stephens's main defense of slavery is that slavery is a natural condition supported by God and that it is a "positive good" for the enslaved, their owners, and all whites—as well as society. Stephens claimed that all Americans and Europeans would eventually recognize the benefits of slavery and adopt the system (Hébert 2021, 224):

> In the conflict so far, success has been on our side, complete throughout the length and breadth of the Confederate States. It is upon this, as I have stated, our social fabric is firmly planted; and I cannot permit myself to doubt the ultimate success of a full recognition of this principle throughout the civilized and enlightened world … The substratum of our society is made of the material fitted by nature for it, and by experience we know, that it is best, not only for the superior, but for the inferior race, that it should be so. It is, indeed, in conformity with the ordinance of the creator. It is not for us to

> inquire into the wisdom of his ordinances, or to question them.

Stephens accepts the divine origin of white supremacy. Of note is the mention that to question the existence of slavery is to question God's actions. To do so, abolitionists become sinners in addition to threatening the Confederacy's well-being.

Diarist Catherine Ann Devereux Edmondston was typical of those rejecting the notion that slaves could be equal to whites in any manner when she declared (Crabtree and Patton 1995, 651), "No! Freedom for whites, slavery for negroes, God has so ordained it!"

The belief in slavery being a "positive good" for the enslaved is best presented in the *De Bow's Review* by Georgian J. A. Turner during 1859:

> The negro slave of the South, if he were enlightened enough to understand his situation, might well thank his master for that slavery which commands his services in such a way as to secure the worse bondage of hunger and poverty, whose chains he would assuredly wear if left to himself.
>
> It follows, therefore, that when the master commands the serve of his negro slave, it does not produce a slavery which is a curse to the bondman, but actually save him from a worse bondage [i.e., poverty].

The "positive good" thesis was so central to Southern ideology and Alexander Stephen's beliefs that it continued into the twentieth century. Poet and novelist Allan Tate (1899–1977) continued this belief (Tate 1998, 41–42):

> On the whole it may be said that out of the great evil of slavery had come a certain good: the master

> and slave were forever bound by ties of association and affection that exceeded all considerations of interest ... For society as a whole the modern system is probably inferior to that of slavery.

Lincoln's Paid Emancipation Attempts

Abraham Lincoln at first completely misjudged the centrality of slavery in the South. Frederick Douglass realized what Lincoln would understand later: "The ties that bind slave-owners together are stronger than all ties." During the early years of the Civil War, Lincoln believed that the most economical way to end slavery in the Union in a manner consistent with the Constitution was to offer compensation to slave owners for the emancipation of their slaves who would then be sent to Africa or central America.

Lincoln hoped that paid emancipation of slaves in the Union slave states (Delaware, Kentucky, Missouri, and Maryland) and in the District of Columbia would legally end slavery in the Union. This plan was similar to the one adopted by the British in their emancipation of Caribbean enslaved persons. Lincoln, on March 6, 1862, asked for a Congressional resolution providing the financial support to free all slaves in the slave states remaining in the Union. This proposal would end slavery in the Union as well as bind more closely to the Union these four slave states remaining in the Union.

Congress enacted the *District of Columbia Emancipation Act*, which would have allocated $300 per slave to owners living in the District of Columbia. None of the representatives from the Union's slave states voted for the bill. Lincoln offered these states a chance for compensated emancipation on October 12, 1862, but it was unanimously rejected. The federal government eventually spent $1,000,000 to emancipate an estimated three thousand slaves in Washington, DC (Seth Kaller, Inc., *Historic Documents and Legacy Collections*, "Lincoln's Emancipation Proposal," 2018).

Monetary offers by Lincoln could never match the economic and cultural significance of owning slaves. By mid-1862, Lincoln realized that slavery could only be eliminated in a fashion other than payment. Lincoln wrote a letter on July 12, 1862, to the governors of the four states in the Union allowing slavery. In "An Appeal to the Border States in Behalf of Compensated Emancipation," Lincoln stated (Roe 1912, 208):

> The institution [i.e., slavery] in your States will be extinguished by mere friction and abrasion—by the mere incidents of the war. It will be gone, and you will have nothing valuable in lieu of it. Much of its value is gone already. How much better for you and for your people to take the step which at once shortens the war and secures substantial compensation for that which is sure to be wholly lost in any other event?

Lincoln's Emancipation Proclamation on January 1, 1863, freeing the slaves in the Confederacy, was in part a recognition that slavery formed a major strength of the Confederacy and also that each freed Black American added to the strength of the Union and weakened the Confederacy. The Union also needed the additional manpower of former enslaved men in its armies. By contrast, the Confederacy lacked the willingness to increase its pool of military-age men by enlisting Black Americans until months before the end of the war.

Winston Churchill summarized the centrality of slavery in Southern culture and its institutions (Churchill 1985, 21):

> It is almost impossible for us nowadays to understand how profoundly and inextricably Negro slavery was interwoven into the whole life, economy, and culture of the Southern states. The tentacles of

> slavery spread widely through the Northern "free" states, along every channel of business dealing and many paths of political influence. One assertion alone reveals the powerlessness of the community to shake itself free from the frightful disease which had become part of its being. It was said that over six hundred and sixty thousand slaves were held by ministers of the Gospel and members of the different Protestant Churches.

George Fitzhugh adds another reason for the importance of slavery in the culture of the South. Fitzhugh states that slave owners were superior because of slavery (McKitrick 1963, 44):

> Domestic slavery in the Southern States has produced the same results in elevating the character of the master that it did in Greece and Rome. He is lofty and independent in his sentiments, generous, affectionate, brave and eloquent; he is superior to the Northerner in every thing but the arts of thrift. History proves this ... Scorpio and Aristides, Calhoun and Washington, are the nobles of domestic slavery.

An additional indication of the centrality of slavery in the Confederate mindset was the almost compulsive illicit capture and kidnapping of more than five hundred Black Americans when Lee's Army of Northern Virginia invaded Pennsylvania during the start of the Gettysburg campaign.

When Lee's army entered Pennsylvania, a major activity of Stuart's cavalry was to capture Black Americans of all ages (Ayers 2017, 46). Supporting Confederate guerilla bands also raided parts of Pennsylvania to kidnap Black Americans to be sold in the South.

Stuart's men and Southerners considered all Black Americans permanent property of whites (Oakes 1982, 134).

Cavalry troopers enthusiastically captured "negroes & horses," as one trooper wrote to his wife (Wynstra 2018, 82). Kidnapped young boys who could not walk long distances were carried on their captors' horses. One trooper entered a home and kidnapped the cook and her two children (Wynstra 2018, 108). These cavalier-like "hunts" indicated that Black Americans and horses were equivalent types of property even though many of the kidnapped were freeborn and had never been enslaved.

Slave Patrols

There were also normative roles for nonslave owners in the culture supporting slavery. The practice of maintaining slave patrols was an important factor in uniting slave owners and poorer nonslaveholding whites. Patrols co-opted white nonslaveholders into defending the institution of slavery. This practice also united plantation owners and the local community by providing locals and planters with common goals.

The purpose of slave patrols was to regulate the behavior of both free and enslaved Black Americans. The major responsibilities of patrols were to capture enslaved fugitives, control the movement of enslaved persons, and be alert for unauthorized meetings.

Patrols consisted of groups of white men, sometimes with dogs, who roamed the countryside on horseback on the alert for enslaved persons. Enslaved persons who did not have written permission from their owners to be away from their owners' plantations or homes were assumed to be escaping. Those without passes would be apprehended and returned to owners. After an attempt to escape, the person would normally be visibly marked as a punishment and as a mark of untrustworthiness.

Patrol members were also allowed to search enslaved persons' cabins for contraband goods such as alcohol, books, and weapons. Searching the enslaved persons' cabins was strictly limited since plantation owners did not want outsiders to limit their control over their enslaved workers. The division of responsibility was primarily that patrols controlled the mobility of enslaved persons away from the plantations while owners and overseers controlled those on the plantation's property (Rosenthal 2018, 115).

Patrol members included members of local militias and cadets attending military schools and academies. Adult white male members of the community could also volunteer for patrol duty. In rural areas, patrol members were selected on a county basis so that members would be neighbors or familiar with one another, further increasing community solidarity. Patrols were essentially locally sanctioned groups of vigilantes organized to control those owned by a wealthy minority of the community. During the postwar Reconstruction period of 1865–1880s and later, slave patrols reemerged as vigilante groups, such as the Ku Klux Klan, with the same purpose of controlling Black Americans.

Patrols generally consisted of three to five mounted men, though patrols were larger during times of racial tension. Patrol members were often rewarded when they caught a fugitive. In the state of Mississippi, the reward was thirty-five dollars for each captured escaping enslaved fugitive. The money was at first paid by local governments, and later, three-fourths of the reward was paid by the enslaved person's owner (Sydnor 1965, 79).

Incorporated towns also maintained patrols to watch over enslaved persons coming to towns on errands for themselves or their owners. The enslaved living on plantations were at times allowed to maintain gardens or fashion handicrafts (baskets, et cetera) to sell their goods in town and buy goods for themselves and their families. Urban patrols enforced curfews and were alert for forbidden behavior among the free and enslaved Black Americans, including drunkenness and suspicious gatherings.

Renting Enslaved Persons

More than owners and their family members benefited from the institution of slavery. Enslaved persons were rented for various periods to those who could not afford to buy enslaved persons or did not want ownership. Renting out enslaved persons could return an annual 6 percent or more of their original cost.

Harriet Tubman was leased by her owner to various families to perform household and child-tending duties beginning when she was five years old. She became a field hand and was rented out when she was in her early teens (McPherson 2007, 23–24). Southern railroad owners used only enslaved labor for the construction and repair of railroads. Some were owned by the companies, but the majority were leased. The Confederate armies also leased enslaved males to build fortifications.

Skilled enslaved workers who were rented out were at times allowed to establish themselves in urban areas and keep some of their incomes. They would pay their owners a certain part of their incomes while practicing professions, such as carpentry or barbering, as well as working in factories or shops. Frederick Douglass, a skilled caulker, was for a time allowed to rent his own urban dwelling and keep any cash he earned over three dollars a week, usually half of his wage (Blight 2018, 80). At times, Douglass earned up to nine dollars in a week, but he was not always allowed to keep his agreed-upon surplus.

Enslaved workers who had learned a trade, such as cooking, blacksmithing, or construction, commanded a premium purchase price, and those who were less skilled were hired as servants. Diarist John B. Jones rented a slave for household duties for an annual fee of $250 in 1864 when inflation had increased prices (Jones 1866, 123).

The Disadvantages of an Enslaved Cotton-Based Economy

The dominance of the institution of slavery in Southern society resulted in a number of negative consequences that contributed to the eventual Confederate defeat.

Mono-cultivation depletes soil fertility. The soil becomes exhausted without the addition of expensive fertilizers, letting acreage fallow for a time, or crop rotation. By 1834, much of the cotton- and tobacco-growing land in the southeast was becoming depleted while the Deep South was producing more cotton per acre. A major industry of the eastern states was the selling of enslaved workers to planters in the Deep South states of Mississippi, Louisiana, Arkansas, and Texas.

Southerners believed slave-growing areas had to expand if they were to survive (targets were the remaining territories, Costa Rica, northern Mexico, Central America, and Cuba). Unlike all Latin American countries except Brazil, Cuba remained a slave-owning country with four hundred thousand slaves (McPherson 2007, 14). Its climate was ideal for the production of slave-driven crops, especially sugar. A Southern fantasy was the colonization of Cuba and dividing it into four slave-supporting states.

The most important reason for the Civil War was the Republican Party's stand that slavery must be geographically restricted and kept out of the territories and any future states. This restriction was seen as an insult to Southerners' honor and "liberty." On their part, Southerners were also convinced cotton production and slavery had to expand geographically. No one had as yet fully realized that enslaved workers could be used in many nonagricultural capacities, such as mining, foundries, factories, and urban occupations.

The profits from cotton, rice, and sugarcane would not be replaced by the substitution to growing other crops. Wheat needed three times the land and more labor to equal the profit from tobacco (Blair 1998, 15). In Virginia's tobacco-growing areas, tobacco growers had little economically rational reason to set aside acreage for food crops except for their own use. The result was that these regions developed neither manufacturing nor much in the way of food crops. Hog production and manufacturing both decreased in the South during the decades before the Civil War. Finished manufactured goods and food crops were increasingly imported by Southerners from the North, northwest, Canada, or Great Britain. Southern seaports and major cities did have a limited number of manufacturing companies. They tended to be entrepôts that received products, mainly cotton, to export elsewhere. The cities of Atlanta, Savannah, and New Orleans were centers that before the Civil War mainly received goods to be sent by rail or ships to markets or factories in the North and eventually to foreign destinations.

At the same time, due to the faster population growth in the then-northwest (Ohio, Indiana, Illinois, Wisconsin, Iowa, and Minnesota), coupled with more extensive transportation systems (including better roads and longer and more integrated railroad and canal systems), farmers in the northwest and the South's border states increasingly sent their food crops east rather than south. The ties were being strengthened among the northwest/New England axis while the economic ties between the northwest and the Southern border states were decreasing. As a result, the South, during the 1840s and 1850s, became increasingly economically isolated from its own border states.

A significant element to these changes in trade relations was the increasing financial dominance of New York City and its port. The city became a key center for the financing and distribution of baled cotton. The city was called "the capital of the South" because of its importance in the cotton trade and its dominance in selling goods to Southerners. Its extensive financial resources offered cheaper loans and higher prices than were available in Southern ports, including New Orleans. At the same time, Southern Atlantic ports decreased in activity.

The tools used to grow cotton and other crops were being increasingly produced outside the South (Cyrus Hall McCormick was born in Virginia but moved north to Chicago, Illinois, and founded the McCormick Harvesting Machine Company). Better-quality tools were available in Great Britain, but tariffs kept American manufacturers competitive. This was a situation that Southerners felt protected Northern goods to the detriment of Southern buyers. These unequal manufacturing developments became unsurpassable deficits during the Civil War and were additional reasons for Confederate defeat.

The Southern cultural values of growing limited amounts of food crops by enslaved workers resulted in the South becoming inferior to the North in food production. Northern farmers, using more expensive free labor, had been encouraged to mechanize their farming production and farm more efficiently. Northern farms became more mechanized during the 1850s, and as a result, food production did not radically decrease when young farmers left to join the military and the war industries. Instead, some crop exports, including the amount of wheat sent to Great Britain, increased.

A number of Southern states, during 1860, passed "stay laws" to delay the payments of planters' debts (usually due on New Year's Day) for one year. This act indicated that planters were already attempting to profit from secession. These debts were owed primarily to New York and London bankers and cotton agents. An *Harper's Weekly* article in the February 16, 1861, issue warned that such an activity would harm the cotton states' credit since "credit is the life and soul of trade, and material prosperity; and laws impairing or postponing the just claims of creditors are necessarily fatal to credit." The *Harper's Weekly* article estimated Southerners owed New York bankers and middlemen between $75,000,000 and $100,000,000 in 1860 dollars. The article concludes with a warning:

> We warn our Southern friends against the perils of the path into which some of their leaders are hurrying them. Their wealth and prosperity and expansion are in a large measure the fruit of the

> credit they have enjoyed. Credit is very sensitive: they should not, for their own sake, subject theirs to any rude ordeals.

Partial or total repudiation of debts for any amount of time would be devastating to New York and British merchants and bankers since they themselves usually borrowed cash to be able to provide planters loans for seeds, tools, and personal luxury items to be repaid after the sale of the next year's cotton, tobacco, rice, and sugar crops. Debt issues in addition to the possible loss of markets were reasons New York financiers considered declaring New York neutral when secession began.

The North also had farm and urban labor supply advantages as a result of immigrants arriving in the United States. Most of the more than 1,651,500 immigrants arrived in the United States during 1856–1865 settled in the Northern states because of the availability of farmland at almost no cost and the expanding industrial sector. Immigrants partly replaced workers who had left their farms to enlist in the military. Most immigrants were young males who could work on farms and factories or enlist in the Union's armies. The Union and state governments offered financial bounties to those who enlisted.

A majority of Southern farmers and foreign immigrants searching for cheaper land moved to free rather than slave states and to the territories. Some had decided they could not compete with enslaved laborers. Good farmland was more available to poorer farmers in the North than in the South. Those leaving the South deprived its society of able, ambitious farmers and their families. Abraham Lincoln's father and his family migrated from the slave state of Kentucky to Illinois where slavery and free Black Americans were both prohibited. Jefferson Davis's father also migrated from Kentucky. As a wealthier slave owner, he settled in the slave state of Mississippi.

The Homestead Act

Migration of poor farmers to Northern states and the territories resulted in an increased concentration of the power and wealth in the South. Planters (those owning twenty enslaved persons or more and more than five hundred acres) had no incentive in encouraging the settlement of small landowners. In 1854, Southern senators and their Northern political allies defeated a homestead bill establishing 160-acre land grants for settlers in the territories and newly formed states.

The 1862 Homestead Act was quickly passed after secession resulted in the departure of Southern representatives in Congress. Two years later, more than one million acres had been allotted to settlers. The conditions stated in the Homestead Act included that up to 160 acres would be granted to those who improved the land and paid a ten-dollar fee five years later to legalize their ownership (Flagel 2010, 68).

Southern Critics of Slavery

There were Southerners who were somewhat critical of the institution of slavery, though these critics wanted to reform or ignore rather than abolish slavery. Critics of the "peculiar institution" saw slavery as a "positive good" for the enslaved as well as for their owners and whites in general. There was also a common support for slavery because the institution made possible the "superior" white-controlled Southern civilization. Edward E. Pollard admitted the system of slavery had its minor faults while it also made possible Southern cultural superiority (Pollard 1866, 50):

> Slavery established in the South a peculiar and noble type of civilization. It was not without attendant vices; but the virtues which followed in its train were numerous and peculiar, and

> asserted the general good effect of the institution on the ideas and manner of the South. If habits of command sometimes degenerated into cruelty and insolence; yet, in the greater number of instances, they inculcated notions of chivalry, polished the manners and produced may noble and generous virtues. If the relief of a large class of whites from the demands of physical labor gave occasion in some instances for idle and dissolute live, yet at the same time it afforded opportunity for extraordinary culture, elevated the standards of scholarship in the South, enlarged and emancipated social intercourse, and established schools of individual refinement.

Slavery, Enlistment, and Secession

A major question in Civil War studies is how important the defense of slavery was to the Confederate population in the states that seceded and how important slave ownership was to fighting for the Confederacy. Was the war "a rich man's war but a poor man's fight"?

We present three major events linking the existence of slavery to secession from the Union. The first event investigates the linkage between the ownership of enslaved persons and the willingness to enlist in the Confederate armies. The second evidence for slavery's centrality in the Confederate culture is found in the Declarations of Secession enacted by the first seven seceded states to explain why secession was necessary for all slave states to protect the institution of slavery.

The third indication for slavery as a reason for secession is the messages made by the commissioners sent by seceded state legislatures to other slave states to encourage them to secede in turn.

Confederate Patriotism and Slavery

Joseph T. Glatthaar (2011) developed a representative sample of those who served in Lee's Army of Northern Virginia. He profiled the six hundred persons in his sample on the basis of fifty-four characteristics (age, wealth, slave ownership, et cetera). This allows for the discovery of the different motivations of Confederate soldiers to enlist and to remain in the Army of Northern Virginia.

Glatthaar's data indicate that slave owners were overrepresented in Lee's army (and presumably in other Confederate armies). Soldiers, regardless of personal or family enslaved persons ownership, were more likely to have enlisted from counties with high-level presence vis-à-vis the white population. The suggests that these recruits were more embedded in the institution of slavery (Glatthaar 2011, 7) than those living in counties with lower slave-to-white population ratios. Such persons were more likely to enlist to protect the slave institution even when they did not own enslaved persons. The data suggest that inhabitants living in counties with high concentrations of enslaved persons were developing different norms from those living in counties with lower percentages of enslaved persons vis-à-vis whites.

The interpretation above is also supported by the fact that, while those who had lived in households owning enslaved persons represented 3.2 percent of the Confederate households, they represented 6.9 percent of the army (Glatthaar 2011, 9). *The planter class did not avoid serving in the military.* They were also dominant in the upper levels of the government and were the ones most likely to invest in Confederate bonds.

Indicating strength of their patriotism, half (43.3 percent) of slave owners were wounded or killed in action (Glatthaar 2011, 162–63). This rate was 27.4 percent higher than that for those who or their families did not own enslaved persons. Glatthaar interprets these differences as indicating a greater strength of Confederate patriotism on the part of those who were involved in owning Black Americans.

Part of this discrepancy may have been that the code of chivalric honor was stronger among slaveholders. This value would also reflect the tendency of officers (overrepresented by owners of enslaved persons) to personally lead their command in battle and exposing themselves to danger. Those who believed themselves to be honorable and courageous knights would be more likely to view engaging in battle as a duty and as an exciting activity. Glatthaar concludes (Glatthaar 2011, 165):

> Soldiers who owned slaves—or lived with family members who did—turned out in great numbers to fight on behalf of their newly created nation. They incurred higher casualties, deserted less frequently, and suffered more for their slaveholding Confederacy than the troops who did not own slaves and were otherwise unconnected to the peculiar institution.

Declarations of Secession

The members of Southern state legislative assemblies discussed and voted on the issue of secession. After a majority supported secession, these assemblies each produced Declarations of Independence to formally announce the breaking of all ties with the Union.

The 1861 Declarations are similar in form to the Declaration of Independence ratified on July 4, 1776, by the Second Continental Congress. Written by Thomas Jefferson and the Committee of Five, the 1776 Declaration listed the reasons for the representatives' rejection of their colonial status. The contents of the 1776 and 1861 Declarations include both general principles as well as specific grievances. The major difference between the earlier declaration for independence and in the 1861 declarations is an emphasis on slavery. The 1776 Declaration states in part:

> That whenever any form of Government becomes destructive of their [inalienable rights], it is the Right of the People to alter or abolish it, and to institute new government …
>
> But when a long train of abuses and usurpations, pursuing invariably the same Object evinces a design to reduce them under absolute Despotism, it is their right, it is their duty, to throw off such Government …
>
> He [i.e., King George III] has combined with others to subject us to a jurisdiction foreign to our constitution, and unacknowledged by our own laws …

Reflecting the format of the 1776 Declaration of Independence by beginning with general grievances and then proceeding to more specific complaints, the Texas 1861 Declaration of Secession included the following:

> In all the non-slave-holding states, in violation of that good faith and comity which should exist between entirely distinct nations, the people have formed themselves into a great sectional party [i.e., the Republican Party], now strong enough in numbers to control the affairs of each of these States and their beneficent and patriarchal system of African slavery, proclaiming the debasing doctrine of the equality of all men, irrespective of race or color—a doctrine at war with nature … They [i.e., Republicans] demand the abolition of negro slavery throughout the confederacy, the

> recognition of political equality between the white and negro races, and avow their determination to press on their crusade against us, so long as a negro slave remain in these states.
>
> They have for years encouraged and sustained lawless organizations to steal our slaves and prevent their recapture, and they repeatedly murdered Southern citizens while lawfully seeking their rendition.

The Mississippi Declaration of Secession similarly reflects a heightened concern to threats to slavery:

> Our position is thoroughly identified with the institution of slavery—the greatest material interest of the word. Its labor supplies the product which constitutes by far the largest and most important portions of commerce of the earth. The products are peculiar to the climate verging on the tropical regions, and by an imperious law of nature, none but the black race can bear exposure to the tropical sun. These products have become necessities of the world, and a blow at slavery is a blow at commerce and civilization. That blow has been long aimed at the institution, and was the point of reaching its consummation. *There was but one choice left us but submission to the mandates of abolition, or a dissolution of the Union, whose principles had been subverted to work out our ruin* [emphasis added].
>
> It [i.e., the federal government] advocates negro equality, socially and politically, and promotes insurrection and incendiarism in our midst.
>
> It [i.e., the federal government] has given indubitable evidence of its design to ruin our

> agriculture, to prostate our industrial pursuits and destroy our social system [i.e., slavery].
>
> We must either submit to degradation, and to the loss of property [i.e., slaves] worth four billion of money, or we must secede from the union framed by our fathers, to secure this as well as every other species of property. For far less cause than this, our fathers separated from the Crown of England.

The Commissioners for Secession

Between December 1860 and April 1861, the first five seceded states—Mississippi, Alabama, South Carolina, Georgia, and Louisiana—sent fifty-five representatives, called commissioners, to encourage (or hasten) the remaining slave states to similarly secede. These commissioners addressed or wrote to legislatures, secession conventions, reporters, governors, friends, and influential politicians and had two general purposes.

The first was to indicate that the establishment of a slave-based Confederacy was now a fact. Second, the commissioners had the authority to present the ideological and existential dangers of staying in the Union. They did so by explaining why secession was necessary to protect the institution of slavery. The commissioners also maintained that the Southern civilization was in danger and that the financial structures of the slave states would collapse if they chose to stay in the Union or secede but not join the Confederacy.

Charles B. Dew (2016) presents compelling descriptions of the themes that the commissioners believed to be the most compelling to fulfill their mission. By doing so, they expressed the major reasons/causes for secession. Their messages show a near-total panic that Lincoln and his administration would support a total abolition of slavery and equality of the races. These would, slave owners understood, destroy the foundation of their society, its culture, and its economy.

An example of this rhetoric is found in the address of Mississippi Commissioner William L. Harris to the Georgia Assembly on December 17, 1860, which was later published in pamphlet form to be distributed to the general public (Dew 2016, 107 and 111):

> Our fathers made this a government for the white man, rejecting the negro, as an ignorant, inferior, barbarian race, incapable of self-government, and not, therefore, entitled to be associated with the white man upon terms of civil, political, or social equality …
>
> She [i.e., the state of Mississippi] had rather see the last of her race, men, women and children, immolated in one common funeral pile, than see them subjected to the degradation of civil, political and social equality with the negro race.

The repetitions of maintaining the belief of Black American inferiority and the continuous emphasis of maintaining white supremacy as the main cause of secession often reoccur in the same speech and from one speech to another. The commissioners also consistently stressed the aggressiveness of "fanatic" abolitionists in spite of the fact that slavery was condoned by the founding fathers and the Constitution. The majority of white Southerners agreed with the commissioners because their messages were already well-known and accepted.

John McQueen of South Carolina is typical of the commissioners when he declares to a Virginian audience (Dew 2016, 48):

> We, of South Carolina, hope soon to greet you in a Southern Confederacy, where white men shall rule our destinies, and from which we may transmit to

> our posterity the rights, privileges and honor left us by our ancestors.

Alabama Commissioner Stephen F. Hale's message is also typical of his colleagues' deliveries. After a discussion of the ideal of a decentralized government protecting the constitutional rights of slaveholders, Halle lists the harm abolitionists have done to the residents of the South. He then, like all commissioners, warns of the probable apocalyptic events under an abolitionist regime (Dew 2016, 119–20):

> It is that the election of Mr. Lincoln cannot be regarded otherwise than a solemn declaration on the part of a great majority of the Northern people, of hostility to the South, her property [i.e., slavery], and other institutions: nothing less than a declaration of war, for the triumph of this new theory of government destroys the property of the South, lays waste her fields, and inaugurates all the horrors of a San Domingo servile insurrection [i.e., the Haitian enslaved persons' successful revolt against France], consigning her citizens to assassinations and her daughters to pollution and violation to gratify the lust of half-civilized Africans.

CHAPTER 3

THE ALPHA COMPLEX

They can talk about their Jackson
And sing of General Lee,
But the one-legged Hood
gave 'em Hell in Tennessee.
—Civil War marching song

The *alpha complex* deals with issues of inequality in the Southern and Confederate subcultures. There was a great concern in the South with dividing persons into inequal ranks rank. There was in addition a fear that one could descend from a higher rank to a higher one. One's honor and self-image were acutely associated with a concern that others were likely to insult a person, thereby reducing his rank in Confederate society. A major reason for Confederate battle losses was the conflict among officers who refused to cooperate with those who had presumably insulted their honor.

Confederate leaders were very concerned with two systems of inequality. The first dealt with maintaining the ranking between whites and Black Americans. A rationale for slavery was that the Southern "civilization" depended on a subordinate position of enslaved non-whites. A reason for secession and the Civil War was the fear that whites could become subordinate to Northerners and freed Black Americans. Another reason for secession was the Southern practice to denigrate Northerners and their subculture as inferior. Northerners therefore would be easily beaten in a war for independence.

The fear of losing one's higher status or position in a social class pyramid resulted in a denial that one's superiority has decreased. Battles that were lost were redefined as victories to maintain the illusion that Southern leaders remained alpha leaders. A consequence for this alpha attitude was a reluctance to change battle tactics even when they failed.

The alpha complex would not have existed had it not been for the existence of slavery because the belief in white supremacy demands a system of a hierarchy of inequality in which one rank is superior to the other. The division between whites and non-whites was so absolute. Any race mingling meant the person was considered a Black American rather than white. Slavery could not exist unless Black Americans were considered absolutely inferior.

The distinctive nature of Southern ranking system is that difference in statuses included a ranking. One could not be different without being also placed in a hierarchical system. Differences among persons become associated with inequality because these status differences are ranked into one or more hierarchies. Differences in lifestyles were not recognized as alternative normative behaviors but rather ranked into marginalized subcultures. This refusal to accept social differences as equal resulted in a Southern demand for conformity.

Those who owned large numbers of enslaved persons became the elites of Southern society. Very few persons could be accepted in the most respected Southern social circles unless they owned enslaved persons. As social leaders, owners of enslaved persons became the models for others to follow. Those who aspired to be upwardly socially mobile copied the ideology and lifestyles of these grand seigneurs along with their absolute power over their enslaved workers.

Winston Churchill realized these elite dominated all institutions. Churchill summarized in his succinct manner the amount power the planters enjoyed (Churchill 1985, 20): "The three or four thousand principal slave-holders generally ruled the politics of the South as effectively as the medieval baronage had ruled England."

The existence of slavery by itself was a source of higher status for all white Southerners as it ensured that there were people (i.e., non-whites) automatically lower in the hierarchy. The thought that slavery might be abolished was frightening to more than just the wealthy planters. Part of the Southern defense of slavery was the belief that slavery resulted in giving all Southern whites an alpha-like superior position in society. In a senatorial speech on March 2, 1859, Jefferson Davis stated:

> I say that the lower race of human beings that constitute the substratum of what is termed the slave population of the South, elevated every white man in our community ... It is the presence of a lower caste, those lower by their mental and physical organization, controlled by the higher intellect of the white man, that gives this superiority to the white laborer.

The alpha complex included a ranking of Northerners and Southerners. It was important for white Southerners to feel superior to Northerners since regional differences had to be ranked rather than accepted as horizontal status differences. The January/February issue of the 1861 *De Bow's Review* included an article by George Fitzhugh. He described Union soldiers as an "unemployed, destitute, agrarian mob," while praising Rebel troops from all ranks as noble and independent thinkers capable of doing what is necessary to win over their enemies (Paskoff and Wilson 1982, 255):

> Our soldiers and our officers have exhibited a noble specimen of the moral sublime, in the patience with which they have submitted to misconstruction, calumny and abuse.

Debasement of Union soldiers into a lower social category resulted in Southerners underestimating the power, courage, and determination of Northerners and foreigners. Since Northerners followed different significant cultural mindsets from Southerners, the alpha complex encouraged the belief that Yankees were culturally different and inferior to Southerners. Southerners considered themselves to be more warlike and braver than those they considered to be their cultural, social, and racial inferiors. By 1860, most Southerners were convinced that Northerners belonged to a different race as well as a different and inferior culture. This belief encouraged the stereotype that Yankees would be inept as well as cowardly battle opponents (Philips 2018, 42).

The central element of the alpha complex is the belief in inequality with the Southern planter elites the apex of the social class pyramid (Northern elites were primarily politicians, merchants, and manufacturers). Nineteenth-century Southern whites defined themselves as superior to all Black Americans and other non-whites. After that, gentlemen were superior to nongentlemen. Southerners were superior to Northerners, and owners of enslaved persons were superior to nonowners. Owners of enslaved persons had their own hierarchy because owners of larger numbers of enslaved persons considered themselves socially superior to those who owned fewer enslaved persons. Enslaved persons had their own social hierarchies. Enslaved house servants felt superior to enslaved field hands.

The Southern aristocracy was composed of the three thousand families that each owned one hundred enslaved persons or more

(Levine 1992, 22). These formed the apex of a seigneurial hierarchy that dominated the economic, social, and political institutions of the South and the Confederacy (Luraghi 1978, 20). Next in superior rank were those who owned between twenty and ninety-nine enslaved persons. Both of these two upper ranks were often defined as "planters" and were the alpha leaders of the Confederacy. Together they dominated the economic, political, and the rest of the South's institutions.

Rank differentiation was a central characteristic of the Southern mindset. A rationale for the declaration and continuation of the Civil War was the fear that the North would "subjugate" Southerners and destroy the Southern way of life and its ranking system. The terms "subjugate," "enslave," and "submit" were commonly used to describe why Confederates fought so tenaciously (McPherson 1995, 13).

To Southerners, if one person were dominant over another, the dependent other must be similar to a slave. This attitude was reported by British journalist William Howard Russell when he was told of the superiority of Southerners compared to Northerners (Russell, n.d., letter 6):

> Nothing on earth shall ever induce us to submit to any union with the brutal, bigoted blackguards of the New England States, who neither comprehend nor regard the feelings of gentlemen! Man, woman and child, we'll die first.

The quote above is typical of many such alpha-type pronouncements by white Southerners. Elite male Southerners are "gentlemen," and resistance to their wishes is an attack on their honor. Compromise with inferiors is seen as total surrender, and gentlemen were expected to defend their positions to the death.

An example of this antagonism to those who might disagree with Southern values is found in the experience of New Yorker

Samuel A. H. Colt, the founder and leader of the Colt's Patent Fire-Arms Manufacturing Company.

After providing arms to Garibaldi—who was leading his own insurrection in Italy—Colt traveled to Charleston, South Carolina, in December 1860 to offer his revolvers and rifles to the emerging Confederacy. Discovered as being a Yankee, Colt was attacked in his hotel lobby and brawled with his assailants. Colt retreated to safety with help of kind strangers and soon left for New York (Starobin 2017, 199).

If the attackers had waited to learn Colt's purpose for being in Charleston, they would have been better able to arm future militia members. At the time, however, Yankees in the South were automatically suspect and driven out of the region, imprisoned, or even worse.

Southern elites believed the white lower classes were socially and morally inferior and potentially threatening to the social status quo. Prolific Southern author George Fitzhugh viewed the white poor as almost a race apart (Fitzhugh 1858, 655):

> The poor must obey the wealthy landholders, and in doing so become civilized, for the skill and capacity to produce the luxuries of life, and to gratify all the wants of the wealthy and intellectual is the essence, the whole civilization.

Fitzhugh was saying that both slaves and poor whites—the "mudsills" and the "greasy mechanics" of society—existed for the benefit of the planter elite. To build a Southern civilization, the poor of both races must be controlled by the elite.

When it was recognized that a large minority of Southerners was against secession, the elite made certain their own interests—in this case the question of secession—were promoted instead of a possible majority's. South Carolinian Alfred P. Aldrich reflected what planters thought (Williams 2008, 10):

> Whoever waited for the common people when a great move [i.e., secession] was to be made—We must make the move and force them to follow.

There were also denials that the poorer elements in the South were respectable and integral parts of the society. A major theorist of the Southern way of life, George Fitzhugh believed poor white Southerners would be better off as chattels of an alpha aristocracy. Fitzhugh claimed a major problem with contemporary English society was that its increasing elements of democracy resulted in a weakened aristocracy and a resulting decline of the society.

No clearer evidence of social class antagonism can be found than in an editorial printed in the Muscogee, Georgia, *Herald* (Stampp 1991, 210):

> Free society! We sicken at the name. What is it but a conglomeration of greasy mechanics, filthy operatives, small-fisted farmers, and moon-struck theorists? All the Northern and especially the New England states, are devoid of society fitted for well-bred gentleman. The prevailing class one meets is that of mechanics struggling to be genteel, and small farmers who do their drudgery, and yet are hardly fit for association with a southern gentleman's servant [i.e., slave].

The lower classes are defined as lower than slaves in terms of their social ranks in Southern culture. The quote above also denounced those who hoped to be upwardly mobile even though they "do their drudgery," that is, unlike the elite, they work. Southerners did not think that hard work ennobled the worker since the ideal was for others to work for members of the elite. To the Southern elite, the blue collars should not be struggling to be "genteel."

Secessionist Edmund Ruffin held a similar elite alpha social class bias. Ruffin defended slavery not only for its support of the Southern economy and white culture but also because slavery would (Ethier 2008, 23) "postpone, if not prevent, the existence, or supremacy, of a destitute class of voters, numerous enough to govern the state." Similar to the sentiments in the above quote from the *Herald*, Ruffin feared both the possible social mobility of members in the lower classes and their possible increased political involvement. Alphas were constantly afraid of losing their power over others—whether poorer whites or all Black Americans.

Military rank did not automatically supersede class superiority. An upper-class trooper had been transferred to Nathan Bedford Forrest's cavalry unit during the end of 1863 after Forrest had been recognized as the foremost cavalry leader (and feared by the Union). The transferee expressed his disgust by writing in his diary (Wills 1992, 145):

> "The Wizard" now commands us ... and I must express my distaste to being commanded by a man having no pretensions to gentility—a Negro trader, gambler ... an ambitious man, careless with his men so long preferment be en prospectu ... [He] may be & no doubt is, the best Cav officer in the West, but I object to a tyrannical, hotheaded vulgarian's commanding me.

It is telling that the author above placed considerations of social class membership above following a man whom he acknowledges as one of the more successful cavalry leaders of the Confederacy.

The wealthy believed themselves superior to everyone else, but they also had their own hierarchies based on genealogy, region of origin, wealth, social polish, education, and land and ownership of enslaved persons. Virginian and South Carolinian families with generations-old wealth and prestige expected to be given more respect from the nouveau riche planters from Texas, Arkansas, or Louisiana—even though the latter were wealthier.

While the ideal ideology in the Southern culture declared that all whites were equally superior vis-à-vis Black Americans, the Southern elites considered themselves to be aristocrats who were superior to members of the white middle and lower classes. Except for successful politicians, lawyers, and physicians, most members of the middle class(es) were also suspected of not being quite respectable and too interested in earning money (Southern merchants were called a pejorative "Yankee Southerners").

Military officers were generally considered part of the upper classes, especially when they were successful. The civilian elite respected military officers, but at times, they considered those originating from lower classes to remain socially inferior. General John Bell Hood courted a young girl from a much higher social class, but her parents refused to accept him as a social equal. She ended her engagement with Hood and later married someone her social equal. There are indications that she was not serious about the relationship with Hood but enjoyed his company when he was a hero.

Former governor of South Carolina James Henry Hammond is another example of the Southern elite's acceptance of inequality. In his "Letter to an English Abolitionist," Hammond claims owners of enslaved persons and Southerners in general are intellectually superior and more religiously pious than the British while the Southern society was more stable because of the presence of slavery. He suggests England could regain its lost glory by instituting slavery and reducing the suffrage of the middle class.

Hammond continues to insult the British and their society in his iconic "King Cotton" letter. Hammond declared Northern and British mill owners (and their workers) would demand a continual supply of cotton, resulting in the recognition of the Confederacy. He assumed, as did Napoleon Bonaparte sixty years earlier, that the British were a "nation of shopkeepers" (a social category with low prestige both in the South and in the eyes of Napoleon) whose sole interest was an honor-lacking interest in moneymaking materialism.

In the same letter, Hammond used the term "mudsill" (i.e., the foundation of a house, building, dam, resting on the earth) for the Union. The Northern and British working classes reflected Southern arrogance of and a dismissive attitude for those who did not own slaves. Hammond's "mudsill" theory states that all societies are based on a lower class existing for the benefit of the wealthier minority.

Feelings of superiority were further reflected when a South Carolinian boasted to British journalist William Howard Russell (Russell 1863, 98), "The Yankees are cowardly rascals. We have proved it by kicking and cuffing till we are tired of it." Boasted another Confederate, "There is not a man in the Southern army who does not in his heart believe that he can whip three Yankees, he would consider it beneath his manhood to count on whipping a less number" (McPherson 1997, 26).

The above boast of being superior to "three Yankees" is a common attitude to those who believe they are innately superior to others. The British stationed in Burma before the Japanese invasion of Burma underestimated the Japanese capability of fighting a modern war because (Smith 1979, 9) "one white soldier was more than capable of seeing off two or three coloured ones."

The North's larger population advantage would have ended if the above boast had been realistic or if "the Yankee is afraid of guns and horses, because he has not been taught to shoot and ride in boyhood" (Daniel 1868, 16). Ignored in this quote was that, during 1863, the Confederacy was losing territory and the control of seaports to Union forces. This alpha attitude among the Confederates includes the refusal to admit their own mistakes and weaknesses.

From the above Southern claims of martial superiority, one could assume that Southerners would be better marksmen than

Northerners. However, this proved to be false like many other claims of superiority. This alpha insistence of natural martial superiority blinded Southerners to reality. Battle statistics indicate Union soldiers were better shots and inflicted a higher kill rate than did Confederates (Adams 1978, 81 and 191). At the battle of First Manassas, Union forces were better marksmen at a time when both sides were equally inexperienced (Weigley 2000, 63):

> Every 1,000 Federals in action suffered about eighty men hit, but hit 100 of the enemy; every 1,000 Confederate in action lost about 100 casualties, while killing and wounding about eighty Federals.

This attitude of superiority over an enemy because of national character was not unique to Confederates. Before the start of World War II, the Japanese military command realized the overwhelming ten times superiority of America's industrial might over Japan's. However, Japanese military leaders also believed their spiritual superiority could overcome America's numbers and "mere" industrial might. General Torashiro Kawabe summed up this belief in the innate Japanese superiority over Americans (Toll 2020, 202):

> The Japanese, to the very end [i.e., of the Pacific War], believed that by spiritual means they could fight on equal terms with you [i.e., Americans]. … We believed spiritual confidence in victory would balance any scientific advantages.

Even those who should have known better raged against the assumed inferior Northerners. Jefferson Davis, during his military and political careers, developed friendships with many Northerners and had fought alongside them during the war with Mexico. He also had respected many of his Northern colleagues while serving in the Senate. As a former secretary of war, Davis knew the character of Northern soldiers and officers. Yet, in a conversation with French observer Charles Girard, Davis described Northerners in this extreme manner (Girard 1962 [1863], 49):

> I am obliged to do violence to my own feeling in order not to give free reign to the just feelings of hate and vengeance which the conduct of our enemies inspires with me. They are people without faith or law, without moral principles, living in the depths of depravity and abjectness so deep that words cannot express it.

In late 1861, after the Confederate victory at the First Bull Run (First Manassas), an anonymous author, writing in the *De Bow's Review*, compared the assumed low quality of Union soldiers to the braver and more noble Confederates (Paskoff and Wilson 1982, 242):

> Our soldiers are not like the miserable hirelings of Lincoln—the scum of infamy and degradation—hunted up from the dens, sewers and filthy prisons of the North, with the low vandalism of foreign importations, picked up wherever they can be found. Yet such are the creatures our brave soldiers have to meet.

If Northern troops had been "hunted up from the dens," then they were subhuman animals without honor and intelligence. They did not deserve respect and would easily be defeated by the more militant and spiritual alpha Confederates.

British historian John Keegan also noted (Keegan 2009, 28):

> Midcentury [i.e., the 1850s] Southerners proclaimed themselves to be a superior breed to Northerners, preserving the agrarian way of life on which the

> republic had been founded at the Revolution and led by a breed of cultivated gentlemen who better resembled the Founding Fathers than the money-grubbing capitalists who dominated public life in the North.

The alpha complex includes the fear of becoming inferior to others. In spite of the presumed superiority of Southern culture and white Southerners, there remained fears that a Northern victory would reduce white Southerners to a subordinate, slave-like subordination. When encouraging the Georgia Assembly to vote for secession in 1861, Georgia Governor Joseph E. Brown declared failure to secede would result in the total destruction of the Southern culture. There was no middle course or compromise for alphas such as Brown and other radical states' right secessionists. The conflicts between abolitionists and leaders of the slave states could only result in a total loss or a total victory; there could be no compromise. Brown warned (Wetherington 2005, 83):

> What is my property worth if I am a slave? If we are conquered, our property is confiscated and we and our children are slaves to Northern avarice and Northern insolence.

The alpha mindset includes the importance of winning over others because losing superiority means becoming inferior to the winner. A consequence of this was a reluctance to admit losing a battle. If one rationalizes a loss into a victory, then there is no need to admit to becoming inferior. The tradition of the Lost Cause—stating that the Civil War was not actually lost—was developed as former Confederates attempted to rationalize that their status rank as superior had been maintained. One rationale of the Lost Cause was that Rebels fought better and more nobly than Yankees and as a result did not lose the war. An example of this aspect of the alpha complex is illustrated by the refusal for Confederates to admit defeat in battle (and later the war). Jason Phillips (2007) calls those who refused to admit defeat "diehard rebels."

These men and women were certain the Union would not lose the Civil War in spite of (near-continuous) Confederate defeats during 1864, in part by redefining a lost battle as a "negative victory" or as a prequel for future victories. A rationalization for maintaining Confederate patriotism was the belief that the loss of further battles or the war itself would result in Confederates becoming "slaves" of the North.

An example of this refusal to admit a battle loss is found in General Pierre Gustave Toutant Beauregard claiming a victory after the battle of Shiloh, which is known as the Battle of Pittsburg Landing (McWhiney 2002, 172): "And after a severe battle of ten hours ... gained a complete victory, driving the enemy from every position." The Union's total casualties of 13,000 at Shiloh was larger than the Confederates' 10,700, though the Confederates lost 27 percent of their forces to the Union's 19 percent. However, the battle is rightly considered a Union victory. The Union army had not retreated and had forced the Confederates to retreat to Corinth, Mississippi, which was captured by Union forces three weeks later.

After Confederate battle defeats and loss of territory during 1864, and a few months before Robert E. Lee's surrender, Reuben Pierson wrote to his father (Phillips 2007, 20):

> We need have no fears of being enslaved by so brutal and cruel enemies as those against whom we are fighting.

Pierson's determination was partly derived by his religious beliefs supporting an unyielding hostility toward Yankees, an unrelenting optimism the Confederacy would gain its independence, and a culturally derived sense of superiority over the Yankees. Pierson did not recognize that the Confederacy needed to change its military tactics if they were to win more battles and experience fewer casualties than it could afford.

The fear of losing prestige included the fear that enslaved men would become dominant. Confederates feared becoming "enslaved" should abolitionists became politically powerful. A common rhetorical technique was to claim that the death of the white Confederate population was preferable to becoming subordinate to Black Americans. The only alternatives to losing the Civil War was to "win or die." An image understood by Southerners was that "the bottom fence rail would become the top rail." By definition, a fence must have top and bottom rails. Southerners could not accept Black Americans as equals or as superiors.

The Alpha Complex and the Dichotomy of Thinking

Southerners often divided groups and ranked divisions into two types. This simplistic practice made evaluating people, as in the case of separating people into a non-white or white dichotomy, much simpler. Another example is the dividing of Southerners as either loyal to the Confederacy or being traitors. There was no consideration of gradations or tolerance of differences.

Southern author George Fitzhugh was a representative of proponents of bipolar racial and class rankings. Society, according to Fitzhugh, was made of an elite class and a subordinate but subservient lower class (Hummel 1996, 23):

> It would be far nearer the truth to say, "that some were born with saddles on their backs, and others booted and spurred to ride them"—and the riding does them good. They need the reins, the bit and the spur.

The writer reminds readers that enslaved persons need to be controlled for their own benefit. The quote above also refers to poor whites who also were seen as needing to be controlled for their own good. The need for the "bit and the spur" also reflects a willingness to use violence to control those believed to be inferiors. The mention of horse paraphernalia reflects the idea that leaders were cavalier born and trained to rule others.

This mindset stressing an either/or dichotomy is illustrated by the execution of twenty-two North Carolinian members of the Union army. Part of the Second North Carolina Volunteers, USA, these men had been members of a local militia but then enlisted as Union soldiers when the war began.

When members of the Second North Carolina Volunteers were captured, the Confederate commander, George Pickett, declared them to be traitors to the Confederacy. A short court-martial declared them guilty of desertion and sentenced to be hung. These Union Southerners should have been treated as any other group of Union soldiers since they wore the Union uniform. Pickett defined them as traitors.

A platform with enough space for three nooses was built in the Kinston's city square (Cordon 1998, 133). They were hung three at a time until all twenty-two were executed (Patterson 2002, 130–32). Pickett allowed his soldiers to strip the bodies of their clothes and shoes and ridicule the family members of the victims. The families of the executed were then allowed to collect the bodies for burial. Similar to Pickett, Confederates did not accept the legitimacy of dissent. Pickett was representative of the Southern elite used to controlling their inferiors through violence and intimidation (Cordon 1998, 134).

Feelings of Inferiority among Cavaliers

The South's cultural emphasis on cavalier honor forced its leaders to defend their inferiority vis-à-vis the North (compared to most European countries, the South as an independent country would present a respectable profile, including literacy rates and miles of railroad tracks). Former Texas Senator Louis T. Wigfall, as did white Southerners in general, defended the Confederacy's shortcomings by turning them into advantages. Wigfall praised Southern society by explaining it to British correspondent William Howard Russell in May 1861 (Russell 1863, 179):

> We are a particular people, Sir. You don't understand us, and you can't understand us, because you are known to us only by Northern writers and Northern papers, who know nothing of us themselves, or misrepresent what they do know. We are a primitive but civilized people. We have no cities—we don't want them. We have no literature—we don't need any yet. We have no press—we are glad of it. We do not require a press. Because we go out and discuss all public questions from the stump with our people [one distinct characteristic of Confederate congressional meetings was that sessions were closed to outsiders. Discussions were kept secret and not formally recorded]. We have no commercial marine—no navy—we don't want them. We are better without them. Your ships [i.e., England's] carry our produce, and you can protect your own vessels. We want no manufactures: we desire no trading, no mechanical or manufacturing classes. *As long as we have our rice, our sugar, our tobacco, and our cotton, we can command wealth to*

> *purchase all we want from those nations with which we are in amity, and lay up money besides* [emphasis added].

Wigfall's attempt to impress a foreign journalist exposed a number of failings of Southern culture. Wigfall was expecting to be able to *force* others to provide the products the South did not produce. This relying on others to help the Confederacy exposes a certain passiveness found in Southern culture. Others, including foreigners, can be legitimately forced to do the bidding of the planters. His use of the word "command" indicates a planter's orientation: the willingness to use force to control others as they did their enslaved laborers. Wigfall seems proud of the South's wealth, though he denies Southerners were concerned with profit. Ironically, Wigfall, in this quote, resembles the despised Yankee merchant's mindset since the South's weaknesses can be overcome by money.

Wigfall's denouncing of cities reflects a typical cavalier value. Cities, to many Southerners, meant commercialism, a focus on profit, and a weakening of the morality and physical character of their inhabitants. By contrast, the plantations of the elites were seen as nurturing alpha values of self-reliance, leadership, and a martial spirit.

Wigfall used the word "amity" in his declaration. Southerners tended to separate others into those who were against them and those who were not. Those considered not *completely* dependable allies become demonized enemies. That is why Wigfall included an implied threat. Those who were not in complete "amity" with the Confederacy would not be offered cotton for their mills. The culture of the Confederacy did not encourage equal cooperation with others. Southern elites preferred ordering others to do their bidding.

Wigfall's comments were commonly held attitudes. A planter from Alabama exhibited the same arrogance when he stated (Fawcett 2011, 8):

> That the North does our trading and manufacturing mostly is true, and we are willing that they should. Ours is an agricultural people, and God grant that we may continue so.

Negative Outcomes of Alpha Diplomacy

Examples of the detrimental influence of the alpha complex are found in the efforts of the Confederates to gain diplomatic and financial support as well as formal recognition from France, England, and Mexico. These diplomatic goals were handicapped in part because Jefferson Davis first appointed inappropriate representatives. Davis sent to France someone who did not speak French correctly, and a consul to Britain (where slavery had been outlawed) had been a vocal defender of slavery. There was no need or time to select more appropriate diplomatic personnel when all that was needed was a show of alpha superiority, in this case by promoting the "Cotton is King" policy and threatening to withdraw access to cotton.

The only strategy of Confederate diplomacy during the first part of the war was to bully foreign nations with the threat of withholding cotton. Reflecting the alpha complex, Southerners assumed they could force foreigners to support their attempts to become independent. The Confederate diplomatic strategy was based on an assumption of their superiority because they viewed the British and the French as merchants whose values were commercial. Foreigners could be bribed with cotton or threatened with a lack of cotton to support the Confederate cause—even though both France and Great Britain had earlier abolished slavery at home and in most of their colonies. In addition, Southerners ignored the fact that these two countries had other global interests and problems to consider.

This policy had drastic consequences. Jefferson Davis was convinced England and France would intervene in the war to the South's benefit in order to maintain a supply of cotton. James Mason, Confederate commissioner in Europe, believed European cotton mills would run out of cotton by February 1862, and then intervention would automatically occur (Fuller 1957, 29). Actually, the Europeans had decided that, by the end of 1861, their dependency on "King Cotton" was less than they had anticipated, but Davis was too rigid to admit he was mistaken. He refused to change the policy of trying to force or bribe Europeans to intervene. Europe valued Confederate cotton less than did the Confederacy.

The sense of alpha superiority weakening the diplomatic policies of the Confederacy is illustrated by Colonel John T. Pickett's prejudice against Mexicans. Pickett was the Confederacy's commissioner to Mexico. His charge was to convince President Benito Juarez and his government to support the Confederacy's access to Mexico's seaports. This would allow Confederates to export cotton and hides from Texas and import needed supplies. Mexicans were pro-Union, and they remembered the results of the Mexican-American War, Texas independence, and the loss of more than half of its territory, including Texas and part or whole sections of nine present-day states.

Pickett was a former filibuster and favored the more conservative Mexican Church Party against the more liberal party in power. Pickett spent thirty days in jail for brawling with an American who was sympathetic to the ruling Juarez party. He was released after bribing a judge (Hubbard 1998, 46–47).

While attempting to cajole Mexican officials into giving their support, Pickett's private correspondence to Robert Toombs, the Confederacy's first secretary of state, described Mexicans as "robbers, assassins, blackguards, and lepers." He noted that, "Mexicans are a race of degenerate monkeys." This was a common view among white Southerners because of the amount of miscegenation in the Mexican population. Pickett also described which parts of Mexico were best for Confederate invasion and colonization. Almost all of Pickett's correspondence to Robert Toombs was intercepted by agents of the Union minister to Mexico and a Union spy in the New Orleans post office. As expected, copies of these letters were shown to Mexican officials.

William Lowndes Yancey was sent to England as an envoy, but he was known to the British government officials as an extreme proslavery supporter, filibuster, and proponent of the reestablishment of the international slave trade. Acting the part of an elite alpha leader of the South and Confederacy, Yancey was noncompromising and arrogant (Hubbard 1998, 31).

The Alpha Complex and the 1861–1862 Cotton Boycott

The Southern cotton boycott during 1861–1862 is another example of Southern alpha bullying those Confederates believed to be culturally inferiors. The boycott was conducted without the Confederacy's formal support and was based upon the mistaken belief that cotton was "king." The assumption was that Great Britain and France could be forced to break the Union blockade in order to obtain cotton because their basic values were mercantile greed and a concern for profit. A bonus for planters was the expectation that a short cotton famine would raise the price of cotton and increase their profits.

Planters and the general public announced that those who were patriots would keep cotton from the market to create an artificial shortage, thereby showing foreigners that they were dependent on a regular supply of cotton.

The withholding of cotton from the international market did result in a European "cotton famine." However, the boycott was ineffective in changing the French or British positions in part because mill owners had an oversupply of cotton at the time. The previous crop had been larger than the mills could process, and Egypt and India were beginning to export cotton. In addition, linen and woolen mills increased their production by adding almost two hundred thousand workers to its labor force.

The Confederacy missed an opportunity to send their cotton on their own initiative before the blockade became effective. Cotton bought for 6–10 cents a pound in the South during the war could be sold in Europe for 50–90 cents a pound. Southern alpha distain of those considered inferiors and their own lack of Yankee business acumen greatly weakened the finances of the Confederacy.

The boycott actually supported the Union's strategy to limit cotton exports as a source of Confederate wealth. The South exported three million bales during 1859–1860. The Union blockade, though inefficient at the time, limited cotton exports during 1860–1861 to fifty thousand bales or 2 percent of the previous period (Foote and Hess 2021, 61).

The boycott was another failure in that it alienated potential allies. The boycott was initiated by the general public, but the British and French refused to accept the Confederate government's declarations that it was not involved. No such activity would have been possible if Confederate government leaders had not allowed and encouraged the boycott. The British assumed that the cotton boycott was an official policy in spite of the denials by Jefferson Davis (Owsley 1959, 30).

The Confederacy's bullying alpha-type tactics alienated potential international allies and limited cotton sales. The Confederate government and state officials should have exported cotton in the early days to provide finances for the war effort. It was only later that the Ordinance Bureau and the Medical Corps purchased five blockade runners to export cotton and import war material and medicines (Vandiver 1984, 115).

Some planters during the boycott avoided the cotton boycott by selling their cotton to Northern agents. The editors of the *Harper's*

Weekly (volume 5, No. 211, January 12, 1861, 18) noted that the sale of cotton bales in Memphis, Tennessee, increased from a former amount of 57,000 bales to 300,000 bales during 1860 and an expected 1,000,000 bales for 1861.

The Southern ports able to receive oceangoing ships, such as Mobile, New Orleans, and Savannah, had been closed to cotton exports, but some planters avoided the boycott by shipping their cotton to Memphis for illegal sale in the North. This pattern of growing and then selling cotton to Northern agents became a common practice. Planters continued to grow cotton instead of growing more food crops, especially corn, to feed the military and the families of those who fought (Woodworth 2000, 44).

By the end of the war, Confederate port cities were overflowing with bales of cotton. Thousands of unsold bales were stored in the streets after the warehouses had been filled. The planters could not stop themselves from growing cotton.

CHAPTER 4

THE CAVALIER MINDSET

The Knightliest of the Knightliest race,
That since the days of old
Have kept the lamp of chivalry
Alight in hearts of gold.
—Francis Orray Ticknor, "The Virginians of the Valley"

The term *cavalier* defined the ideal behavior and character of Southern white men and became a significant additional label to an already established Southern identity. The traditional term "gentleman" as a public identity denoted a social designation of superiority based on refined behavior as well as inheritance of high social class membership. The image of the cavalier added to the gentleman ideal the attributes of a medieval knight: courage, duty, willingness to gamble, militancy, leadership, and a ruler over others.

Confederate Cavaliers were impatient with mundane affairs such as administration and were more comfortable with short-term goals and immediate action. Jefferson Davis realized Southerners needed quick victories reflecting a "quixotic devotion to protocols of the *geste*."

An 1833 critic of Virginians complained Virginian leaders were enthusiastic for a short time but abandoned mundane tasks because they were easily bored (Ruffin 1834, 201):

> A remarkable and notorious characteristic of Virginians, is to commence the support of any good and popular scheme, with vehement and overflowing zeal—and having thus wasted our energy in the outset ... finally cease entirely to make them ... We act more from feeling, than from reasoning. We start forward to aid a good cause, as most of us would rush to a joyous festival—the wearisomeness and lassitude which always follow the pursuit and enjoyment of mere pleasure.

William Alexander Carruthers (1802–1846) was the first to use the term "cavalier" in a publication. Carruthers wrote a number of popular novels promoting the cavalier image, including *The Cavaliers of Virginia, or The Recluse of Jamestown: An Historical Romance of the Old Dominion.* The heroic cavalier image was usually presented as a young, wealthy gentleman who was noble in character as well as gallant and knightly in behavior. Virginians considered themselves to be superior cavaliers.

Robert E. Lee became the most respected cavalier in the Confederacy in part because he looked the part. After meeting Lee for the first time, and before he became a famous warrior, diarist and member of the Southern elite Mary Chesnut described him (Woodward 1981, 116):

> A man riding a beautiful horse joined us. He wore a hat with somehow a military look to it. He sat on his horse gracefully, and he was so distinguished.

The terms *cavalier, knight,* and *gallant* include the notion of being a gentleman with the addition of a superior (and imagined) genealogy of Norman (knightly conquerors of England), French, and Scottish ancestry. The term includes being imagined descendants of valiant and chivalrous knights. The latter includes an ancestry of honorable patriots fighting the more numerous British to remain independent (Schivelbusch 2003, 48). The addition of the cavalier-related nomenclature adds a warlike, aggressively military dimension to the Southern self-image.

This mindset was reflected in the description by a participant in a minor cavalry engagement during what is now called the East Cavalry Field engagement taking place during the third day of the Battle of Gettysburg (Gragg 2013, 289):

> A joust or tournament, where the knights, advancing from their respective sides, charge full tilt upon each other in the middle of the field.

The epitome of the cavalier image as a gentleman and warrior is found in the person of Robert E. Lee. Lee realized he had a temper and fought to control himself. He was always conscious of his public image and maintained a dignified image while in public. He was a good horseman, ever courteous, and had the correct social credentials. Lee could relax, as did many cavaliers, only when in the company of women, children, and enslaved persons. These were persons who could not challenge a gentleman's reputation as a noble cavalier.

The apex of his cavalier behavior is illustrated by Lee's demeanor during his surrender of his army at the Appomattox Court House on April 9, 1865. Lee, dressed in his best uniform, carried his formal sword for the occasion and gently guided his conversation with Grant to the topic of surrender. After Grant had offered very liberal surrender terms that did not damage Lee's and his army's honor,

Lee calmly and with dignity rode his horse back to his troops. This behavior continued until his death on October 12, 1870.

Lee viewed gentlemanlike behavior as an important personality attribute. When he became president of Washington College, Lee instituted three major reforms. He de-emphasized the classics as irrelevant to a modern education. Instead, he introduced more practical subjects, such as civil engineering and journalism. Lee discarded the student behavior code. He informed new arrivals that there would be no formal rules of behavior and instead expected all students to behave as gentlemen.

Opposite the status of "cavalier" was the Southerners' stereotype of Northerners as intolerant and uncouth merchants concerned only with business and profit. A joke enjoyed among Confederates during the Civil War is the account of a Rebel who was about to be shot by a federal soldier. Instead of waiting to be shot, the Rebel pulled out his pocketbook and offered to buy the man's gun, which was duly offered up by the Northerner (Rable 2015, 35)! Member of the South Carolina elite Mary Chesnut reflected this view (Woodward 1981, 410), "Yankees do not undertake anything that does not pay." An 1861 poem enjoyed by Southerners stressed the amoral, greedy behavior of Yankees in general (Vandiver 1999, 9):

> Yankee Doodle is a knave,
> And everybody knows it,
> And swindling is his natural trade,
> For by his tricks he shows it.

The term *gentleman* continued to be used with the addition of the more militant term *cavalier,* though both differentiated the superiority of elite Southerners from both Southern inferiors and Northerners.

The Emergence of the Cavalier Ideal

There were many reasons why the cavalier image emerged as a dominant cultural ideal during the first part of the nineteenth century. The development of a slave economy necessitated a concept of the social superiority of whites. Wealth per se in the South was not as openly respected as it was in the North, but in its place was the inheritance of cultural superiority and ownership of enslaved persons. Racism, white supremacy, and elitism are also core elements of the cavalier ideology.

Nostalgia for a Superior Past

Parts of the South had declined economically during the first half of the 1800s, especially when compared to the developing Northern economy and urban centers (Watson 1985, 45). The North was outstripping the South in population, industrialization, wealth, urbanization, most agricultural and industrial products, and intellectual productions. As important, much of the agricultural land in the upper South was becoming less productive because the constant growing of crops, such as tobacco and cotton, destroys the fertility of the soil. A consequence of this decline was the past becoming more attractive than the present. It was more comfortable to be part of a mystical heroic past and adopt more idealistic and flattering medieval values than to accept more problematic and modern self-images.

By contrast, the more dynamic North promoted the "Promethean impulse" where the past was denigrated vis-à-vis the future. Southerners promoted a heroic past as a model for their society and themselves (Watson 1985, 31).

Southern authors began to emphasize these regional differences by developing the myth of a superior society dominated by the images of the slave-owning cavalier and gentleman in contrast to the presumed unrefined money-grubbing Northerner. A new vision (or stereotype) of Southern society centered on what Watson characterizes as (1985, ix) "idealized fictional landscapes … [and a] larger-than-life figure of the Southern aristocrat, or Cavalier."

The Lack of External Intellectual Influences

The development of the cavalier stereotype was facilitated by the fact that white Southerners were intellectually isolated. Relatively few Southerners read books or magazines. Few books were published in the South, and first-rate authors from the South were rare. The most common themes of Southern intellectuals were defenses of slavery or descriptions of an idealized South. The books found in plantation libraries were commonly medical references, almanacs, the Bible, and works by Shakespeare and Sir Walter Scott. Scott wrote a series of novels based on the theme of heroic knights winning over villains and saving damsels in distress. Mark Twain (Twain 1883, 349) called the Southern fascination with medieval themes and the South's lack of modern industry "the Scott disease."

Athleticism More Important than Learning

Some Southerners were highly educated and could speak and read one or two foreign languages. They were also superficially familiar with the Greek and Roman classics, but most reading was restricted to novelists such as Charles Dickens and Sir Walter Scott. Nationally respected Southern scholar Basil Gildersleeve explained this general lack of readership by noting that the Southern elite preferred politics to scholarship. It was better to rule and orate than to read (Briggs 1998, 8). Teachers and tutors were given low levels of prestige in the South.

Literate pursuits were not part of the cavalier requirements. Horsemanship and theatric courage were more respected than knowledge. Southern politicians excelled in a Victorian rhetorical style that was flowery and emotional. The public expected a high level of oratory, which included long speeches dealing with analyses of current issues and heated oratory. Speeches at the time were major entertainments and a source of information.

Basil Gildersleeve was a partial exception to the lack of intellectuals in the South. He received a doctorate in the classics from Germany and became a nationally respected scholar in Greek studies. He was one of the few Southern scholars who gained respect outside of the South. Basil and his three brothers enlisted soon after the fall of Fort Sumter. He explained his rationale for his support for secession and his enlistment (Briggs 1998, 11):

> The cause [i.e., secession] was one for which I wrote, prayed, fought, suffered but in the long agony [i.e., the war] I never was haunted by a doubt as to the righteousness of the course which we followed and even if there had been a doubt as to the justice of our cause, the command of the state would have sufficed.

For Gildersleeve, his state identity trumped any logic or reason to secede. He was able to teach the Greek classics at the University of Virginia during the winters and rejoin the Army of Northern Virginia during the summers to take part in the spring campaigns. As a defender of slavery, Gildersleeve's rationale for the war was the defense of states' rights and the refusal to surrender any personal right or freedom that would have been seen as a dishonorable "submission" resulting in his own slavery. This rationale was supported by his view that the Southern elite were cavaliers and paragons of honor (*sans peur et sans reproche*). His vision of Southern society was the commonly held view of a superior society because of and based on slavery.

At times, a Confederate hero would not meet these impossible social demands, yet he might be considered a cavalier if his behavior were admirable. The vice president of the Confederacy, Alexander Stephens, was short in stature, suffered from a number of physical ailments, looked boyish, and had a high-pitched voice. However, Stephens was once lauded as "a Knight in chivalry and in courage" (Hébert 2021, 23). Southerners developed a unique, quasi-medieval nomenclature to describe and praise their heroes even when they did not completely fit the cavalier image.

The Importance of Bravery for Cavalier Status

In addition to ignoring physical ailments of those designated as cavaliers, there was a tendency to ignore other weaknesses of those deemed brave and honorable. Edward Alfred Pollard, journalist and author, noted (Pollard 1869, 262–63):

> There is an excess of admiration in the world for the courage that despises physical dangers. More than this there appears to be a certain indulgence for all the weaknesses of men accounted brave … The people of the South are excessive in their admiration of low physical courage. A certain amount of animal combativeness has been often vulgarly taken for a type of "Southern Chivalry."

Pollard criticized Jefferson Davis for being a bad president of the Confederacy, though he was admittedly brave and knightly in posture. Pollard believed that Davis (Pollard 1869, 107) "of all men in the South—ruined this cause [i.e., Confederate independence]." Pollard criticized other Confederate leaders for the same reason, that courage excused many weaknesses.

Cavalier Denial of Failure

Cavaliers feared that defeats would be defined by the public as personal moral failures and the result of cowardice. A consequence of this fear of failure was to ignore defeats, define them as victories, or blame others for their own failures (Thrasher 2021, 38). A major element of the cavalier mindset was blaming scapegoats for their own failures. The consequence of these denials was a lack of recognizing the reasons for battle defeats or other failures. Failures were not analyzed to avoid them in the future.

Two Types of Cavaliers

Two general mindsets contrast cavalier ways of behaving: the *Spanish* and the *Italian* types (Wilson 1990, 55). Most of the Southern elites were a mixture of both cavalier types, though some exhibited extreme characteristics of one or the other. All cavaliers, however, exhibited the values of courage, social superiority, gambling and taking chances, leadership, and militancy. The differences between the Spanish and Italian cavaliers were in how they expressed these values. A description of each cavalier type in its extreme form allows for a better understanding of the behavior of the leaders of the Confederacy and their counterproductive behaviors.

The Spanish Cavalier

The first type of cavalier is the *Spanish*. Opposite to the Italian type, the *Spanish* cavalier prefers an austere lifestyle of self-sacrifice and ascetic in behavior, including an avoidance of foul language, tobacco, and alcohol. This cavalier sees duty as a dominating force in his actions. Many seem haughty and intolerant because they evaluate others by their own high standards of behavior. Their sense of duty often results in Spanish cavaliers becoming workaholics and a refusal to delegate work tasks to others. Spanish cavaliers are able to plan for the long term and are less likely to rush into action without planning.

The most effective Confederate military and civilian leaders were Spanish cavaliers. Jefferson Davis, Robert E. Lee, Thomas "Stonewall" Jackson, and Nathan Bedford Forrest were cavaliers of the Spanish type. In an earlier era, Virginians George Washington and Thomas Jefferson represented the Spanish cavalier ideal, though the latter was not a soldier.

Spanish cavaliers were more dubious about the wisdom and necessity for the secession of the slave states in large part because they were better able to plan for the long term and evaluate the consequences of their behavior and the behavior of others. Many feared the consequences of secession, including Robert E. Lee. Spanish cavaliers supported secession as a duty to their states after the Confederacy was established and their states had seceded.

Self-sacrifice, attention to detail, dedication to work, and a sense of duty are core values for the Spanish cavalier. An example of a high sense of duty as well as sacrifice is the explanation David Pierson gave his father for having enlisted on April 22, 1861 (Kreiser and Browne 2011, 34):

> I have volunteered because I thought it my duty to do so … and if I perish it will be but a sacrifice which duty impels every patriot to make upon the altar of his Country's Glory.

Spanish Cavalier Nathan Forrest

Though from a poor family background, Nathan Bedford Forrest is a representative of the Spanish type of cavalier. Six feet one inches tall and Puritan in behavior, he was single-minded in finding and defeating the enemy as if the war were a personal venture. Forrest was wounded four times and personally killed thirty Union soldiers (Woodworth 1990, 132).

Forrest looked partly like a cavalier, though he also exhibited signs of his lower-class origins. He seldom drank alcohol and did not smoke. He was an avid gambler (a cavalier trait), and he always dressed well—but not in a flamboyant manner. He cursed fluently when angry, but he did not curse in front of women.

Forrest had a temper he did not always control, and he often verbally abused others, though he was capable of apologizing for his behavior. Forrest once insulted an acquaintance, and a duel was immediately arranged for the next day. Forrest reconsidered and went to the other man that evening and apologized, though he had remarked to friends he knew he "could beat him."

Forrest's military style was similar to "Stonewall" Jackson's and William Tecumseh Sherman's (all from non-elite backgrounds, though Sherman belonged to a politically prominent family). They avoided frontal attacks and used ambush, maneuvers, and surprise. Their tactics belonged more to guerrilla-style warfare than to Napoleonic tactics and the grand gestures favored by cavaliers.

Forrest exhibited a strong sense of duty to the Confederacy. He quarreled with most of his superiors because he believed they were incompetent and less dedicated to the Southern cause. He was especially antagonistic toward those he thought were not willing to fight at a strongly dedicated level. Needing recruits, Forrest once rode into a town and conscripted all the military-age men who had not already enlisted. When one man asked to be allowed to go home to settle his affairs, Forrest pistol-whipped him in response (Daniel 1991, 118).

In another situation, Forrest asked that Lieutenant Andrew Gould be transferred from his command because of his alleged cowardice. When they next met, they began to curse each other. Forrest pulled out a penknife, and Gould drew his revolver. Forrest stabbed Gould in a lung, and Gould shot Forrest above the hip. A doctor tending Forrest told him he would probably die from his wound. Forrest then rose from his sickbed and chased after Gould because no one, Forrest declared, could kill him without also dying in turn.

Making certain he was better armed, Forrest found Gould and shot at him. He missed and accidently hit a bystander. Ironically, Gould died of his previous wound, and Forrest was able to ride his horse in less than two weeks (Daniel 1991, 114). The Spanish cavalier could be as violent as anyone, but his violence was often associated with anger at the lack of duty of others.

Spanish Cavalier Jefferson Davis

Jefferson Davis was a model of a Spanish cavalier, reflecting its strengths as well as its weaknesses. Like most Spanish cavaliers, Davis was a workaholic, but he couldn't delegate. He believed he and only he was competent enough to fulfill his duties. His sense of duty was absolute. Davis continued to work while in his bed when his health failed. He often suffered from bouts of malaria and corneal ulceration, which caused debilitating headaches and recurrent pain. He nevertheless worked at home or while in his sickbed when these diseases attacked (McPherson 2014, 7).

Davis considered himself a skilled warrior and strategist. He once admitted, "If I could take one wing and Lee take the other, I think we could between us wrest a victory from those people." Many of Davis's generals, such as P. G. T. Beauregard, preferred more aggressive behavior, though their plans were often unrealistic.

Davis also exhibited a too-strong cavalier sense of superiority. He reacted with a lack of diplomacy and tact to those he considered having opinions different from his. Davis believed he was superior to everyone except his close friends. He disliked being told anything and especially being criticized by others. His wife admitted he was not diplomatic enough to become a successful politician, and Davis felt threatened by those who offered him advice or stated their own opinions too openly.

Those who avoided criticizing Davis and continuously praised him, as did Lee and Judah Benjamin, maintained his friendship. Sam Houston described him as (Foote 1958, 13) "ambitious as Lucifer and cold as a lizard."

Similar to other Spanish cavaliers, Davis had a martial personality. He was a West Point graduate, and his best friends, such as Braxton Bragg and Albert Sidney Johnston, were fellow graduates. To others' dismay, Davis considered himself a superior military strategist. Davis had been honored (breveted) for his action and courage during the Mexican War, had received a wound that bothered him for the rest of his life, and had been an effective and innovative secretary of war. He may have been the best candidate for the presidency in spite of his egoism.

Unlike the general Confederate public and Italian cavaliers, Davis was able to plan for the long term, and he realized that a war with the Union would last longer than most Confederates believed. He began to develop a war-based infrastructure even before the war officially began. Davis was the linchpin in the development of the Confederacy into a nation capable of fighting a premodern war for four years.

A Formerly Enslaved Spanish Cavalier

William Ellison reflected the Spanish cavalier type, though he was never accepted as such by the local white community. Born enslaved in 1790, twelve-year old Black American Ellison was apprenticed by his owner to a gin manufacturer (enslaved children began to work at ages nine to twelve). His father was either his owner or his owner's son (Johnson and Roark 1984), and working in a shop and learning a trade would be preferred to becoming a field hand.

Ellison earned his freedom and opened a cotton gin and blacksmith shop in cotton-producing Sumterville, South Carolina. He quickly became successful, but he needed slave labor to expand his gin production and repair. At the time, the most common way to expand a business or plantation while also gaining prestige was to own or hire enslaved workers. In a similar fashion, Ellison bought both land and slaves as his wealth and local credit increased.

As was done by freed Black Americans, Ellison's first purchases included family members and then enslaved workers. By 1860, he had become one of the 3,776 free Black Americans owning an estimated four thousand slaves. Owning two slaves in 1820, Ellison owned sixty-three slaves as well as nine hundred acres in 1860, one year before his death (Johnson and Roak 1984, 340).

Ellison was single-minded in his pursuit of wealth and security. He did so in large part by developing a reputation among local whites for honesty and quality work in an area where making and repairing cotton gins was in great demand. He was not seen as a threat to the white community because Ellison's ownership of enslaved persons indicated an acceptance of the institution of slavery. Ellison also maintained a humble and upright reputation among the white leaders of the community. Ellison became one of the wealthiest enslaved-owning landowners in the area.

Ellison's road to success necessitated behavior reflected in the Spanish cavalier mindset, and he had no other choice than to maintain a reputation for honesty and hard work. Ellison also conformed to neighboring white planters' expected behavior of Black Americans by behaving in a humble manner. Not doing so would have lost his white sponsors' protection and sponsorship.

Ellison's owning of enslaved workers showed how the institution of slavery permeated Southern culture. It was almost necessary to own enslaved persons in order to be economically successful—even for Black Americans. There were almost no other avenues for high levels of social mobility and wealth.

The Italian Cavalier

The second type of cavalier is the *Italian* model, which is defined as someone demonstrating a self-indulgent, generally theatrical lifestyle. Lavish living and an emphasis on hospitality are its more positive elements. Negative characteristics include gambling, excessive drinking, and acting before thinking. Italian cavaliers considered their own desires for glory and excitement over the demands of others, including their military superiors.

Miguel de Cervantes's title character in his novel *Don Quixote* saw the world from a personal, romantic perspective. The major theme of the work is an attack on the Italian type of chivalry as unrealistic. A barmaid could become a lady in Don Quixote's mind, and a windmill could be transformed into a ferocious giant. The author denounced the Italian mode of chivalry as a type of insanity, though at times, it was a noble one.

In the military, Italian cavaliers could be recognized by their ostentatious dress. Their uniforms were ornate and embellished with ribbons and lace, their hair would be perfumed, and their hats would be capped with feathers. Such "peacock generals," as they were called, originated from the upper classes and could afford tailored uniforms and personal servants. They viewed battles as romantic opportunities for gaining personal honor and fame. These peacock officers were often more concerned with their own self-image than the more practical and the immediate goals of the Confederacy. Their major characteristics of impulsive, flamboyant, and theatrical behavior can best be described by the French word *panache* or the Italian word *brio*.

A feature of the Italian cavalier type is a lack of concern for the consequences of his behavior. This indicates an aristocratic distain for practical concerns, including losing large sums of money. Gambling on horses and cards and land speculation were major entertainment. The Italian cavalier ideally experienced financial losses with aplomb and a seeming disinterest. Italian cavaliers were also likely to gamble in military situations to augment their self-image.

It was primarily this type of cavalier that Edward C. Pollard complained that their "juvenile mind" made Southerners "deficient in the practical application of means to end" (Maddox 1974, 66). It is also because of the widespread presence of the Italian cavaliers that Frank E. Vandiver (1987, 172) described Southern culture as "a way of life already in decay."

This "decay," also recorded by Henry Adams, included the behavior of Southern scions while attending universities. University attendance was often an extension of their previous idleness and offered new opportunities for pleasure (Johnson and Roark 1984, 87). In the Italian cavalier fashion, many Southern university students brought their own horses for recreation. The expulsion rates for Southern students were high because of their riotous behavior, inadequate preparation, and lack of interest in their courses. The West Point curriculum was primarily focused on engineering. If prepared at all, Southern cadets, like many others, were well versed in the classics rather in the sciences.

Disorderly conduct and lack of study consistently placed Lewis Addison Armistead at the bottom of his West Point class. Armistead failed to pass the first year of instruction three times, but he was allowed to remain at West Point because of his family's political and military connections. He finally resigned from West Point in order to avoid a second court-martial because he had been accused of breaking a dinner plate over a fellow cadet's head (McMillan 2021, 23). Armistead, like many Italian cavaliers, was both aggressive and an underperforming scholar.

Italian cavaliers were typically egotistical and concerned more for their reputations than the Confederacy they served. General Earl Van Dorn dressed in a flamboyant and "dapper" manner, but he was also an erratic, "unsteady" leader (McMurry 1989, 114). Van

Dorn was obsessed with gaining fame and glory (Carter 1999, xii). Ever the romantic cavalier, Van Dorn was a superb horseman and an aggressive warrior as well as reckless in love. Dorn maintained a secret five-year affair with Martha Goodbread, and she bore Van Dorn three children (Carter 1999, 32–33). His flirtations were well-known, and one affair resulted in the involved husband fatally shooting him.

Typical of Italian cavaliers, Van Dorn did not easily accept the demands of rigid discipline. As a West Point cadet, Van Dorn annually accumulated large amounts of demerits for violating rules. During his third year, he accumulated 193 demerits when two hundred demerits would have resulted in his automatic dismissal. Van Dorn was also a mediocre student and graduated fifty-second in his class of fifty-six (Hartje 1967, 14–15).

Van Dorn lost the battle of Pea Ridge in March 1862 to a smaller force partly because he had ignored logistics and left his men underequipped and underfed. Van Dorn lost another battle through his failure of reconnaissance. Italian cavaliers often failed by ignoring such mundane details as logistics and reconnaissance and refusing to cooperate with colleagues and superiors.

Van Dorn nevertheless became successful as a cavalry commander in part because less-disciplined cavalry raids were more acceptable to Italian cavaliers. Van Dorn's cavalry division traveled into enemy territory to destroy a vital Union supply depot at Holly Springs as well as bridges and telegraph communications. Van Dorn also claimed to have captured 1,800 prisoners (Carter 1999, 157).

With the cooperation of Nathan Bedford Forrest, Van Dorn forced Ulysses S. Grant to retreat and end one of his campaigns to capture Vicksburg. At the high point of his reputation, Van Dorn was killed by a husband claiming Van Dorn had seduced his wife. The angry husband was acquitted because Van Dorn was a known philanderer, and the aggrieved husband was obviously defending his honor against a known seducer. It was discovered later that Van Dorn had also seduced and impregnated the husband's fourteen-year-old daughter (Mitcham 2022, 665).

Assuming their own superiority, Italian cavaliers were often considered too haughty and self-involved though they were sociable and enjoyed parties and social gatherings. A more serious colleague of Earl Van Dorn described him as a (Carter 1999, 77) "coxcomb, dandy, fop, ball-room beau, and such a thing of paint, perfume and feathers." Italian cavaliers often did wear their hair long and perfumed, and they were consistently well-uniformed with extra gold braids, feathers, fancy gloves, and shiny boots. They were careful to ride the most attractive horses.

Italian cavaliers reflected the general attitude of focusing on the short term rather than planning for the future. Immediate victories and fame were common goals for Italian cavaliers, but they ignored the long-term consequences of their actions. Like many Southerners, Italian cavaliers reacted to crises and current conditions rather than preparing for future demands (DeCredico 1990, 67).

The Aggressive Courage of Cavaliers

Author Steven Hardesty (Hardesty 2016, 2) noted, "People go to war for many reasons but culture decides how they will make war." The South failed to gain its independence because "its military and political leaders could not recognize and transcend the limits of the culture that made them."

Courage and calmness under fire were paramount traits of both types of cavaliers. Jefferson Davis was correct when he claimed that Southerners glorified war and the warrior spirit. The practical consequences of this attitude were that bravery under all circumstances was a major element of the cavalier personality—even when such activities were not productive and resulted in unnecessary casualties. Cavaliers also preferred aggressive military strategies, such as frontal charges—even against fortified enemies—over defensive military campaigns.

Instead of favoring a more defensive policy where casualties would be fewer, Confederate soldiers preferred offensive tactics. During the last part of the war, Union and Rebel frontline soldiers dug rifle pits (i.e., foxholes) and fortifications when reaching a battle site. However, Confederate soldiers preferred more aggressive charges rather than waiting for the Federals to attack.

Few commanders on either side realized that recent development in firearms afforded a three-time advantage to the defensive over the offensive (McWhiney 2002, 125). There were even more advantages to defensive positions when Union forces were able to obtain breech-loading and repeating rifles. Soldiers of that era received little target practice. The rapidity of firing gave protected forces an advantage over enemies charging toward them for two hundred yards or more.

Consequences of the Cavalier Self-image

The Southern elite considered themselves descendants of British cavaliers and Norman knights. A consequence of this mythology was the belief that Southerners were innate warriors. No training was necessary to conduct war. All one needed for military success was personal courage, gallantry, and the will to attack (Davis 2002, 91). This mindset was successful often enough to encourage frontal attacks—even though the casualties were high.

Southern cavaliers often imagined themselves to be literal cavaliers excelling in war, a reputation believed by Northerners during the first part of the year (Adams 1978, 100). This myth encouraged many of the Southern elite to join the cavalry and resulted in an excess of cavalry troopers in comparison to the infantry. Two Prussian observers, von Borcke and Justus Scheibert, observed (Borcke and Scheibert 1976, 37):

> The Confederate cavalry was made up of those valiant country men who were able to provide their own horses. Almost every large plantation, even small farms, had contributed their sons to the cavalry. *For it was precisely this arm of the service that suited the taste and character of the Southerner best* [emphasis added].

Men in the Union also rode horses, and there were more horses per capita in the North than in the South (Adams 1978, 43). However, the Federal cavalry was considered inferior and did not, in fact, perform well during the first years of the war. The fault with the Union cavalry was most likely a lack of adequate leadership and inferior horses and not because of a general characteristic of Northerners. With training and better selection of horses, the Union cavalry became a formidable adjunct to Union infantry. The Union enjoyed a larger number of horses than did the Confederacy. The Confederacy began to lack horses by 1863.

Experience taught that the midwestern northern horse was a better steed than the more cavalier-owned thoroughbred. The Morgan was developed in New England and was a hardy animal. "Stonewall" Jackson's favorite steed, Little Sorel, was from Connecticut and had been captured in a raid by John Hunt.

The cavalier mindset was romanticized and unrealistic. As dangerous to the Confederate chances of victory was the cultural characteristic of, according to Vandiver (1992, 32), the tendency of ignoring truth (i.e., facts) and relying on "wishes." This tendency was a dysfunctional element of the romantic element of the cavalier mindset.

Consistent with the belief that military training was less important than bravery and boldness, the Confederate cavalier showed a tendency to go against orders and engage in rash forays into enemy territory. The most successful Confederate raider was Brigadier General John Hunt Morgan. Morgan's forte was raiding and guerilla tactics, which allowed for heroic and theatrical activities and the possibility of personal fame (Woodworth 1990, 134).

Italian Cavalier John Hunt Morgan

John Hunt "Thunderbolt" Morgan was representative of the Italian cavalier. Known as a gambler, a womanizer, and a father of at least one child by an enslaved woman, he was also known as an argumentative person and a daring cavalry leader. Morgan attended two years of college until he was suspended for dueling.

His first raid into Kentucky during 1862 resulted in more than one thousand captured Union horses, hundreds of captive Union soldiers, and large quantities of destroyed supplies. His most famous raid took place a year later during June 11–July 26, 1863, when Morgan and his command reached into Indiana and Ohio while suffering casualties from local militias. Morgan and his surviving men were eventually captured. His escape from prison became legendary. The raid was nevertheless romanticized as a daring and heroic example of the Confederate cavalier culture, though it accomplished little long-term advantage for the Confederacy.

Typical of cavalier behavior, Morgan's raid was conducted against orders with little lasting result except that he became one of the most admired Confederate heroes. While his raids at times did not fulfill their official purposes, the Confederate public expected their generals to be aggressive as well as theatrical. One form of praise after his most famous raid was the poem celebrating his exploits (it was a rare admired Confederate general who did not receive a poem or song describing his exploits):

> Morgan, Morgan, the raider, and Morgan's
> Terrible men,

With Bowie knives and pistols are galloping
Up the glen.

Morgan had become a Celtic knight! The reference to "Bowie knives and pistols" highlights a Confederate romancing of personal combat. It would have been more effective had the Confederacy invested in repeating Spencer carbines for its cavalry.

A Negative Example of a Cavalier

Major General George Edward Pickett exemplified to a considerable extent the negative characteristics of the Confederate cavalier image. Used to commanding others, Pickett did not like to follow orders. Graduating last in his West Point class (traditionally called the "goat"), Pickett was a lazy student and gathered almost enough demerits to be automatically expelled. He can be best described as "indolent" (Guelzo 2013, 378).

Egotistical, the adult Pickett was, cavalier-like, concerned with his appearance. He wore a tailored uniform with a double row of gold buttons and gold spurs. His riding crop, which he carried with him when riding and walking, was a symbol of his superiority over others. His hair and beard were carefully combed and perfumed. In spite of a commendable record, Pickett was more likely to tell his command to advance than to lead them. He also was absent without leave whenever it suited him.

Pickett spent part of Pickett's Charge behind a large tree while he, his younger brother, and his staff spent some time drinking whiskey. Pickett was the only general of his grade who did not personally lead his men in the iconic Pickett's Charge (Tucker 2016, 233–34).

The Romance of War: Pickett's Charge

The romantic mindset of both types of cavaliers is illustrated by how Southern historians described battles, especially Pickett's Charge (ideally named the Pickett-Pettigrew-Trimble Charge) during the third day of the Battle of Gettysburg on July 3, 1863. This aspect of the iconic Battle of Gettysburg has been romanticized by Southern historians. No other battle of the Civil War captured the imagination and interest of historians and the general public. Even the very controlled historian Harry Hansen devoted twenty-two pages to the battle and described the beginning of Pickett's Charge (Hansen 2002, 386):

> Then the Confederate guns stopped firing after two hours of bombardment, the smoke lifted, and the regiments and brigades came forward to take part in *the most thrilling and tragic spectacle ever seen on the American continent* [emphasis added].

No better example of Southern military romanticism is found than in E. A. Pollard's description of Pickett's Charge. While Pollard's account contains factual errors, he attains a high level of rhetorical romanticism typical of midcentury Southern historians and commentators (Pollard 1866, volume 2, 38–40):

> The enemy replied with terrific spirit, from their batteries posted along the heights. Never had been heard such tremendous artillery firing in the war. The warm and sultry air was hideous with discord. Dense columns of smoke hung over the beautiful valley. The lurid flame leaps madly from the cannon's mouth, each moment the roar grows more intense; now chime in volleys of small arms. For one hour and a half this most terrific fire was

continued, during which time the shrieking of shells, the crashing of falling timber, the fragments of rock flying through the air, shattered from the cliffs by solid shot, the heavy muttering from the valley between the opposing armies, the *splash* of bursting shrapnel, and the fierce neighing of wounded artillery-horses made a picture terribly grand and sublime [emphasis in the original].

But there was now to occur a scene of moral sublimity and heroism unequalled in the war. The storming party was moved up—Pickett's brigade, and on the left by Heth's division, commanded by Pettigrew. With steady measured tread the division of Pickett advanced upon the foe. Never did troops enter a fight in such splendid order. Their banners floated defiantly in the breeze as they pressed across the plain. The flags which had waved amid the wild tempest of battle of Gaines' Mill, Frazer's Farm, and Manassas, never rose more proudly. Kemper, with his gallant men, leads the right; Garnett brings up the left; and the veteran Armistead, with his brave troops, moved forward in support. The distance is more than half a mile. As they advance the enemy fire with great rapidity—shell and solid shot give place to grape and canister—the very earth quivers beneath the heavy roar—wide gaps are made in this regiment and that brigade. The line moves onward, cannons roaring, grape and canister plunging and ploughing through the ranks, bullets whizzing as thick as hail-stones in winter, and men falling as leaves in the blasts of autumn.

As Pickett got well under the enemy's fire, our batteries ceased firing, for want, it is said, of ammunition. It was a fearful moment—one in which was to be tested the pride and mettle of glorious Virginia. Into the sheets of artillery fire advanced the unbroken lines of Pickett' [*sic*] brave Virginians. They have reached Emmitsburg road, and here they meet a severe fire from heavy masses of the enemy's infantry, posted behind the stone fence, while their artillery, now free from the annoyance of our artillery, turn their whole fire upon this devoted band. Still they remain firm. Now again they advance. They reach the works—the contest rages with intense fury—men fight almost hand to hand—the red cross and the "stars and stripes" wave defiantly in close proximity. A Federal officer dashed forward in front of his shrinking columns, and with flashing sword, urges them to stand. General Pickett, seeing the splendid valor of his troops, moves among them as if courting death. The noble Garnett is dead, Armistead wounded, and the brave Kemper, with hat in hand, still cheering on his men falls from his horse. But Kemper and Armistead have already planted their banners in the enemy's work. The glad shout of victory is already heard.

But where is Pettigrew's division—where are the supports? The raw troops had faltered and the gallant Pettigrew himself had been wounded in vain attempts to rally them. The order is given to fall back, and our men commence the movement, doggedly contesting for every inch of ground. The enemy press heavily our retreating line, and many noble spirits who had passed safely through the fiery ordeal of the advance and charge, now fall on the right and on the left.

Pollard concludes his description of Pickett's Charge and then offers a series of excuses for why the campaign failed. Pollard next presents his analysis to claim neither army won a victory, though he does admit Lee's campaign had ended. Pollard then dismisses the consequences of the Battle of Gettysburg and mentions the Union capture of the city of Vicksburg as the real tragedy of the week. This second loss could not be blamed on Virginian troops and Lee but rather on distant western troops. The commander in charge of Vicksburg was John C. Pemberton (sent west because of his quarrelsome personality) who had been born in the North. The blame for Confederacy battle losses and hardships tended to be placed on "others" and anonymous outsiders. Jefferson Davis had given Pemberton the order to protect the city from Grant's attacks and to also protect his army. These orders were contradictory since Pemberton could not do both without help from other Confederate commands. The lack of cooperation from Lee and those generals stationed in the western theater left Pemberton helpless. Again, the Confederacy was weakened by confusion of aims and a lack of cooperation.

R. C. Horton expressed a similar reaction as Pollard's to Lee's loss at Gettysburg. Like Pollard, Horton was a secessionist, a propagandist, and an early proslavery historian of the Lost Cause. The quote below is found in a publication authored by Horton meant for children. Horton describes Pickett's Charge as heroic while ignoring its human and tactical losses (Horton 1866, 281–82):

> About three o'clock the Confederates prepared for a grand charge upon the position [i.e., Cemetery Hill]. Never was there a braver or more gallant charge. Though hundreds of cannons mowed through their ranks a swath of death, these war-worn veterans heeded them not. They thought themselves invincible, and rushed into the very jaws of death, if thereby they could themselves save

> their beloved land from the abolition destroyer. But in vain. No mortal men could withstand this tempest of leaden and iron hail. Slowly they fell back, but without dismay or confusion … *indeed, so far as the battle was concerned, it was a drawn game.* It was only in its effects that it was disastrous to the Confederates. General Lee was short of ammunition. He had expected to capture it from his enemies. But failing in that, was forced to fall back for supplies [emphasis added].

Note the term "a drawn game" in the above quote. Southern cavalier vocabulary often described battle as a "game" and that Confederates were often willing to gamble in order to win. The expectation (i.e., gamble) that supplies would be available from a beaten enemy did not seem to Horton to be a failure in logistics. After all, Lee could have assumed that Union forces would also be short of ammunition after three days of battle. As expected, Horton uses the romantic term "gallant" to describe the men in Pickett's Charge.

Pickett's Charge, known as "Longstreet's Charge" for a short time after the event (Tucker 2016, xxii), was still viewed sixty years after the event as a heroic event by one of Lee's biographers. James C. Young was very favorable toward Lee, and he refused to criticize Lee in any way because he considered Lee both a military genius and a perfect cavalier. Young's description of Pickett's Charge is sparse and curiously bloodless as he exonerates "Marse Robert" as a knight free of any blame for the consequences of his failure in Pennsylvania (Young 1929, 247–48):

> On, the steady ranks go, withering under fire. Within five minutes it is clear that their task is beyond the human. Yet on they go. Lee has ordered it. Longstreet will not call them back. Perhaps—in

> the great scheme of the Fates—it had been written that they must fail … Longstreet—unexplainable man—has failed to throw in two strong divisions to the right.

Young concludes by saying, "Magnificent futility." As was common, Young believed the Battle of Gettysburg was "a victory in the negative sense" (Young 1929, 251), and he blames Longstreet for its failures. There is a disturbing element in the above quote that many Southern authors mention without admitting any criticism of Lee. The quote claims the charge might have been fated to fail. This strategy prevents Confederates from learning from their mistakes. Southerners were culturally conservative, and this attribute inhibited a mindset unable to seek and accept change.

Lee is seldom personally blamed for his mistakes by Southern authors but rather on "the fates" or other reasons external to Lee, including inadequate subordinate officers. Some modern historians do the same (Tucker 2016, 349 and 369). This fatalism allows Confederates to maintain hope of an eventual victory after numerous battle losses (Phillip's 2007).

Another description of the Pickett's Charge also emphasized its romantic elements rather than its consequences. Brigadier General Gilbert Moxley Sorrel was a member of Lee's army and de-emphasized the failure of the charge while stressing its glory (Sorrel 2019, 74):

> If there was repulse and its usual result, a quick flight for cover, there was also something else. A charge that, considering the difficulties of position, comparison of numbers, was so steady to the objective point, and so near success as to make it one of the greatest feats of arms in all the annals of war … To-day, the detail of the great charge, not as barely hinted at here, but as described in

> full with ample particulars, mounts one's blood, stirs all hearts with deep tragedy and pride ... The memory of Pickett's charge will forever live in song and story of that fair land for which the Southern soldier poured out his blood like water.

Sorrel was unique among Southern authors in that he begins his description of Pickett's Charge by admitting there was a retreat—a "repulse." He nevertheless devotes only one sentence to those who retreated and then conventionally stresses the romantic elements of "one of the greatest feats of arms in the annals of war."

The British and French newspapers also viewed the Battle of Gettysburg through rose-colored romanticism. *The Examiner* described the South's loss as "no more than a repulse." Confederate supporters in England also described the results of the battle as a minor "gleam of success" on the part of the North (Grant 2000, 48). Pro-Confederacy French observer Charles Girard noted (Girard 1962, 78):

> The battle of Gettysburg is presented [in Lee's report] as having been an unforeseen event in the campaign. General Lee had intended to have no battles whatever; his plan was to avoid fighting during the summer and rout the enemy with his tactics ... Nevertheless, a battle having started unexpectedly on July 1, he had to continue it until the evening of the third. On July 4 began that able retreat which the enemy could not harass.

Girard ignores the failure of Pickett's Charge and continues to stress the brilliancy of Lee's retreat—as do most Southern historians. Girard then notes that the casualties were easily replaceable and the battle itself was of little importance. Again, a lost battle was seen as a minor event with little consequence.

The Cavalier's Love of Gambling

Southerners gambled on cards, horses, cockfights, dice, and more. Cavaliers disliked professional gamblers and labeled them without honor since they gambled for money rather than for pleasure and excitement. By contrast, a gentleman who gambled as an act of recreation or daring was respected as long as he won or lost with equal nonchalance. This attitude continued under battle conditions.

Kenneth S. Greenberg presents the observation that the passion among cavaliers for gambling was repeated on the battlefield. Southern military strategists and tacticians gambled and took unreasonable risks. This acceptance of gambling resulted in unnecessarily high casualty rates even when these gambles won raids and battles. A trait of cavaliers in addition to gambling was bravery, which became an aggressive attitude to be exposed to danger. Most Confederate generals seemed to be willing to gamble their own lives to show their bravery and chivalric sangfroid coolness when under fire, and 55 percent of the 425 Confederate generals were either wounded in combat, killed, or both. This cultural necessity to show others their aggressive bravery was partly responsible for the fact that of those Confederate generals who were killed in battle, 70 percent fell during offensive maneuvers (McWhiney 2002, 34 and 132). Cowardice was a cultural fault most Confederates could not forgive. By contrast, facing danger was considered a sign of nobility and character.

Inappropriate attacks in the face of overwhelming odds were gambles that honorable Italian cavaliers could not resist (Greenberg 1996, 138):

> The Confederacy may have well have lost the Civil War as a result of lessons learned at Southern card tables and racetracks.

Robert E. Lee, a combination of both cavalier types, provides an example of the Spanish cavalier's acceptance of gambling. Spanish cavalier General James Longstreet argued with Lee that a frontal attack on the third afternoon of the Battle of Gettysburg could not succeed. Lee answered (Tucker 1983, 187), "They [i.e., the Union forces] are in position and I am going to whip them or they are going to whip me." The phrase "or they are going to whip me" reflects a willingness to gamble for victory or defeat. Lee was called "audacious," a term used to describe Spanish cavaliers.

Similar gambles by Lee had been successful in the past and may be classified as calculated risks. In this instance, however, Lee's gamble in ordering Pickett's Charge was a "winner-take-all" gamble that he almost won. If the charge had been successful, Lee's forces might have been able to divide Mead's command in two and attack the Union troops from the rear. Such a charge might also have been impossible to continue. The Rebels would have been exhausted and low in ammunition, and reinforcements might not have been available. The Union infantry and cavalry might have also blunted the charge after it reached its goals. Both Confederates and historians have considered "what-ifs" involving Pickett's Charge.

Lee's well-prepared tactics (Tucker 2016, 8) also involved a gamble he was willing to make. Although primarily a Spanish cavalier, Lee's behavior at times reflected Italian cavalier elements.

This attitude favoring military gambles stands in contrast to Ulysses S. Grant's beliefs (Fuller 1957, 82):

> I do not believe in luck in war any more than luck in business. Luck is a small matter, may effect a battle or a movement, but not a campaign or a career.

A central part of Grant's personality, such an attitude was a more common culture-based characteristic among Federals than

Confederates. Confederate officers would never mention luck as a "small matter" or admit there was a similarity between war and business. Grant's statement above also indicates a willingness to think about the long term.

In a sense, the commonly stated belief that God would decide whether a battle would be won or lost placed God in the role of "Lady Luck." John Bell Hood was typical of those who combined fatalistic and gambling attitudes that God was the ultimate arbiter:

> I am going to fight. The odds are against us, but I leave the issue with the God of battles.

Unsurprisingly, Hood was a cavalier general who preferred to attack whenever possible. He tended to use "sheer audacity" rather than planning and strategy when in command (Sword 1992, 375). Hood believed that an army that did not constantly attack would become cowardly with low morale.

Robert E. Lee's father, "Lighthorse" Harry Lee, was another example of an Italian cavalier. He was a brave warrior and one of Washington's favorite officers. The elder Lee was a self-indulgent gambler and land speculator, and he was dishonest as well. He mortgaged the same properties to different lenders and dissipated his two wives' fortunes (Lee men always married well).

He fled to Jamaica to avoid his debtors and another period in debtor's prison. Harry was also in bad health due to a beating and torture he received while protecting a friend from a mob. Harry was beaten and had hot wax poured in his eyes in an attempt to blind him. While Robert E. Lee adored his father, his dignified and disciplined behavior must have been influenced by his father's activities.

Italian Cavalier Captain Raphael Semmes

To the detriment of the Confederacy, the Italian cavalier culture encouraged symbolic victories over practical results, and the Confederate commerce raiders are superlative examples. The Confederate commerce raiders were symbolically and theatrically successful. The purpose of the Confederate commercial raiders was the destruction of the Union's commercial shipping. Their efforts were so successful that American commercial shipping did not recover for nearly one hundred years. However, the success of the Confederate commerce raiders had no practical result other than pleasing the British who now dominated commercial shipping. Foreign trade during the Civil War increased British shipping profits by one-third, and the Union continued to receive supplies as before (Owsley 1959, 554).

The captains of these commerce raiders became heroes in the Italian cavalier tradition, but the resources they used could have been used for better purposes (Fuller 1957, 33). Though the Union lost cargo, ransom gold, and merchant ships, the commerce raiders produced little direct harm to the Union's war capabilities. The strategy promising the most harm to the Union was the near destruction of the US whaling fleet because whale oil was used as a lubricant in the Union's factories and as lamp fuel. The attacks on unarmed whalers, however, occurred too late in the war to be effective (Vandiver 1984, 68).

A better alternative would have been to invest in building blockade runners or additional ironclads to attack the blockade itself and defend the major Confederate rivers. The Confederate secretary of the navy, Stephen R. Mallory, and his staff were more innovative than their army counterparts or the Union navy establishment. Mallory and his personnel could have better used the resources wasted by the commerce raiders.

The major benefit of the Confederate commerce raiders was to temporarily increase morale among the Confederate population

(Marvel 1996, 265). The false image of dueling dashing sea captains wreaking havoc among Yankee merchant ships fit the Southern mentality of manly knights besting an inferior enemy. Each ship sank, unlike land-based battles with their resulting casualties, was a distinct victory easily imagined and clearly understood. Ignored was the fact that the armed Confederate raiders attacked unarmed merchant vessels.

Though of little value to the successful pursuit of the war, naval victories falsely reinforced the Confederate belief that the destruction of Northern economic resources would force the assumed commercial and monetary-oriented Yankees to cease fighting the Confederacy.

Rafael Semmes, captain of the CSS *Sumter* and later the CSS *Alabama*, became one of the most celebrated and successful commerce raiders (Johnson 1997, 238–43) during his two-year attacks on Union merchant shipping. He was a superb navigator and was responsible for the capture or destruction of sixty-four merchant and whaling ships (Marvel 1996, 71). In January 1863, Semmes sank one Union warship in the first sea battle involving steamboats when he was captain of the CSS *Sumter*.

Semmes was cornered at the French port of Cherbourg by Captain John Winslow, a former shipmate and Union commander of the USS *Kearsarge*. The two ships were almost equal in terms of size, engine horsepower, and armament, though the CSS *Alabama* needed repairs (Keegan 2009, 282).

The only significant difference between the two ships was that the *Kearsarge's* sides had been covered with spare anchor chains to provide protection of its boilers from exploding shells. The chains had been covered by pine planks and painted black for concealment and aesthetic reasons. This action was also used to protect the sides of the *Kearsarge* from increasingly efficient and destructive naval cannons.

The *Alabama*'s gunpowder was old, and its gunners were unskilled. Their opponents had been unarmed ships, and

Semmes did not see the need to regularly expend hard-to-obtain gunpowder in firing practice. The Confederate practice of "what-if" to rationalize losses is found in the comments of an anonymous *Alabama* sailor in 1864. He claimed the *Alabama* would have won had its gunpowder been of better quality and if the fuses in the shells had ignited. The author did admit that the *Alabama's* gunners lacked training (Ferapontov 2017, 34).

Semmes had been ordered by the Confederate naval command to abandon the *Alabama* and return home via France and England. Instead, Italian cavalier-like, Semmes challenged Captain Winslow to a sea fight in the tradition of two knights jousting with each other. Semmes was disobeying orders not to attack the USS *Kearsarge,* but he did so because a formal duel would have been evaluated as more heroic by the public. Similar to many Italian cavaliers, Semmes was more interested in maintaining his honor than in strictly following orders. Semmes believed a heroic contest would show he was neither a pirate nor only a sea captain preying on unarmed merchantmen (Taylor 1994, 198). Semmes wanted the world to recognize that the CSS *Alabama* was "a real ship of war" (Holzer 2011, 843). When told of his ship's lack of proper gunpowder or fuses, Semmes answered he was willing—cavalier-like—to gamble for the sake of his honor.

Semmes sent his former cabinmate, Winslow, a note issuing a formal challenge although he had been ordered not to engage in battle but try to escape (Bradley 1921, 5):

> Sir:—I am undergoing a few repairs here which, I hope, will not take longer than the morrow.
> Then I will come ont [*sic*] and fight you a fair and square fight.
> Most respectfully yours,
> Captain R. Semmes

The challenge became public, and a special excursion train brought spectators from Paris to the coast. An estimated fifteen thousand people watched the battle, or tournament (Keegan 2009, 283). The pro-Confederate French were interested in the battle, and "the fight was the conversation of Paris for more than a week" (Holzer 2011, 857). The sea battle was later commemorated in paintings by a number of artists, including Edouard Manet, who witnessed the sea battle (Marvel 1996, 262). The battle promised to be lengthy since a 10 percent accuracy of naval cannons was considered acceptable (Taylor 1994, 204).

On June 19, 1864, the CSS *Alabama* sailed out of the port of Cherbourg and into international waters. Semmes refused to surrender and again formally issued his challenge. When almost five hundred yards apart, the two ships circled one another and began firing their cannons. The conflict lasted a little over an hour before the CSS *Alabama* sank. The better-trained Union crew rate of fire was twice as fast (Marvel 1996, 251). The *Alabama's* cannon fire was too high and resulted in relatively little damage to the USS *Kearsarge*. One Rebel shell lodged near the USS *Kearsarge's* rudder, but it failed to explode. The battle would have ended with a crippled ship had it exploded.

Semmes later claimed he did not know that the USS *Kearsarge*'s captain had draped camouflaged anchor chains along its sides and considered this act unchivalrous. He wrote in his 1869 memoirs (Ferapontov 2017, 11–12):

> But he [Winslow] did not show me a fair fight, for, as it afterward turned out, his ship was iron-clad. It was the same thing, as if two men were to go out to fight a duel, and one of them, unknown to the other, were to put a shirt of mail under his outer garment. The days of chivalry being past, perhaps it would be unfair to charge Captain Winslow with deceit in withholding from me the fact that

> he meant to wear armor in the fight ... So far from having any condemnation to offer, the [Union] press, that chivalrous exponent of the opinion's icons of a chivalrous people, was rather pleased at the "Yankee trick." It was characteristic, "cute," "smart."

Semmes believed that the "Yankee trick" was dishonorable and typical of Yankees. He, on the other hand, had followed the cavalier's chivalrous code of honor (Taylor 1994, 213–14). As usual among cavaliers, Semmes blamed others for his own failings. Semmes defined the battle as a duel guided by the code duello. He expected a "fair" fight without unexpected technical improvements. This attitude was hypocritical since Semmes had made a career of attacking unarmed vessels. He would also raise a neutral nation's flag to lure potential victims closer (Marvel 1996, 7, 66–67). There is also evidence that Semmes had been told a number of times of the anchor chain protection but had ignored the information.

After surrendering while his ship was sinking, Semmes and some of his officers were picked up by a yacht that had sailed close to the ships to witness the sea battle. The British owner of the yacht was a supporter of the Confederacy (Bradley 1921, 10). Having surrendered, Semmes should have been taken to the USS *Kearsarge* to become a prisoner; instead, he asked to be taken to England and safety. Semmes left the rest of his crew to be rescued by his opponent. A naval captain who did not do his best to protect his ship and crew would be quickly court-martialed and cashiered. Semmes should not have blamed Winslow for protecting his ship as best he could.

Like many cavaliers, Semmes confused the goals of war. Becoming a hero or achieving the reputation of being a gallant knight was often seen as more important than winning the war by many Confederates. Semmes lost his ship, but he became a cavalier martyr who had been unfairly beaten.

While Semmes became a hero—and as a commerce raider helped to destroy the Federal merchant marine—his actions did not materially help the Confederacy. The Union loss of sea transport was more than compensated for by its increased industrial capacity and British vessels importing and exporting goods (Taylor 1994, 275–76).

Italian Cavalier J. E. B. Stuart

Flamboyant General James Ewell Brown "Jeb" Stuart is another example of the Italian type of cavalier. Stuart was one of the Confederacy's most prominent cavalry officers and was respected by both Confederates and Yankees. Stuart dressed extravagantly. He wore a cloak with a scarlet lining and a hat with an ostrich plume. He wore a red rose when in season on his jacket or a ribbon tied with a love knot. The jacket carried gold buttons that were always in danger of being pulled off for souvenirs by admiring ladies (Matteson 2021, 156). His attire was completed with kid gloves, a red sash, thigh-high boots, and golden spurs. He called himself the "Knight of the Golden Spurs." Stuart was described as "young, gay, and handsome, dressed out in his newest uniform, his polished sword … the personification of grace and gallantry combined."

Stuart enjoyed music. Band members followed him everywhere, including Mulatto Bob who played the bones and a banjo player, Sam Sweeney. Sweeney was a private, but he was made an official staff member, a position limited to officers (Matteson 2021, 159). He loved to entertain—especially young ladies with whom he innocently flirted—and he enjoyed organizing military spectacles and formal military balls.

Before the June 1862 Seven Days Battle, Lee ordered Stuart to locate the Army of the Potomac's flanks. Stuart "expanded" his orders, as he called it, and led his troopers around McClellan's army, gathering information and prisoners. Circling the enemy resulted in Stuart becoming a hero to the Confederate public and an embarrassment to the North. He became as famous as "Stonewall" Jackson since he had humiliated the enemy in a cavalier horse-riding fashion. The accolades he received encouraged Stuart to consider repeating this knightly heroism.

Stuart decided to circle the Army of the Potomac a second time during October 10–12, 1862. Stuart and his troopers again captured supplies and horses, but they gathered little information. Aside from gaining supplies and horses, Stuart added little information to where the Union army was located, and he tired his limited number of available horses. Jubal Early sarcastically called Stuart's second ride "the greatest horse stealing expedition."

Jeb Stuart's mindset reflected the cavalier enjoyment of the romance of war. During another raid, Stuart's troops surprised and captured a Union telegraph station fifteen miles from Washington, DC. The proper reaction would have been to send false messages to confuse and distract enemy forces. Stuart, using his own telegraph operator, could also have sent messages asking for information about the location and plans of local Federal forces. A third option would have been to send Federal forces into an ambush.

Instead, Stuart used the occasion to enjoy a joke and gratify his pride. He sent a telegraph message to Union Quartermaster Montgomery C. Meigs, telling him that the Union's mules he captured were of such bad quality that they had difficulty moving the supply wagons he had also captured. Stuart then signed his name to the message to finish his boasting (Matteson 2021, 363). This foolish act informed the Union of Stuart's location and let the enemy realize that its telegraph system had been compromised. Stuart's cavalier ego had contributed to a lost opportunity.

Stuart was later ordered to Brandy Station, Virginia, to gather his command in preparation for the coming Gettysburg campaign. In all, Stuart ordered three reviews of his troopers while stationed at Brandy Station (Wittenberg and Davis 2016). The second involved a review of all his command in maneuvers lasting three hours, including a "sham fight and charge [and] artillery loaded with blank cartridges." There was also a "Sabers and Roses ball."

The third review took place on June 8 with Lee in attendance. The review began with a cavalry line, stretching roughly three miles, engaging in maneuvers and ended with almost ten thousand troopers passing in review in front of Lee and civilians with their "sabers flashing in the sun light."

Stuart did not concern himself with maintaining his force's horses, equipment, and men in peak condition for the upcoming campaign. He did not worry about the wasted powder he used in his theatrical charges to impress his audiences, especially young ladies. Some of his admiring ladies appropriately fainted when the cavalry raced toward them at a gallop. Stuart's *fantasias* were successful as theater.

Disaster struck Stuart at Brandy Station, Virginia, on June 9, 1863. The Union cavalry located Jeb Stuart's units and began the largest cavalry battle of the war. The Union cavalry withdrew when commander Alfred Pleasanton decided he had won a victory and achieved his goal of locating part of Lee's army. The fact that Confederate infantry had arrived to protect Stuart's cavalry was another reason to withdraw. Stuart's headquarters had been overtaken, and vital papers may have been taken (Roland 1995, 59). Stuart had been more concerned with organizing reviews and celebrations than with his scouting duties.

Stuart was embarrassed that the infantry had to drive the Union cavalry from the battlefield and that his forces had been surprised, though the battle was technically a victory for the Confederate forces. The Union cavalry was first to leave the field, and their casualties (860) were larger than the Confederates' (523). The major losses were to Stuart's ego and Lee's attempt to conceal his forces and intensions. The opposing Federals knew that Lee was concentrating his forces in a specific area.

The battle was significant for a number of psychological reasons. The battle showed the Union cavalry had matured and was now as good or better than the Confederate cavalry units, though there had been earlier Union cavalry victories. The quality of Union cavalry was a shock to those who considered Confederate cavaliers superior to Yankees. Just as important, Stuart's forces had been surprised by presumed inferiors. The Confederate public and newspapers accused Stuart of failing to win a clear victory. The loss of his heroic image made Stuart determined to regain his reputation as a knightly cavalier—regardless of other concerns.

Upon reaching Pennsylvania during the Gettysburg campaign, Lee again ordered Stuart and part of his command to discover where the Army of the Potomac was located, destroy Union communications, and protect his flanks. As usual, Lee's orders were politely vague (Fuller 1957, 195). Stuart, in response, again decided to "expand" his orders and circle the Union army. Stuart wanted to reclaim his honor and the reputation he had lost at Brandy Station. Repairing his cavalier reputation was more important than following more mundane but practical orders. He chose, as many Italian cavaliers would have, to consider his own reputation as more important than the larger good.

The first success of Stuart's movements was to capture a large Union wagon train of supplies because supplies would be needed when the army returned to its winter quarters. However, Stuart's capture of wagons, mules, and horses slowed his cavalry's advance and delayed the completion of his official mission. Stuart did not return to Lee's army until the second day of the Battle of Gettysburg, July 2, 1863, with the consequence of Lee being ignorant to the enemy's movements and location for five days.

The Battle of Gettysburg was fought on a location not chosen by Lee—where the Confederates were at a disadvantage—and it was a battle that Lee did not want at the time. Stuart was blamed for the campaign's defeat. Ignored was the fact that the first two days of the battle were won by the Confederates and that Lee could have withdrawn and declared the raid into Pennsylvania a success. Lee also had at his disposal cavalry units he could have used until Stuart's return. While blaming Stuart for the battle's loss is unrealistic, Stuart was guilty of at least repairing his cavalier reputation instead of following his official orders.

CHAPTER 5

HONOR

Mine honor is my mine life;
Both grow in one;
Take honor from me and my life is done.
—Shakespeare

The concept of honor is central to the understanding of Southern and Confederate behavior. In a survey of Civil War soldiers' letters, James McPherson (1997, 25) found that while the importance of honor was mentioned by soldiers on both sides, Confederate rank-and-file soldiers and officers were more likely to mention the importance of honor as a motivator to enlist and continue to fight. In 1864, after the Confederacy had suffered numerous defeats, a Tennessee cavalry officer declared that surrendering to the Union meant (McPherson 1997, 169): "disgrace, dishonor, and slavery [i.e., for white male Southerners] forever."

Honor as Good Manners

The concept of honor is culturally complex and is defined a number of ways. The first definition is honor as the refinement of manners and good conduct (as defined by the group) necessary to be socially accepted by one group or another (Fischer 1989, 396–97). Being polite and gracious to others acknowledges they are deserving of respect. Honor as good manners cements relationships among equals and reinforces community ties.

Groups usually have periods when new members are expected to learn the group's customs or norms. The more extreme the normative differences between a group and the new members, the more extreme the learning.

Being recognized as an honorable person was important among both Southerners and Northerners and was a prerequisite for being defined as a member of the middle or upper classes. This demanded correct deportment (good manners, proper clothing, a modicum of education) and a correct lifestyle. A consequence of the pressure to maintain "correct" behavior was the tendency of elite Southerners to live so lavishly that most were in constant debt. Often the death of a patriarch was accompanied with the paying of massive debts, and the inheritors were forced to sell both land and enslaved persons to pay debts.

There were differences in the concept of honor—in this case behaving as a gentleman or lady—between the North and South. This concept of honor-as-good-manners among Northerners allowed for social mobility. A person could learn to act according to the cultural expectations of a higher social class. Economic success and proper deportment were avenues for social mobility (Foote 2010, 43). Though there were exceptions, Southern values did not encourage or accept social mobility from a lower class to a higher one.

David R. Hundley was typical of white Southerners who held that few persons could completely adapt to a higher social class (Hundley 1860, 9):

> New England was settled mainly by persons in the humbler walks of life ... whereas the early pioneers in the occupancy of the South possessed no such

> homogeneal [*sic*] characteristics, but differed … widely—the two extremes being, in one hand, the high-bred English courtier of aristocratic mien and faultless manners, and on the other, the thick-lipped African … while between these were some half-dozen other classes, possessing different degrees of culture and refinement—all of whom yet have their descendants in the South, changed in many particulars from their aboriginal ancestors, but for all that, *distinctly the representatives of the several classes whence they derive their origin* [emphasis added].

According to Hundley and other elite Southerners, few, if any, members of the lower classes could achieve acceptance into the upper class. Southerners who did not already enjoy "aristocratic mien and faultless manners" could seldom become accepted members of the Southern upper class. Hundley ignores the fact that Southerners did experience upward mobility. Jefferson Davis's father's social position was middle class, yet his sons became members of the Mississippi elite. Samuel Davis enrolled Jefferson in the best schools available and sent him to West Point. Jefferson Davis's older brother also mentored him in political theory. Nathan Forrest and his brother became part of the elite during their lifetimes even though they began life in a very poor environment and began their wealth by dealing in enslaved persons. Professional enslaved persons traders were held in very low esteem in the South.

An 1860 popular guide of the era for social mobility, *Beadle's Dime Book of Practical Etiquette for Ladies and Gentleman: Being a Guide to True Gentility and Good Breeding*, illustrated how a would-be lady or gentleman was expected to behave in order to be accepted. Northerners could learn "good breeding," considered as good manners, because the knowledge for social mobility was available to everyone. This guidebook offered a democratic guide to the knowledge and behavior necessary to be recognized as a lady or gentleman.

While much of the advice of the hundred-page book demands a level of wealth, the emphasis is on obtaining the knowledge of the proper minutiae of correct behavior (Beadle 2019). Anyone could learn the appropriate manners and customs reflecting "good breeding." One could then hopefully join what poet laureate Allan Tate (1899–1979) favorably designated the Southern ruling class as a "squireocracy" (Tate 1998, 51).

Social Mobility in the South

Southerners were supporters of a static and a more stratified society than Northerners by using the concept of honor to place barriers on social mobility. While the behavior expected of gentlemen was similar between the two regions (except for a more Southern aggressive defense of one's honor), the Southern sense of honor was limited to those from the middle and upper classes, ideally those who could trace their lineage for several or more generations. There was little opportunity for social mobility in the South unless one enjoyed wealth based on the ownership of plantations and enslaved persons.

While few persons could achieve entry into the upper levels of Confederate society, a number of Southern intellectuals and politicians promoted the increase in the number of owners of enslaved persons. New owners would support the institution of slavery and were more likely to support the status quo. The increase of owners of a few enslaved persons also would enjoy more leisurely and/or more prosperous lives. J. D. B. De Bow promoted the increased leisure for those who owned a limited number of enslaved persons (Carpenter 1990, 10):

> The non-slaveholder knows that as soon as his savings will admit, he can become a slaveholder, and thus relieve his wife from the necessities of the

> kitchen and the laundry, and his children from the labors of the field.

Southerners could achieve middle-class respectability by attending military academies of one type or another as well as universities, though tuition for these were too expensive for most potential social climbers. A significant exception was enrollment at the United States Military Academy, commonly known as West Point. While tuition and other costs were mostly free, the entrance requirements generally demanded tutors and previous attendance in expensive schools.

West Point teachers expected cadets to become gentlemen as well as military professionals (cadets were given dancing lessons to polish their social graces), but appointments were based on political connections. Attendance at West Point was usually encouraged for boys from branches of elite families too poor to afford tuition to a university. The immediate families of Robert E. Lee, Thomas "Stonewall" Jackson, Ulysses S. Grant, and William Tecumseh Sherman could not afford the tuition for educating their sons beyond a few years of basic education at local schools.

West Point also taught cadets to be disciplined. A cadet's life was rigorously controlled. Cadets were not allowed to enjoy the lives they had previously enjoyed. Food was bad, rooms were small and spartan, and few luxuries were available. Cadets were allowed one bath a week using cold water.

A last avenue for social mobility was to read law with a successful lawyer, but such apprenticeships were usually given to young men from elite families. While lawyers were respected as professionals, they were not considered part of the elite unless they owned plantations and enslaved persons or became well-known politicians.

While a sense of honor motivated young (the average age of recruits in 1861 was twenty-five) Southerners to enlist, a sense of honor was coupled with the belief that an honorable man should protect his family and homeland from Yankee invasion. Family, honor, and loyalty to the homeland (defined as home, county, state, South, Confederacy) formed a potent—though eventually contradictory—mixture of values as the foundations for Confederate patriotism.

Below is the advice a father gave his son as he departed for the war. The son thought the war would be short and winnable in spite of his father's beliefs (Fletcher 1908, 5):

> William, I have long years since seen this [i.e., the war] had to come and it is a foolish undertaking, as there is no earthly show for Southern success, as our ports will be blocked and the North will not only have advantage of men and means, but the world to draw from, and if you live to return, you will see my predictions are right. While I have opposed it, but as it is here, *I will say that you are doing the only honorable thing and that is defending your country* [emphasis added].

Young William's honor was attached to the Southern sense of fatalism. Even if the cause were doomed, he must enlist to maintain his honor. Defending one's honor was more important than considerations of winning, losing, or dying. The father, formerly a Unionist, became a fervent Confederate when the war began. Loyal to the Union, he was not loyal to the North (Ural 2017, 19). The Northern stance on slavery inadvertently insulted the Southern sense of honor that ultimately contributed to secession and the Civil War.

The Courtesy of Robert E. Lee

The most courteous Confederate general was Robert E. Lee. He maintained his reputation as a dignified and honorable gentleman throughout his life. His notable courtesy was exhibited when he dealt with Jefferson Davis and his own staff and generals. Lee realized one of his roles as general was to communicate fully with his commander in chief while accepting a subordinate position. Few other generals felt the same way, thereby creating personal and dysfunctional conflicts among generals, the Confederate president, and his supporters. Note also that Lee was the Confederacy's major hero and a member of one of the Confederacy's most respected families. Any praise from Lee would be welcomed by a western social parvenu such as Davis.

Lee spent an inordinate amount of time reporting to Davis. His messages were invariably polite and nonthreatening because he realized Davis could not accept being criticized or told what he should do. The introductions of Lee's letters to Davis began politely with conventional phrases such as, "I have had the honour to receive your letter" or "In reference to my conversation with you when I had the honour of seeing you."

Lee was also careful not to openly criticize or communicate to Davis what should be done. Lee complained numerous times about the lack of replacements and supplies, but he never directly blamed Davis or his policies for these shortcomings. In the letter below, Lee gently asks Davis to hurry the enlistment of Black Americans into the Confederate armies. There is no suggestion of Lee demanding Davis to act in this letter. He instead presents his needs in a nonthreatening, polite manner (Freeman 1957, 373–74):

> I do not know whether the law authorizing the use of negro troops has received your sanction, but if it has, I respectfully recommend that measures be taken to carry it into effect as soon as practical …

> I hope that if you have approved the law, you will cause the necessary steps to carry it into effect to be taken as soon as possible.

In another letter to Davis dated August 17, 1862, Lee proposes a plan of action and indirectly asks for more action and cooperation from the incompetent Commissary General Lucius B. Northrop, a friend of Davis (Dowdy and Manarin 1961, 258–59):

> I beg you will excuse my troubling you with my opinions, and especially these details [i.e., what Northrop must do], but your kindness had led you to receive them without objection so often that I know I am tempted to trespass.

He closes "With high respect, your obedient servant." Lee's diplomacy is also illustrated by the courtesy he exhibits in the following letter, dated January 6, 1863, sent at the peak of Lee's popularity. Lee flatters Davis with his concern for Davis's health, the suggestion that Davis increased morale, and implying that Davis was partially responsible for victory in a battle in which he did not participate (Freeman 1957, 68–70):

> Allow me to congratulate you & the country upon your safe return to Richmond. I trust your health has been invigorated, & that you have enjoyed great satisfaction as well as comfort from the condition of affairs in the great west. I know that your visit has inspired the people with confidence, & encouraged them to renewed exertions & greater sacrifices in the defense of the Country, & I attribute mainly the great victory of Genl Bragg to the courage diffused by your cheering words & presence ... I know you will have much to occupy

> your attention. I will not trespass farther on your time, but wishing you all happiness & prosperity, & many returns of the New Year, remain with great esteem, your obt. Servt, ...

Robert E. Lee was also reluctant to upset the sense of honor and dignity of others even when they deserved strong criticism. Once he had organized his battle plans and issued his orders, Lee became a "nonfactor," and he seldom interfered once a battle had begun (Tucker 2016, 305). He assumed the officers at the battlefront would be better able to decide what needed to be done. Lee issued mild criticisms when his officers failed (as they often did), but he seldom punished them. His most extreme punishment was to transfer the offender to another army.

Lee's same diplomatic practice when giving military orders made it possible for subordinates to ignore their objectives (Fuller 1957, 226–27). That is why Lee complained to Davis (Fuller 1957, 121), "The greatest difficulty I find is in causing orders and regulations to be obeyed."

Lee felt that both rank-and-file soldiers and officers were lacking in discipline and were too independent. This sense of independence irked Lee, and he complained to Jefferson Davis (Freeman 1957, 369):

> Many officers have too many selfish views to promote to induce them to undertake the task of instructing & disciplining their Commands.

Lee found that officers did not want to spend time drilling their commands because doing so "deprives them of pleasant visits, dinners, &." Southerners did not enjoy the minutiae of their military duties.

Only Thomas "Stonewall" Jackson was able to understand Lee's orders and be willing to carry them out. Jackson knew what was expected of him and his army during his historic Shenandoah

Valley Campaign when Lee suggested, "Should there be nothing requiring your attention ... you can make arrangements to deceive the enemy."

Lee felt obligated to treat his staff as fellow gentlemen rather than as subordinates because gentlemen did not give orders to other gentlemen. Lee's orders were couched as polite suggestions (as was his advice to Jefferson Davis). The result was that orders were often ambiguous and allowed for multiple interpretations (Weigley 2000, 244). Jeb Stuart reinterpreted ("expanded") his orders, resulting in his and his command's disappearance for five days before and during the Battle of Gettysburg. Another significant error was Lee's vagueness in ordering Richard Stoddert Ewell to capture and hold Cemetery Hill "if possible."

A Virginian who survived Pickett's Charge claimed (Tucker: 2016, 36): "Our failure to a great extent can be laid to General Lee's fault—he left too much to his subordinates," and his "battlefield control was minimal." Lee surrounded himself with a staff and commanders who were Virginians and fellow West Point graduates—a group known for their adherence to social protocols and the rituals of war and insisting on the privileges of their rank. It was easy for such cavalier elites to feel insulted or slighted.

Honor as Theatrical Patriotism

Honor was often projected as patriotism since only those who were loyal to the Confederacy could be honorable. Those who were not loyal Rebels were defined as dishonorable cowards, traitors, speculators, and worse. The result was a tendency to prove one's patriotism and honorable courage by facing danger irrespective of its effectiveness. Showing public loyalty was a "theater of patriotism" as an end of itself.

Examples of this "theater of patriotism" include the behavior of both men and women after the Union's easy capture of New

Orleans. A mob almost killed the two Federal generals who were in New Orleans to negotiate the terms of the city's surrender. One man raised the Confederate flag on top of a building after the surrender of the city.

Women were determined to show both their patriotism and honor by publicly insulting the occupying Yankee soldiers. Like the men, the women were angry that there had not been a more forceful and successful defense during the invasion of the city of New Orleans. A source of this anger was that the war had been distant before the arrival of Union forces. A group of women was reputed to be "all in favor of resistance *no matter how hopeless* that resistance might be" (Eaton 1954, 177, emphasis in the original). The result was a series of theatrical insults by women to the Union occupiers, which changed nothing but was symbolically satisfying in the short run.

Chamber pots were emptied on officers (Admiral David Farragut was a victim of the contents of a chamber pot). Women crossed the street to avoid passing near anyone wearing a Union uniform. Women refused to acknowledge soldiers' presence. There were cursing and spitting at uniform wearers. Women refused to talk to the military and answer their questions and turned their backs when a Yankee officer approached. Part of the anger felt by Confederate civilians was that Black American troops (many recruited from the area) led by Black American officers were part of Butler's occupying army.

Shortly after entering New Orleans, the military governor, Benjamin F. Butler, was walking near a balcony occupied by four women. As Butler passed, the four turned around, lifted their skirts, and exposed themselves. Butler walked away and remarked (Lowry 1994, 152), "Those women evidently know which end of them looks best."

More serious to Butler, however, were the women's continued insults to Union officers. Ignored was the fact that the occupation was benign and beneficial to the residents. Butler ended endemic theft by Southerners and repaired the sewer system, which ended the recurrent cycles of yellow fever. He also distributed to the city's poor food supplies stored in Confederate warehouses.

As a result of the continued insults to his officers, Butler issued his infamous General Order 28, announcing that any woman showing disrespect toward any Union soldier or officer would be considered a prostitute, fined, and jailed:

> As the officers and soldiers of the United States have been subject to repeated insults from women (calling themselves ladies) of New Orleans in return for the most scrupulous non-interference and courtesy on our part, it is ordered that hereafter any female shall by word, gesture, or movement insult or show contempt for any officer or soldier of the United States she shall be regarded and held liable to be treated as a woman of the town plying her avocation.

It was then that Butler was called "Beast Butler" or "the Beast." Butler had violated the rituals (norms) of how civilians should be treated by the military and had insulted Confederate women.

The Confederate population responded with outrage (as did many in France and England), and "Beast" Butler was threatened with lynching or immediate execution if captured. His face was painted on the inside of chamber pots.

Insults to Union soldiers ceased because the New Orleans middle-class ladies did not want to be defined as or treated as prostitutes. Butler, a wily politician, had found a way to control the behavior of insulting women and still avoid making them into martyrs through imprisonment or physical punishment. In this case, the women's fear of losing their honor proved to be a weakness exploited by "Beast" Butler.

The outrage toward Butler was in large part a reaction to his actions that Confederates could not protect white women from being insulted. A major element of both the Southern mindset and the cavalier ethic was that (decent white) women were to be respected and protected. Women were also showing by their behavior that they were more patriotic than men. The Confederacy was exposed as unable to defend its largest city and its women. Men had been emasculated and insulted as weaker and more helpless than women.

Honor as Courage

An honorable white male adult was expected to face danger with courage and nonchalance. A cultural dichotomy exists that a person is either brave or an honorless coward. One way a man could determine whether or not he was honorable was to face fire during battle without showing fear. Even those who were not completely loyal to the Confederacy would want to be recognized as courageously performing their duty. The pressure to maintain honor by being courageous warriors was a major reason for the successes of the Confederate armies (Linderman 1987, 60).

Charles Davis was typical of this attitude. Davis was a successful Tennessean farmer with thirteen children from two wives and was the owner of twelve enslaved persons. Davis taught his sons (Phifer 1967, 33) "the wisdom of holding one's tongue, keeping the peace, and *never yielding an inch when honor was involved* [emphasis added]."

Charles Davis's oldest son, Sam, enlisted when he was eighteen and served under Stonewall Jackson, Albert Sidney Johnston, and P. G. T. Beauregard. Captured during 1863 during a spying mission in Middle Tennessee, Sam was offered the choice of giving his captors the source of his information on Federal installations or being hanged. Sam chose hanging. When the Federal general in charge pleaded with Sam to give him the information, Sam replied, "I know, General, I will have to die; but I will not tell where I got the information and there is no power on earth that can make me tell. You are doing your duty as a soldier, and if I have to die, I shall be doing my duty to God and my country" (Phifer 1967, 109).

Sam's death is an example of the strength of the Southern values of honor and duty. At times counterproductive, the Southern code was also an encouragement to perform bravely.

Honor as Reputation

Honor includes a man's reputation for being able to defend himself and his family from insult and injury. Related to the concept of valor, the defense of one's honor demands physical courage and aggression. This type of honor is illustrated by William O'Brian Yancey. He fought a number of duels and stated, after he killed his opponent in one such duel (Quigley 2012, 61), "I have done my duty as a man, & he who grossly insulted me, lies now, with the clod upon his bosom." Yancey concludes that his successful defense of his honor would become a "warning to others who feel like browbeating a Yancey."

The term "warning" in the quote above identifies honor as public reputation. In the same manner, radical secessionists were described as "a set of young enthusiasts inspired with notions of personal honor to be defended and individual glory, fame and military laurels to be acquired."

A similar but dysfunctional defense of honor occurred between Major General John A. Wharton and Colonel George Wythe Baylor (Selcer 2020, 51–55). Wharton's family belonged to the South Carolina elite and was Baylor's social and military superior. Baylor's family was politically important—but not part of the elite social class.

Baylor felt he had been insulted by Wharton when the latter transferred Baylor to the command of an elderly and inept commander. Baylor and Wharton quarreled during April 1865, the last month of the war, and Baylor accused his military superior Wharton of being a "a liar and a demagogue." Wharton had Baylor arrested and ordered him to report to their headquarters for a court-martial. The next day, Wharton struck Baylor with his fist. Baylor drew his revolver, shot Wharton in the heart, and killed him. It probably never occurred to Wharton that a socially inferior person would dare strike a superior alpha individual.

A civil trial took place three years later. Baylor's defense was that no Southern gentleman would accept being struck on his face with a fist. It was also argued that Wharton should have been armed and prepared to defend his own honor. The jury delivered a verdict of "not guilty" after half an hour of deliberation.

The Southern elite was not the only social class to defend honor by aggressive behavior. A poorer neighbor who had been insulted by an arrogant planter might react by burning the latter's barn, destroying fences, or having a planter's prized horse shot. A poor white was as likely to react violently to being shamed or insulted as a wealthy planter (Wyatt-Brown 2001, 304). The defense of honor by a fistfight or an eye-gouging wrestling match versus a ritualized duel by pistol was a matter of social class, though both groups were expected to defend their reputations and honor. Bertram Wyatt-Brown (Wyatt-Brown 1986, chapter 2) calls this mindset "primal honor." Primal honor is characterized by a "ferocity of will" to defend one's reputation against real or potential enemies.

Honor as Conformity

Honor is a public phenomenon. A white male is expected to have a publicly recognized reputation of being brave and ready to defend his honor. A public show of cowardice or physical weakness destroys a reputation that most likely could never be regained. Aggressive behavior is most likely initiated in a public situation where witnesses are present to gain a reputation of being aggressive and thereby honorable. There is a strong theatrical element to maintaining honor.

The defense of one's honor encourages the public conformity to social values. Sociologist David Riesman found that a major element of the modern American character was "other-directedness." The other-directed person seeks guidance for their behavior from other persons rather than their conscience (Riesman 2001, 137): "He seeks ... the respect and, more than the respect, the affection, of an amorphous and shifting, though contemporary, jury of peers."

The concern for others' acceptance—or being other directed—was a central cultural aspect of Southern culture. A man worthy of respect must publicly represent the elements of honor as when a secessionist claimed a Rebel was worth five or more Yankees. Honor requires the public's perception that personal bravery and prowess be recognized by others (Wyatt-Brown 1986, 27).

The self-directed morality (defined by Riesman as an inner-directed trait) of the New England Puritans is contrasted by the Southern elite's need to conform to dominant local values and the acceptance of the others they respected. By contrast, Puritan values stressed that behavior is directed by one's inner conscience—irrespective of the demands of others. Southerners were more sensitive to the wishes and guidance of others (Riesman 2001, 21–22) even though Southerners believed themselves to be independent in character.

The other-directed person is more traditional and unwilling to accept change that alienates him from others. By contrast, the inner-directed personality encourages change. During the nineteenth century, the North became more dynamic in terms of behaviors and beliefs. The faster pace of industrialization and mechanization, the emergence of religious cults and fads such as spiritualism, the extension of education and political movements (i.e., abolitionism, women suffrage, and a new political party) were more prevalent in the North than in the South. Even authors were more likely to develop new styles of literature in the North.

Southerners were recognized as social persons more sensitive and conforming to the signals as early as Tocqueville's observations during the 1830s. While more inner-directed Northerners were more likely to feel shame and guilt when they failed to act according to their standards of behavior, other-directed Southerners felt rejected by others when they failed to conform. It is no wonder that Southerners could become violent when they disagreed with others. The threat of disagreement threatened a person's place in society.

The Caning of Charles Sumner

An example of a very public instance of Southern defense of honor was the caning of Charles Sumner by Preston S. Brooks on May 22, 1856. Brooks, a member of the South Carolina elite, had a reputation for violent behavior and a hypersensitive sense of honor.

Sumner was a leader of the extreme wing of the antislavery Republican Party and a leader in the attempts to establish Kansas as a free state. He was also a believer that a Slave Power conspiracy existed to protect and expand the institution of slavery. A popular speaker, Sumner used an emotional and dramatic rhetorical style respected and enjoyed by mid-century audiences.

On May 19–20, 1856, Sumner delivered what can only be called a very intemperate diatribe against slavery, slave owners, and Southern culture in general: "Crime Against Kansas." The reason for Brooks's attack of Sumner was Sumner's personal attack of Senator Andrew Butler, a cousin of Brooks. The part of the speech that especially enraged Brooks is quoted below ("Charles Sumner," Wikipedia, July 27, 2018):

> The senator from South Carolina [i.e., Andrew Butler], has read many books of chivalry, and

> believes himself a chivalrous knight with sentiments of honor and courage. Of course, he has chosen a mistress to whom he has made his vows, and who, though ugly to others, is always lovely to him; though polluted in the sight of the world, is chaste on his sight—I mean the harlot, slavery.

Brooks was incensed over the insults delivered by Sumner. Sumner had ridiculed Butler as a false knight and demeaned chivalry, and the speech also clearly stated slavery was not a "positive good," as well as not the God-given institution defended by Southerners. There was also the reference to the fact that the civilized world was ending slavery. England, France, and most of Latin America had already abolished slavery. This reminded Southerners they were becoming increasingly isolated because of their support of slavery "in the sight of the world."

It was also insulting when Sumner referred to the sexual practices of slave owners, a theme dramatically described by Harriet Beecher Stowe in her book *Uncle Tom's Cabin*. The book had been published four years earlier, and the reference to the link between slavery and forced sexuality would be recognized by all, though public mention of miscegenation was taboo among Southerners. Yet Sumner had spoken of slavery as Andrew Butler's "polluted" mistress. To mention publicly a man had a mistress was another insult.

Brooks debated with his friends as to what his response should be. A challenge to a duel would indicate Brooks considered Sumner his social equal. Under the popular North Carolina code duello, only gentlemen were allowed the honor of erasing an insult through a formal one-on-one duel. Brooks and his friends decided Sumner's insults proved he was no gentleman and that other means besides a duel should be used to avenge the insults made to Andrew Butler and Southern culture.

Brooks's friends also reminded him that an earlier duel had left Brooks with a limp and that reaching Sumner in the Senate chambers demanded climbing several sets of stairs. Doing so would tire him and leave him at a disadvantage should an immediate confrontation take place. Another friend mentioned to Brooks that Sumner was taller, healthier, and stronger (Donald 2009, 245). An ambush would be both symbolically preferable and physically safer. A fair face-to-face confrontation in public was therefore rejected as impractical.

They decided the most appropriate response would be a beating using a gutta-percha cane. Gutta-percha canes were used to punish slaves and dogs and were also symbols of superiority. Such a weapon would physically punish Brooks, and its use would insult him and publicly deprive Sumner of honor. Brooks would show the public that Sumner was beneath the contempt of a Southerner and was socially on the level of an honorless slave or dog. Shaming an opponent was a central value in the cavalier mindset.

Brooks found Sumner writing at his desk on the Senate floor (there were no private offices at the time). Waiting until female visitors had left (women were protected from seeing violence according to the Southern code), Brooks began to beat Sumner with his cane. Sumner became entangled in his desk and could neither escape nor defend himself. The beating continued until Brooks's cane broke into pieces. Brooks then ferociously beat Sumner with the cane's handle and continued to beat him after he became unconscious. Brooks even injured himself with a backswing that cut his forehead.

The reaction among Southerners was swift and positive: a Southerner's honor had been vindicated, an antislavery Northerner had been whipped, and the institution of slavery had been violently defended. At the time, firebrand Laurence Keith wrote to a friend (Berry II 2003, 249), "Brooks that day flogged Sumner of Massachusetts, and he did it well and soundly." Brooks received a number of canes to replace the one he had broken.

A few days after the beating, Massachusetts Representative Anson Burlingame publicly called Brooks "the vilest sort of coward" on the House floor. Brooks felt forced to respond by challenging Burlingame to a duel. Burlingame, a known marksman, accepted the challenge and chose rifles as weapons. He also selected the Canadian side of Niagara Falls as the location for the duel since dueling was against the law in the United States. Brooks canceled the duel on the grounds that traveling through Northern states to reach the Canadian border was too dangerous for a Southerner who might be met by mobs. Burlingame was lauded for defying the "Slave Power," was celebrated with parades, and was in demand for lectures (Freeman 2018, 227).

Northerners defined Brooks as a coward and a barbarian. The New York *Evening Post* published a poem about the caning and his refusal to take part in a fair duel (cited in Donald 2009, 260):

> To Canada Brooks was asked to go,
> To waste a pound of powder or so,
> But he answered, No, No, No.
> For I am afraid, afraid, afraid,
> Bully Brooks's afraid.

The caning of Sumner on May 22, 1856, had two general consequences vis-à-vis the push toward Civil War. The caning proved to many Northerners that Southern slaveholders were violent "barbarians" and aggressively violent on the issue of slavery. Further debate on the topic was seen as futile. Southerners were also increasingly demonized as a unified Slave Power refusing to compromise on the issue of slavery while demanding its geographic expansion. For their part, Southerners reveled in their superior use of violence while they further defined Northerners as men without honor and cowards.

Southern Rejection of Criticism

Southerners, as self-defined cavaliers, found it difficult to calmly and rationally discuss an issue because they understood disagreement as personally insulting. That is why the House of Representatives in 1836, on the insistence of Southerners, established a nine-year gag rule that no petition to weaken or limit the institution of slavery would be considered even though the Constitution included the clause that citizens had the right "to petition the government for a redress of grievances."

There was a rejection in the South for free speech when the contents disagreed with Southern elites' interests in addition to negative comments concerning slavery. Southern postmasters censured the mail to prevent abolitionist literature from being distributed in the South. Antislavery French observer Count Agénor de Gasparin criticized the Confederacy for its enforced other-directed conformity (Gasparin 1862, 230):

> Such has been the influence exercised in the United States by the institution of slavery; it has forbidden authors to write, clergymen to preach, and almost [all] individuals to think any thing that displeases it; it has invented the right of secession in order to have at its disposal a formidable means of intimidation, and to place a threat behind its demands.

Honor and Masculinity

A white male Southerner's sense of honor was also associated with his sense of masculinity. The traits of honor, aggressiveness, and masculinity were closely linked together. A perceived attack on one of the above values was also an attack on the other traits. This personality trait, also called "toxic masculinity," encouraged white male Confederates to unnecessarily expose themselves to danger during battles to show themselves and others their masculinity.

The desire to be evaluated by others as masculine encouraged Southern male elites to become comfortable in the saddle, shoot well with both rifle and pistols, become experienced hunters (Wade Hampton III hunted bears with a knife), and endure hardships without complaint. The training of boys to be aggressive knights began early.

The defense of masculinity encouraged violence in general because masculinity was publicly earned and defended by violence. Ownby summarizes the link of masculinity and honor (1990, 13):

> Men liked to see battles of many sorts, especially those with an element of chance and the possibility of danger. Honor came from winning; momentary shame came from losing; identification with the male community came from participating in the competition.

Southern white women from the middle and upper classes were especially adept in using threats of rejecting a man's masculinity to encourage their enlistment. Eighteen-year-old diarist Kate Stone wrote during early 1862 that failure for men to enlist resulted in them being defined as traitors lacking in masculinity. Kate Stone maintained that honor did not allow for nuances: one was either an honorable conformist or a rejected nonperson (Anderson 1995, 92):

> In the present sad condition of affairs traitors are springing up in every direction, … I would not trust any man now who stays at home instead of going out to fight for his country.

Men's masculinity was challenged by the practice by young unmarried women of sending packages of petticoats to men who hesitated to enlist during the early days of the war. If they were unwilling to defend the Confederacy, these "men" lacked both honor and masculinity and should dress as women. Men defined as without courage or honor became emasculated as well as traitors.

A group of women advertised they were forming a Ladies Home Guard to protect men of military age who refused to enlist. A woman about to be married called the wedding off and sent her (now former) fiancé women's clothes when he did not enlist (Williams 2008, 43). In the same manner, the *Raleigh Register* approvingly reported, perhaps truthfully, during 1863 how a woman engaged to a soldier rejected him when he left the army (Clinton 1995, 58):

> A young lady was engaged to be married to a soldier in the army. "Why have you left the army?" she inquired of him. "I have found a substitute," he replied. "Well, sir, I can follow your example, and find a substitute, too. Good morning."

The pressures to maintain a reputation for masculinity were difficult to resist in an other-directed society that emphasized the importance of the link between honor and masculinity. Similar to the pressures experienced by the young man in the above quote, Henry M. Walker of Arkansas received a package of a chemise and a petticoat from an anonymous sender. Walker enlisted soon after. Those who did not enlist had their honor, masculinity, and patriotism challenged (Neal and Kremm 1997, 47).

The necessity to be recognized as courageous motivated men to remain steady while under fire or willing to attack against great odds. The fear of being accused of cowardice also resulted in higher casualty rates than necessary among Confederate officers. The battle mortality rates for Confederate and Union generals were 18 and 8.7 percent, respectively. To be respected, Confederate officers were expected to exhibit their courage by leading their men into battle, sharing their hardships, and stoically facing enemy fire (McPherson: 1997, 53).

Honor and Pride of Rank

The often-exaggerated sense of honor among Confederates was also associated with the fear of not receiving the level of honor to which one feels entitled. When Confederate President Jefferson Davis began organizing the Confederate armies, he appointed five generals to the highest levels in the Confederate armies based on their previous levels of rank and seniority in the antebellum Old Army.

The five highest-ranked were, in descending rank, Samuel Cooper, Albert Sidney Johnston, Robert E. Lee, Joseph E. Johnston, and Pierre G. T. Beauregard. The rankings above could be legitimately changed according to how promotion protocols were interpreted and on considerations of talent rather than seniority. Cooper, for example, was senior to the others, but he did not have field experience. At sixty-three, Cooper was a bureaucrat, but he had no other positive qualities.

On another location, Beauregard felt he had not been adequately promoted or given an independent command. He complained that the commanders in the nearby districts had higher ranks (Hattaway and Jones 1991, 153). Both he and Joseph E. Johnston developed animosities toward Jefferson Davis because of hurt pride. They later refused to communicate with Davis. The pride and feelings of hurt honor among these two generals and others inhibited interdistrict and interdepartmental cooperation.

Pride deprived the Confederacy of effective leaders. General Gustavus Woodson Smith resigned his commission during October 1862 because he had not been promoted to lieutenant general over seven others, four of which were his previous subordinates (Younger 1985, 38). Smith then worked as a volunteer aide to Beauregard and later commanded a division in the Georgia state militia as a major general.

Joseph E. Johnston was also outraged when he was not given the highest rank in the Confederate military since he was senior in terms of field experience. He wrote a formal letter to President Davis explaining in great detail why Davis had made a grave error in his rankings and why he deserved the highest rank. Davis, in turn, formally wrote Johnston that he completely rejected his argument and the tone of his letter.

Neither correspondent could admit the other was in the right since doing so would threaten his honor. Later, Johnston quarreled with the then-Confederacy's secretary of war, Judah Benjamin. Johnston believed Benjamin was issuing inappropriate orders and refused to communicate with Benjamin or even submit required reports to the Confederate War Department (Hattaway and Jones 1991, 110).

Lack of Honor and Social Death

Those who lacked honor or failed to act honorably in the South were often ostracized. Honor was a public attribute, and the public endowed or rejected the honor of an individual. A major fear of those who valued being defined as honorable was to lose the respect of others.

An example of the *social death* of a nonconformist was the treatment of George H. Thomas, a Union general. Thomas was born in Virginia, joined the military as a career, and became a recognized hero during the Mexican War. He had lived on a plantation, owned enslaved persons, and was a member of Virginia's elite. In 1855, Jefferson Davis, then secretary of war of the United States, promoted Thomas to the rank of major general.

Thomas was expected to be given a similar high-level command when Virginia seceded since his reputation at the time was one of the highest and equal to Robert E. Lee's. Instead, Thomas kept his military oath and stayed with the Union. As a Southerner with a strong sense of honor, he decided that honor demanded he remain with the Union. Thomas became one of the finest generals of the Union. His leadership saved the retreating Army of the Cumberland during the battle of Chickamauga. He later destroyed what was left of John Bell Hood's Army of Tennessee at the Battle of Nashville. No one else during the Civil War achieved a similar feat of destroying an army.

The reaction to Thomas remaining with the Union was immediate. He was declared a traitor by the general public, and the Confederate leaders denounced him. J. B. Stuart, one of Thomas's former students, declared that he should be hanged. His two sisters burned his letters and turned his picture to the wall. They hid the ornamental sword presented to him in 1848 for his honorable behavior during the Mexican War and refused to ever mention his name. The sisters rejected his letters and packages and never spoke to him again. Their brother was socially dead to them. In contrast, George and his two brothers reconciled after the end of the war.

A minor but symbolic example of social death was Jeb Stuart changing the name of his son (Wert 2008, 76). His son was originally named after his father-in-law, Philip St. George Cooke. However, Virginian Brigadier General Cooke remained in the Union military (Cooke served for fifty-six years and authored a work on cavalry tactics that became the standard during the Civil War). Stuart changed his son's name to James Ewell Brown Stuart Jr.

Retribution for nonconformity could take the form of community-involved murder. During 1840–1860, there were more than three hundred lynchings of white males in the South who expressed antislavery attitudes (Tanner 2001, 89). Others were tarred and feathered and sent out of town.

This emphasis on conformity to Southern values makes it surprising that any Southern officer refused to join the Confederacy. An estimated eighty of the three hundred Southern officers in service when the war began kept their commissions and served in the Union's military. Seldom mentioned are the more than one hundred thousand white Southerners who served in the Northern armies. An additional 112,000 Southern Black Americans also served in Union armies.

Effects of Honor on the War

A dominant characteristic of Confederate's leaders was the lack of cooperation on the battlefield, in politics, and in other areas when the situation did not involve friends or family members. It is valid to declare that "the Confederacy died of a lack of cooperation." This weakness existed in all levels of the Confederacy.

At the highest governmental level, President Jefferson Davis and all but two members of his cabinet were replaced at least once. Almost immediately after his election to the presidency, Davis quarreled with Vice President Alexander Stephens, and they became antagonists. Stephens spent most of the Civil War at his plantation in Crawfordville, Georgia. Stephens continuously disagreed with Davis's policies. Stephens remained an advocate of states' rights, and Davis had a more centrist national orientation. Stephens once delivered a three-hour speech against Davis's policies, which he described as unconstitutional and dictatorial. Neither man was capable of compromise.

A major incident involving lack of cooperation involved the protection of the city of New Orleans from Federal invasion. Jefferson Davis and his colleagues were convinced that an invasion would come from the upper Mississippi, and the city of Vicksburg's cannons blocked the Union navy from descending to New Orleans. By contrast, the local military officers located in or near New Orleans insisted that a more probable strategy would be for a Union navy to attack from the south and up the Mississippi River. They asked that the forts south of New Orleans be strengthened and manned by additional troops. The governor of Louisiana asked Davis to send more troops to the area. Instead, Davis ordered locally stationed units sent elsewhere. When the governor enlisted more men to defend New Orleans, he found that the units sent east had taken their state-provided arms with them. The new volunteers had no arms!

The local Confederate infantry and naval leaders quarreled among themselves and refused to present a unified command (Bielski 2021, 77). In 1861, a commander was sent to replace the current leader, General David Emmanuel Twiggs. Twiggs was seventy-two years old at the time and in poor health. He had refused to personally inspect the surrounding military installations and did little to improve the fortifications. Twiggs died two years later of several illnesses. His successor, Major General Mansfield Lovell, was much more dynamic and improved the fortifications. However, Lovell found many of the current officers inadequate, including one to whom he refused to delegate any responsibility (Bielski 2021, 73).

The precipitating cause for the start of the war was the bombardment of Fort Sumter on April 12, 1861. The location of the fort and its defenders could not threaten the city of Charleston, South Carolina, since its guns were aimed out toward the sea rather than toward the city. However, the control of the fort by the Union and its display of the American (now Union) flag was seen as insulting the honor of the nascent Confederacy by Charlestonians.

Confederate officials had been told the fort would soon run out of food, and it was unlikely that a Union ship carrying food would arrive in time. The commander of Fort Sumter, Robert Anderson, had indicated he would surrender at that time. The fort could have been captured without a bombardment if the Confederates had waited a few days. Allowing a Union ship to resupply the fort would have shown a peaceful intent of the Confederacy. Southern passion and impatience in responding to perceived insults to Southern honor unnecessarily began the Civil War. The only honorable reactions possible to this attack on Southern honor were aggression and violence. The fort was attacked and captured, and the war came.

Fatal Heroism

Troops respected officers who led them into battle. Such men showed honor, bravery, gallantry, and masculinity. Courageous acts by officers similarly motivated their commands to face enemy fire or to attack fortified forces. These feats of honor also resulted in an unnecessarily high casualty rate among officers. John S. "The Gray Ghost" Mosby once rode back and forth in front a Union regiment taunting the Yankees to shoot. They did so and seriously wounded Mosby, but he returned to duty in three weeks.

Joseph T. Glatthaar analyzed a sample of six hundred men from the Confederate Army of Northern Virginia. Glatthaar reported that officers had a mortality rate of 24.7 percent in contrast to the 10.7 percent mortality rate among enlisted men (Glatthaar 2011, 95). Officers were expected to show their courage by personally facing fire and leading their troops since behaving otherwise would result in a loss of honor.

Confederate Brigadier General Lewis Addison Armistead's heroic actions during the Battle of Gettysburg are a typical example of fatal heroism. Armistead had attended West Point, but he had resigned for allegedly breaking a dinner plate over the head of a fellow cadet and a future Confederate general: Jubal Early. An alternate explanation for Armistead's resignation was his inability to pass French. Though he failed to graduate, he later managed to receive a commission through the efforts of his wife's social and political connections. His wife was a distant relation of Robert E. Lee and a member of Virginia's First Families (VFF). The Confederate eastern elite centering on Virginia and South Carolina was densely interconnected in part because marriage among cousins was a common feature.

During the third day of the Battle of Gettysburg, Armistead led his brigade as part of Pickett's Charge to the farthest point reached by those taking part in the battle, which was later known as the "high-water point of the Confederacy." Leading his men and waving his saber with his hat stuck on its point, Armistead and what remained of his command reached their destination of a stone wall and copse of trees. A counterattack by the Union stopped the Confederate attack as it was almost successful. Armistead received two slight wounds, was captured, and died two days later of infection in a Union field hospital.

Armistead was a courageous and honorable member of the Confederate elite and personally led his brigade in an appropriately dramatic and theatrical manner. Armistead is reported to have told his command before the battle, "Remember what you are fighting for—your homes, your friends, your sweethearts."

His last speech to his brigade did not directly mention honor as a motivation (by July 1863, there was no doubt as to both the courage and honor of the men in Lee's army), though Armistead did mention in the above quote the major reasons most of his command had enlisted. It was understood that an honorable man protects his home [i.e., family], friends, and sweethearts—and women in general.

Honor and Owners of Enslaved Persons

There were exemptions from the drafts for those owning or managing twenty or more enslaved persons in large part because of fear of enslaved persons rebelling. Later exemptions were enacted for plantation owners with ten enslaved persons or more to ensure men would be present on plantations to supervise the enslaved workers. Other wealthy Confederates were at first able to buy substitutes for themselves or their sons. However, contrary to popular opinion, slave owners and those from slave-owning families did take part in the war and seldom took advantage of the legal exemptions. As would be expected, members of the Southern elite were willing to join the higher levels of the Confederate government and military. The more prestigious positions were given to the new nation's elite.

Joseph T. Glatthaar conducted an empirical test to determine whether or not adult males living in households containing enslaved persons avoided joining the military. By comparing the proportion of households containing slaves (25 percent) in the South from the 1860 census and the same for men in Lee's army (37 percent), it is obvious that the social class that was motivated to start the Civil War to protect their control of the institution of slavery also fought in the war (Glatthaar 2011, 154). This overrepresentation was influenced by the elite's code of honor as evidenced by their letters and diaries.

Glatthaar (2011, 164–65) also found that men from enslaved-holding households were less likely to desert. Similarly, men from the upper classes were less likely to desert (18 percent) than men from the poorer classes (52 percent). Owners of enslaved persons were also slightly more likely (72.4 percent) to be killed in action, die of other causes, be wounded, or captured than nonslave owners (67.8 percent).

As significant, Glatthaar reported that nonowners of enslaved persons were also overrepresented in Lee's army when their homes were located in counties with higher concentrations of enslaved persons. These enlistees would be more conscious of the existence of slavery because of the high percentage of the population of the county who were enslaved. Since secession was promoted as a reason to protect slavery, whites living in these locations would be more concerned with protecting their higher status in comparison to the enslaved. In addition, whites in counties where there also lived higher than average non-whites would be more aware of the dangers—to whites—of slave insurrections.

CHAPTER 6

FIVE BLOWS TO SOUTHERN HONOR

I love the name of honor, more than I fear death.
—Julius Caesar

Five significant events taking place between 1840 and 1860 increased the South's animosity toward the North and increased the likelihood of a civil war. These events were attacks on the institution of slavery and therefore on the Southern sense of honor. The events that increased regional distrust, fear, and hostility were: (1) the publication of Frederick Douglass's autobiography in 1841; (2) the Northern reaction to the 1850 Fugitive Slave Law; (3) the 1852 publication of *Uncle Tom's Cabin* by Harriet Beecher Stowe; (4) the 1857 publication of *The Impending Crisis of the South: How to Meet It* by Hinton Rowan Helper; and (5) John Brown's 1859 attempt to lead a slave insurrection in Virginia.

These five events created a crisis of honor among Southerners. Each involved denunciations of slavery and clear challenges to the institution of slavery and Southern honor. They are also representative of similar events raising Southerners' anxiety over their increasing political and cultural isolation. These events showed Southerners their ability to control events was deceasing and led to feelings of helplessness, victimization, and demonization of Northerners.

These five events also had repercussions among Northerners. These five events radicalized opponents of slavery while Northerners became more sympathetic to the sufferings of the enslaved and were less willing to ignore the issue. Abolitionists became more determined to end slavery. And their numbers increased. The first three events encouraged many to join the newly established Republican Party in 1854. For the Southern elite, there was no other feeling that threatened the Southern sense of honor more than the perceived of loss of power and threat of changes to the institution of slavery.

Frederick Douglass's Autobiography

Frederick Douglass became one of the most famous antislavery representatives of the abolitionist movement. Born enslaved in 1818, Douglass worked on his, perhaps, white father's plantation and was later given to a relative of his owner living in Baltimore, Maryland, where he learned how to read. Sent first to work in the fields as a young adult and then later sent back to Baltimore, Douglass attempted twice to escape. With the help of a free Black American woman—whom he later married—Douglass escaped to the North in 1838 and eventually settled in Bedford, Massachusetts.

Northern abolitionists quickly recognized his oratorical talents, and Douglass began to lecture for the Massachusetts Anti-Slavery Society. He became a respected member of the abolitionist movement. Douglass published his first autobiography in 1845, and it became an instant bestseller. The book sold thirteen thousand copies the first year and thirty thousand copies within five years (Douglass 2014, vii).

Douglass became a respected symbol of a former enslaved person who became both literate and an eloquent orator. He was also an authentic witness of the inhumanity of slavery and the owners of enslaved persons. Douglass emphasized the immoral elements of slavery within the context of the constitutional promise of citizenship and social equality. He disproved the argument that slavery was necessary because of Black American inferiority. Douglass's successes were instead an indication that slavery was cruel and counter to basic American values.

His autobiography, newspaper columns, and lectures resulted in making him such a celebrity that there were fears his former owner might attempt to recapture him. His sponsors sent him to Great Britain for what became a successful two-year lecture tour. While in England, two admirers collected enough money to pay Douglass's master $711.66 for his liberty, and he legally became a free man. He was no longer under the threat of a forced return to slavery as allowed by the Fugitive Slave Act of 1793 (later strengthened in 1850).

Douglass's autobiographies included descriptions of the very negative and violent elements of slavery. His *Narrative of the Life of Frederick Douglass, An American Slave* published in 1845 showed the savagery and brutality of slavery from a personal perspective. As important, Douglass described the dehumanization of the enslaved. Even minor events described the degradation of slavery. Douglass recounts how enslaved children were fed on a large plantation, and he also remarks he always suffered from hunger (Douglass 2014, 37–38):

> [Boiled coarse cornmeal, called mush] … was put into a large wooden tray or trough, and set down on the ground. The children were then called, like so many pigs, and like so many pigs they would come and devour the mush; some with oyster-shells, others with pieces of shingle, and none with

> spoons ... [H]e that was strongest secured the best place; and few left the trough satisfied.

Douglass was also adept at describing from personal experience the brutal elements of slavers' personalities. These descriptions offered a picture of owners of enslaved persons as being morally corrupt, hypocritical, and cowards. These were opposites of the noble cavalier self-image among elite whites (Blight 2018, 58).

There were two notable experiences among many described by Douglass. The first incident Douglass recorded was his separation from his mother before he was less than one year old. She was hired out to a plantation owner twelve miles away, and she would walk the distance to put Douglass to sleep and then return to her master's plantation. Since she visited her son without permission, she would have been whipped if caught (Douglass 2014, 18). Douglass's mother was eventually sent to a plantation that was farther away. The lesson of this account was to point out how slavery destroyed families.

This account of Douglass's separation from his mother was especially effective because the nation during the 1800s was developing a more sentimental view of the institution of the family in which children became more central. In addition, the ties between mother and children also became increasingly more emotional. Northern women reading Douglass's autobiography or attending his lectures were affected by his descriptions of the cruelty of separating mothers from their children and the sexual treatment by owners of enslaved young women.

The 1800s increasingly defined the family as central and as a model of society; consequently, the destruction of a family was thought to weaken the society in a corresponding manner. The family was also seen increasingly as God-ordained, including the ties among parents (especially mothers) and children.

The second notable event Douglass recorded was witnessing the beating of his aunt Hester. His first master's overseer was a "savage monster." Both master and overseer enjoyed being cruel and frequently whipped the enslaved. Douglass recounts (Douglass 2014, 20):

> I have often been awakened at the dawn of day by the most heart-rending shrieks of an aunt of mine, whom he used to tie up to a joist, and whip upon her naked back till she was literally covered with blood … The louder she screamed, the harder he whipped; and where the blood ran fastest, there he whipped longest.

The reason the overseer treated the aunt harshly was that he wanted to use her sexually. Whipping at times seemed to be linked to sexual and sadistic issues among slave owners and overseers (Blight 2018, 15).

Douglass gained fame through his writings in his mentor's abolitionist newspaper *The Liberator.* The newspaper's publisher, William Lloyd Garrison, distrusted all the US institutions (political, economic, and religious) and their leaders. He also believed the Constitution defended slavery and once burned a copy before an audience. Douglass eventually broke away from the Garrisonian wing of abolitionism. Garrison and his followers believed the best strategy for eliminating slavery was moral persuasion, reflecting a belief in the Higher Law, to denounce the existence of slavery.

In contrast, Douglass believed the United States Constitution could be used to eliminate slavery. In his powerful lecture "What to the Slave is the Fourth of July?" delivered before an audience of white abolitionists, Douglass reassured his audience (Douglass 2014, 144–45):

> Now, take the constitution according to its plain reading, and I defy the presentation of a single pro-slavery clause in it. On the other hand, it will be

> found to contain principles and purposes, entirely hostile to the existence of slavery.

Douglass founded his own weekly newspaper, the *North Star,* in 1848. In 1851, he changed the name of his newspaper to *Frederick Douglass' Paper,* which was possible because of his fame as a foremost orator and lecturer (Colaiaco 2006, 23).

In addition to his belief that the US Constitution was an antislavery document, Douglass encouraged abolitionists to engage in politics to seek reforms. Douglass encouraged abolitionists to work within the legal and religious systems.

A pragmatic, Douglass believed abolitionists should seek support wherever it could be found—even if the support were not as strong as he wished. He was an early supporter of the Republican Party because—though it did not propose full citizen rights for Black Americans—the leaders were antislavery.

Unlike Garrison, Douglass was willing to urge church members to support the cause of abolitionism. Being familiar with the Bible, Douglass used scriptures to define slavery as anti-Christian. Seeing slavery as an evil, Douglass warned audiences that there would be divine retribution if slavery were not eliminated (Colaiaco 2006, 2). A favorite example used by Douglass was the biblical story of the enslaved ancient Hebrews in Egypt when God intervened to free the Hebrews from their slavery.

A common belief since the founders of American independence was that the unalienable rights of freedom and civil rights were derived from God. Douglass warned that depriving Black Americans of rights was anti-American, against natural law, and against basic religious values. Slaves were equally justified to rebel against being enslaved as the colonists were to rebel against England or the enslaved Hebrews were to rebel against Egypt (Colaiaco 2006, 36–37). These references were familiar and understandable to Northern audiences.

The 1850 Fugitive Slave Law

Planters were highly angered that many Northerners supported and aided escaping enslaved persons and refused to return them to their owners. Since they were considered property, owners of enslaved persons experienced an economic loss—though an escaped enslaved worker was more than an economic entity. An escaped enslaved person (most were males) was an insult to the owner's honor. He had failed to secure his "property."

In addition, each fugitive contradicted the propaganda that the enslaved were happy and wanted to be slaves, or as Frenchman Gasparin argued (Gasparin 1862, 15):

> It is enough for me to see these *happy* slaves expose themselves to a thousand deaths to escape a situation declared "preferable to that of our workmen" [emphasis in the original].

Each escaped enslaved worker was a denunciation of slavery, an attack on the owner's honor, a sense of a loss of control, and an economic loss. A number of fugitives, including Frederick Douglass, became well-known lecturers and authors, adding to the insult of former enslaved persons showing the general public their intelligence as well as their scars. Northerners' willingness to help and protect fugitive enslaved persons increased the Southern antagonism toward the North and increased feelings of victimization.

The psychological importance of the Fugitive Slave Law to slaveholders is indicated by a letter the governor of Virginia, John Letcher, wrote to a Northern newspaper (*Harper's Weekly* volume 4, December 1, 1860, 759):

> The South asks only for the fair and faithful execution according of the laws passed for the

> recovery and protection of her property—that you will cease to *embarrass* and lend your aid to effect their execution according to their letter and spirit: that if her property shall escape and be found in the non-slaveholding states, you will see that it is promptly restored to its rightful owner. ... *especially when the preservation of the Union depends on it* [emphasis added].

In the quote above, Letcher described an enslaved person as "it," meaning the enslaved were property and less than human. There is also an implicit threat that Southerners will secede from the Union if they do not get their way. This reflects the tendency of cavaliers to demand obedience from others.

The economic loss due to fugitives was real, but the percentage of slaves able to escape from their owners was overestimated by owners of enslaved persons. The 1850 census reported that an estimated one thousand enslaved persons each year escaped to the North. Assuming an average cost of enslaved persons (including women and children) of $1,000 each, a thousand slaves would cost the South an annual $1,000,000 or more. If the enslaved had escaped from an owner with five or fewer slaves, the economic loss would be significant. There were also the minor costs involved in attempting to recapture fugitives, which involved hiring professional slave hunters, paying a reward, jailing the escapee, and legal and transportation costs.

Northern whites—especially women—became more sympathetic toward fugitives and more antislavery when they witnessed or read about Black Americans being brutally dragged away into slavery without proper legal representation. In 1854, President Franklin Pierce ordered 1,500 troops to escort escaped Anthony Burns back to his master in Virginia while mobs attempted to liberate the fugitive. The outrage caused by Burns's treatment encouraged abolitionists and others to demand a trial for Burns; they were certain that a local jury would acquit the fugitive. The Republican Party was increasingly recognized as the antislavery political party and gained popular support when such reenslavements were publicized.

The Virginia governor and owner of enslaved persons, Letcher, and fellow owners were angry that some Northerners as well as Southerners were "conductors" of the Underground Railroad. The Underground Railroad was established to guide escaping slaves to slave-free states where Black Americans could disappear into Northern cities or Canada. Activists such as Harriett Tubman and Sojourner Truth became cultural heroes for their support of escaping slaves, further angering Southerners. An unexpected result of the Underground Railroad is that it was used to guide escaped Union prisoners to safety during the Civil War (Foote 2016).

The Fugitive Slave Act of 1793 regulated how fugitives were to be returned. Captured escapees were to be taken by their capturers to any federal, state, or local judge and show proof of ownership. Those who interfered with the process were to be fined five hundred dollars plus court costs.

In response to attempts to capture fugitives and return them to their owners, Northern states enacted "personal liberty laws," which made the return of escaped individuals more expensive due to legal expenses and time-consuming legal delays involving a demand for jury trials (Levine 1992, 186–87). Some of these laws banned professional slave catchers from entering a state. Laws enacted in other Northern states banned bounty hunters from the use of local jails to keep recaptured enslaved persons in custody until they could be returned to their owners.

The 1850 Fugitive Slave Law strengthened the original 1793 act. The new law prevented fugitives from testifying on their own behalf or allowed jury trials. Federal commissioners were appointed in every county in the Northern states to judge the validity of a claimant's charges. The commissioners were awarded five dollars if they decided for the alleged fugitive and received ten dollars when the decision was for the claimant. In practical terms, the 1850 Fugitive Slave Law was a significantly important federal subsidy to slave owners since the legal and other costs of returning fugitives were paid by the federal government (Hummel 1996, 51). A British minister denounced the act as forming "the whole of the United States and its free citizens ... into a huge slave-making mob" (Chater 2020, 85).

The 1850 Fugitive Slave Law came to an inglorious end on March 23, 1861. Three enslaved fugitives constructing Confederate coastal batteries escaped to Union-occupied Fort Monroe in Virginia. Confederate Colonel Charles Mallory went to the fort to demand the return of his enslaved workers on the basis of the 1850 Fugitive Slave Act. The Union commander, Major Benjamin Butler, a radical abolitionist from Massachusetts, refused Mallory's request on the basis that the act did not apply to citizens from a foreign country, which Virginia became after it had seceded from the United States. Mallory and the Confederacy as a whole learned that the Constitution no longer protected their rights to have their escaped human property returned since they were no longer citizens of the Union.

These fugitives were among the first to self-emancipate themselves and reach Union protection. An estimated half a million enslaved Americans managed to escape to freedom during the Civil War (Foote and Hess 2021, 7).

Butler was later given official permission to keep escaped enslaved males and employ them in building Union military projects. The rationale was that keeping fugitives deprived the Confederacy of workers—while the Union gained the same number.

Consequences of the 1850 Fugitive Slave Law

The 1850 Fugitive Slave Law resulted in making slavery and its abuses a personal matter Northerners could no longer ignore. It was impossible to ignore its existence because the law forced Northern citizens to help slave catchers or else be penalized. In addition, those who helped fugitives could face heavy penalties, including fines and imprisonment. The 1850 Fugitive Slave Law both individualized and nationalized slavery by making the recapture of fugitives the personal responsibilities of Northerners as well as co-opting local law enforcement officials and facilities (Levine 1992, 189).

A result of the 1850 Fugitive Act was riots in many Northern cities as abolitionists protested the active intervention of the federal government over local laws and sentiments. Jailed fugitives were liberated from jails by mobs before they could be sent south to slavery. The Act was affirmed by the Supreme Court, and an estimated nine hundred fugitive slaves were returned to their likely owners during 1850–1862 (Salzman 1993, 287–89).

The anger caused by the 1850 Act also forced Northerners to consider disobeying the law and replacing legal conformity with a moral responsibility to disobey certain laws that ran counter to a person's moral beliefs. The moral disobedience of laws is called the Higher Law. Although the original fugitive law was mandated in the Constitution, the law was superseded by natural law and morality, which were both supported by God. The Higher Law concept negated any law or local statute opposing ethical, religious, and moral standards. Many Northerners were culturally conflicted and felt a strong attraction to the Constitution but also were against the institution of slavery (Potter 1976, 46).

A minority of Northerners increasingly decided that slavery would not disappear on its own over time because it was becoming too economically important in the slave states and legalized in newly established states. Those who were antislavery experienced a cultural conflict. Their religious and ethical values were in conflict with their political and citizenship values (Potter 1976, 46).

There were numerous responses to this conflict. One was to accept the constitutional protection of slavery while limiting its geographic expansion. This was a position taken by moderates, including Abraham Lincoln. This position had historical precedents since slavery had been barred from the Northwest Territories, and the international slave trade had been abolished in 1808.

The solution to this moral conflict was the acceptance of a Higher Law that rejected slavery irrespective of its legality. When a Higher Law is accepted, the legal institution of slavery no longer has its constitutional support. This appeal to a law more legitimate than one enacted by men encouraged law-abiding Northerners to resist bounty hunters attempting to capture escaped enslaved persons. Antislavery advocates could more easily rationalize violating the law of the land when helping escaping and escaped fugitives. The Higher Law reduced the efficacy of proslavery laws.

The Experiences of Henry Box Brown

A dramatic consequence of the 1850 Fugitive Slave Law involved the fugitive Henry "Box" Brown (1815–1897). Henry Brown was a self-employed enslaved man living in Richmond, Virginia. At age fifteen, Brown was separated from his family and leased to work in a tobacco factory. Brown later married, and he and his wife and two children were able to live in a rented house near his workplace.

Brown paid his master part of his wage as well as an added monthly fee for an agreement not to sell his family. This promise was not kept. Brown, in 1859, witnessed his family being shackled and taken away by their new owner, a Methodist minister. Brown then decided to escape to Pennsylvania (Foner 2015, 103). A sympathetic white shoemaker, Samuel "Red Boot" Smith, helped him escape. Smith was taking the chance of being jailed if he were caught helping a fugitive slave. His property would also have been confiscated (Delbanco 2018, 113). Smith was caught soon after Brown's escape as he attempted to mail two other fugitives (Diemer 2022, 71). After a very public trial, Smith was sentenced to a penitentiary for an almost eight years. The Philadelphia Black American community raised funds for Smith to settle in New York (Diemer 2022, 155).

Smith and Brown constructed a ventilated wooden crate that was three feet long, two feet wide, and thirty inches deep. Brown (five foot eight inches tall) climbed inside, and then Smith mailed the crate, labeled "dry goods" to James Miller McKim, a Quaker abolitionist living near Philadelphia (Pierson 2009, 24). The two-hundred-mile journey took twenty-seven hours. The crate was sent by wagon, railroad, steamship, wagon, a second railroad, ferry, and finally delivery by another wagon to its destination. Though the crate was labeled "handle with care," the crate was turned upside down several times.

It Is reported that Brown arrived at his destination, was uncrated, and sang a psalm he had composed for the occasion as he was welcomed by leading abolitionists. Brown became a popular lecturer, showman, and publicist in the United States and Great Britain. Brown was then known as Henry "Box" Brown and later legalized his new middle name. The wide publicity given to Brown's escape became another example to Southerners that the North was determined to liberate enslaved property from their owners (Pierson 2009, 25). Brown's escape also showed Southerners the determination of enslaved persons to escape to freedom.

Brown fled to Great Britain after the passing of the 1850 Fugitive Slave Act. He became a successful lecturer and later a showman and manager of a traveling show. At times, he would arrive in a town and climb into a crate to be transported by wagon through the town to the local theater. Brown would then climb out of the crate, deliver a short speech, and promote his future shows and presentations. Brown later returned to the United States to lead tours as an entertainer and lecturer. Brown retired in Canada. For decades, Brown was a symbol of a talented former enslaved person who openly criticized slavery in the United States and Great Britain.

Harriet Beecher Stowe's *Uncle Tom's Cabin*

Uncle Tom's Cabin: or, Life Among the Lowly, was published on March 20, 1852, after its serialization in the magazine *The National Review* during 1851. Stowe began the work as a reaction to the 1850 Fugitive Slave Law. She wanted to show the inhumanity of slavery and argue that it must be ended even though the institution was legal and supported by the Constitution. With the book's sentimentality, complex characters, humor, and detailed imagery of the cruel nature of slavery, Stowe characterized slavery as an anti-Christian and antifamily institution that debased both the enslaved as well as their owners and their own families.

Stowe humanized the enslaved by describing them as individuals with human feelings that were negative as well as positive. An especially effective element of the work was its descriptions of the enslaved religiosity, feelings of love, and family loyalty. There were also vivid scenes of the brutality and sexual exploitation of slaveholders.

The book touched the conscience of the North and the world. The work made Northerners more antislavery and more willing to consider and approve of its abolishment. The book convinced many of the legitimacy and necessity of the Higher Law as a rationale to end slavery. Stowe's emphasis on slavery's destructive effects on families was especially affecting during an era when families were becoming an increasingly emotional significance.

Stowe gave a human face to enslaved Black Americans and the cruelty of slavery as an institution (and slave owners). The sadistic and debauched Simon Legree, the sexually exploited young enslaved female, and other enslaved victims pictured as loving their families and very human feelings reinforced the humanity of Black Americans. A major and innovative theme of the book is that most, though not all, Black Americans deserved respect.

Motivated by the 1850 Fugitive Slave Law, Stowe overcame many readers' reluctance to commit illegal acts related to slavery by promoting the alternative ethical standard of the Higher Law. The Higher Law states that some laws should be disobeyed if they clashed with God's precepts. Morality and religious beliefs supersede legal demands.

Harriett Beecher Stowe was an influential proponent of the Higher Law concept. Abolitionist Frederick Douglass described his reaction to her book (Reynolds 2011, 118):

> We doubt if abler arguments have ever been presented in favor of the "Higher Law" than may be found [in] Mrs. Stowe's truly great work.

A number of themes in Stowe's book dealt with escaping fugitives. Few readers would be inclined to support the 1850 Fugitive Slave Act after reading *Uncle Tom's Cabin*. Stowe's intent in writing her book was to convince readers that disobeying the "unholy" laws supporting slavery was a godly act. Faithful Christians now had the responsibility to resist laws that were contrary to their religious and moral dictates. Those who helped escaping slaves in *Uncle Tom's Cabin* were characterized as honorable and godly persons. Those who chased after fugitives to reenslave them were described as legalistic villains using laws for nefarious and ungodly personal advantages (Reynolds 2011, 133).

Stowe's book sold more than three hundred thousand copies during its first year of publication. Three different editions were sold for $1.00, $1.50, and $3.00, an equivalent of $45–48 in today's currency and expensive for that the era (Reynolds 2011, 128). The work became America's first international bestseller. Many of the book's scenes became iconic and were reproduced in silent movies, theaters, and traveling shows.

The book's unforgettable scenes include the fatal beating of the Christlike Uncle Tom, the depiction of the flight of Eliza Harris carrying her child across the ice-covered Ohio River while fleeing slave traders and their slave-hunting dogs, and the slow death of the angelic Little Eva. These and other emotional scenes made the work unforgettable for generations across the world. The book brought home to its readers the personal agonies and injustices of slavery.

The Response of Southerners to *Uncle Tom's Cabin*

Southerners found subversive Stowe's insistence that Black Americans had the same feelings, loyalties, and attitudes as whites. There were also in the book enslaved characters whose attempts to escape from their masters showed that the enslaved preferred freedom over enslavement.

The first response from Southerners was to attack Stowe, and she was denounced as a shrew or as masculine. Other critics called her a "termagant virago" and a "foul-mouth hag." A major criticism was that a female author shouldn't write such incendiary and "intimate" material. A representative critic faulted Stowe for including "scenes of license and impurity, and ideas of loathsome depravity and habitual prostitution" (Reynolds 2011, 44).

The work was banned in the South, and having a copy of *Uncle Tom's Cabin* could result in punishment. A free Black American minister was discovered with a copy of the book and was sentenced to ten years in prison. He served five years and was only freed during the Civil War (Reynolds 2011, 151).

Another Southern response to *Uncle Tom's Cabin* was the publication of books with the purpose of showing how slavery was a benign system. In one such novel, Tom had escaped to the North but asked his former owner to reenslave him because economic conditions in the North were too harsh, and his poverty made him miserable (Reynolds 2011, 154).

A common Southern reaction to the book was to declare the descriptions of slavery false and misleading. In 1853, Stowe responded by publishing *Uncle Tom's Cabin & The Key to Uncle Tom's Cabin.* She explained in this work why she described her characters as she did. Her sources upon which the novel was based included court reports, personal experience, letters, various reports, and newspaper advertisements for fugitives. Stowe presented two newspaper advertisements of owners of fugitives. The first announcement is found in the *New Orleans Picayune* in 1852. The second was published in the *Republican Banner and Nashville Whig* in 1836 (Stowe 1853, 176):

> Run away from the plantation of the undersigned the negro man Shedrick, a preacher, 5 feet 9 inches high, about 40 years old, but looking not over 23, stamped N. E. *on the breast and having both small toes cut off.* He is of a very dark complexion, with eyes small but bright, and a look quite insolent [emphasis added by Stowe].

> 100 DOLLARS REWARD WILL be given for the apprehension of my negro Edmund Kenny. *He has straight hair, and complexion so nearly white that it is believed a stranger would suppose there was no African blood in him* … [He] was apprehended, *but escaped under pretense of being a white man!* [emphasis and exclamation mark added by Stowe]

Helper's *The Impending Crisis of the South*

In 1857, Hinton Rowan Helper published a work as devastating to Southern honor as Stowe's *Uncle Tom's Cabin,* but Helper's work was devoid of sentimentality, and the readership was aimed at both the Southern elite and poorer white Southerners. Helper's *The Impending Crisis of the South: How to Meet It* presents census data, financial reports, and other statistics, including the value of farm crops and trade data. While Stowe's book attacked slavery using emotions, Helper's approach was rational, comparative, and factual.

The book's thesis was that slavery impoverished both the South and Southerners, especially the white poorer social classes. Slavery enriched only the wealthier enslaved persons' owners to the disadvantage of the rest of the Southern population. Helper's data were based partly on selective parts of the 1850 census and were difficult to disprove because the director of that census was Southerner J. D. B. De Bow, a well-respected promoter of Southern economic development and a supporter of slavery.

Helper's book became an instant success in the North, and it eventually sold 140,000 copies. Part of its success in the North and notoriety in the South was based on the fact that the author was a Virginian. It was also difficult to argue against census and economic data.

The book became well-known among Northern abolitionists and white Southerners. A senator from Massachusetts read several paragraphs from Helper's book during a speech in the Senate. In response, a senator from North Carolina responded with an ad hominem attack by denouncing Helper as a traitor to the South (Brown 2006, 135):

> He is a dishonest, degraded man, and although—
> much to be regretted—a native of the State, yet he
> is an apostate son, ruined in fortune and character,

> and catering to a diseased appetite at the North, to obtain a miserable living, by slanders upon the land of his birth.

Helper experienced his social death and social rejection because he dared to criticize the institution of slavery. He also proposed that the white social classes were being exploited by slavery for the benefit of the few elites.

The view that slavery retarded local economies and impoverished whites was not an original proposition proposed by Helper. Kentuckian abolitionist Cassius Marcellus Clay (1810–1903) lectured during the 1840s and 1850s that slavery was a cruel institution that harmed poorer whites as well as Southern society in general.

Helper presented the example that two hundred enslaved persons in a large plantation added nothing to the local economy. By contrast, two hundred free workers working for wages would contribute to the financial prosperity of their county and state. Clay also pointed out that more slaves in an area resulted in fewer jobs for whites (Ellison 2005, 47). Similar to Helper's methodological contrasts between slave and free states, Clay also compared the demographic and economic differences between slave state Kentucky and free state of Ohio. Clay pointed out that during 1830–1840, the population of Ohio increased by 60 percent compared to Kentucky's 33 percent.

Clay's comparisons were not original. Alexis de Tocqueville, during the 1830s, also compared two states to show the detrimental economic effects of the presence of slavery. Frederick Olmsted continued this tradition of finding that slavery was a dysfunctional system of labor (Olmsted 2017, 11 and 243):

> Most of the people [i.e., Southerners] lived very poorly; that the proportion of men improving their condition was much less than in any Northern

> community; and that the natural resources of the land were strangely unused, or were used with poor economy ... Slavery is a great evil, morally and economically. It was a curse upon the South.

In addition to focusing on the decreasing economic conditions of poor whites, Helper suggested that poor whites should demand more political and economic power as well as access to better education. The fear of revolts among poor whites was a constant worry among the Southern elite. Helper also showed that slavery was beneficial to slave owners and detrimental to everyone else in the South (Williams 2008, 35). Helper's arguments, based on census data, threatened the social order of the Southern elite, whom he called the "Lords of the Lash." Helper denounced the Slave Power as detrimental to all but themselves.

Helper also noted in numerous passages that the extensive dependencies on Northern manufacturers and culture (including books and education) were insults to the South. Few other accusations, aside from the threat of poor whites' rebellion, could anger slave owners to a great degree (Helper 1859, Kindle location 252–53):

> In one way or another we are more or less *subservient* to the North every day of our lives ... But it can hardly be necessary to say more in illustration of the *unmanly* and *unnatural dependence*, which is so glaring that it cannot fail to be apparent to even the most careless and superficial observer. All the world sees, or ought to see, that in a commercial, mechanical, manufactural, financial, and literary point of view, we are as *helpless* as babes; that, in comparison with the Free States, our agricultural resources have been greatly exaggerated, misunderstood and mismanaged; and that, instead

> of cultivating among ourselves a wise policy of mutual assistance and co-operation with respect to individuals, and of self-reliance with respect to the South at large, … we have been spending our substance at the North, and are daily augmenting and strengthening the very power which now has us so *completely under its thumb* [emphasis added].

Helper's methodology of comparing states was used by modern research that reinforced Helper's findings. William H. Pease and Jane H. Pease (1991) compared the economic development of the cities of Boston and Charleston during 1828–1843. The authors found that the lack of Charleston's economic development as compared to the more prosperous Boston was influenced by the institution of slavery.

John Brown's Attack on Slavery

During October 16–18, 1859, one of the greatest fears among Southerners almost came true. John Brown and a band of twenty-two men attempted to lead an armed slave insurrection. Included in his arsenal were 950 pikes made from bowie knife blades attached to six-foot poles to be distributed to formerly enslaved persons expected to join his band. His choice of Harpers Ferry was in part due to the arsenal's hundred thousand weapons. Brown and his followers, augmented by future Black volunteers, believed they could establish hidden refuges in the nearby mountains.

The pikes and the arsenal's firearms would be used to arm both Black and sympathetic whites willing to serve as antislavery guerrillas. They would periodically attack nearby plantations to steal supplies and liberate more enslaved persons until the institution of slavery collapsed.

John Brown was already notorious. He had sought for decades to end slavery. He had traveled to the Kansas Territory with a band of volunteers to help the antislavery forces attempting to establish a slave-free state. Proslavery forces had previously killed a number of abolitionists and threatened to kill more (Reynolds 2006, 166).

The incident galvanizing Brown was the destruction of the town of Lawrence, Kansas, by a proslavery band of 750 led by Henry Clay Pate. Lawrence was a town located in an area dominated by abolitionists. After months of threats by proslavery Missouri "border ruffians," as they were called, Pate and his men entered Lawrence on May 21, 1856. The raiders used a cannon to destroy the town's hotel. They destroyed two abolitionist printing presses and looted the town.

In revenge, Brown sought out proslavery men at the Pottawatomie Creek settlement, killed five men, and hacked their bodies with a broadsword. Brown's reason for these murders was to avenge the earlier murder of six abolitionists and the burning of the city of Lawrence.

Deeply religious in an Old Testament manner, Brown believed certain sins demanded the shedding of blood in retribution. He also believed that harsh responses to the violence and threats of Southern violence were necessary. Brown was angry with Pate and his followers, but he was disappointed that the town's residents had not fought back. Brown believed that blood must be shed to destroy slavery and protect abolitionists. Abolitionists should be as violent as those who were proslavery.

Soon after the five murders, Brown, his band, and members of the Free-State Party located a camp of Missourian slavery supporters led by Henry Clay Pate. Pate had promised to chase and capture Brown. Brown's band of thirty attacked Pate's band of more than fifty men, and the battle of Black Jack began. The battle, the first in "Bleeding Kansas" fought by organized opponents, has been called the first battle of the Civil War (Brands 2020, 93).

Captain Brown, as he was now called, learned that a band of proslavers was planning to attack the town of Osawatomie, which was located in an antislavery area. Brown and his band of thirty "Kansas Regulars" rushed to Osawatomie and waited for the attackers. A firefight began on August 30, 1856, when the two forces met near the town. The first to die was John Brown's son Fred. Outnumbered, Brown's men soon retreated and left the scene. Rather than pursue Brown, the proslavers burned Osawatomie (Brands 2020, 100). Brown was called "Osawatomie" Brown after the battle.

Brown's fame rests not on his earlier struggles against slavery but on his Harpers Ferry raid. Under Brown's leadership, his followers would attack slavery and live according to his definition of Christian principles guaranteed by a constitution—written by Brown—that guaranteed freedom to all members (Current 1998, 265). In these communities, whites and Blacks were to be equal in all ways.

Brown's constitution, "The Provisional Constitution," promoted total racial equality and complete citizenship rights for Black Americans. The document describes the minutia of a government, including the establishment of offices and elected officials as well as the behavior expected of the new republic's citizens. Article 11 of the forty-eight articles constituting the Provisional Constitution reflects Brown's strict Puritan values:

> Profane swearing, filthy conversation, indecent behavior, or indecent exposure of the person, or intoxication or quarreling, shall not be allowed or tolerated, neither unlawful intercourse of the sexes.

A more rational terrorist would have seized arms and immediately hidden in the mountains, but Brown remained surprisingly passive and inactive while local armed residents, the local militia, and a militia from Maryland arrived and surrounded the building where the band had been forced to seek shelter. Brown had earlier stopped and then released a train. The train's engineers rapidly telegraphed the authorities the news of the arsenal's takeover.

A marine unit led by Robert E. Lee and Jeb Stuart arrived thirty-six hours after the beginning of the raid and forced themselves into the building where Brown and his followers were trapped. Brown surrendered after ten of his followers had been killed—including two of his sons—and he was wounded. Four local civilians, including the mayor and a marine, were also fatalities. A week later, Brown was tried for treason and then executed by hanging on December 2, 1859.

While being led to the gallows, Brown was asked whether he wanted to be accompanied by a clergyman. Brown answered that he would rather be accompanied by "barefooted, barelegged, ragged slave children and their old gray-headed slave mother" (Puleo 2012, 282).

Brown's last message was a note saying in part, "I, John Brown, am now quite certain that the crimes of this guilty land will never be purged away but with blood."

The Southern Response to Brown's Raid

Brown's death became a boon for Southern radicals. Southern secessionists claimed the raid proved that Northerners wanted to violently end slavery and the Southern way of life (Sheehan-Dean 2018, 26). Radical secessionist Edward Ruffin, who later sent Brown's pikes to selected politicians to warn them of Brown's and the North's goals, declared happily (Current 1998, 264): "Such a practical exercise of abolition principles is needed to stir the sluggish blood of the South."

A more practical reaction to Brown's raid was an increased militarization of the South that had begun in earnest during the 1850s. Reflecting a near hysteria, militias were organized or given new life. The slave states began preparing for war (Franklin 2002, 289).

Southerners admitted to a grudging respect for Brown. He had followed his conscience and carried out a bold cavalier-like act of violence while gambling his life—and his son's lives (Wyatt-Brown 1985, 124). Brown's raid was also cavalier-like in that it was not well planned and was based on emotions rather than a rational strategy.

Brown's promoting of an act of violence was the slaveholders' major fear. They could no longer assume that abolitionists could be intimidated by threatening personal violence or secession. They had to recognize the possible aggressive attitudes of abolitionists. This was reinforced by the way Northerners idolized John Brown after his death.

The Northern Response to Brown's Raid

The most important consequence for Northerners of John Brown's failed raid was the fact that he was willing to use violence to end slavery. Most Northern abolitionists did not yet accept the use of violence as a means to end slavery, but they hoped instead that slavery would disappear when slaves were no longer economically necessary or when slaveholders themselves saw the moral unfairness of slavery. These abolitionists preferred moral persuasion over violence (Reynolds 2006, 195).

Northerners now had a martyr who had sacrificed himself for the abolitionist cause and was willing to use violence to combat slavery. He had insisted that slavery was sinful and that it was the responsibility of honorable Christians to use any means, including violence, to combat slavery. This belief was a radical use of the

Higher Law in which violence is an honorable tactic to destroy slavery. As Wyatt-Brown (1985, 127) concluded:

> He [i.e., Brown] became exactly what he wished to be: a Christ-like figure for the North and an avenging angel for the South.

Henry David Thoreau used similar imagery during a prayer service to honor Brown (Puleo 2012, 283):

> Eighteen-hundred years ago, Christ was crucified. This morning … John Brown was hung. These are two ends of a chain which is not without its links.

Wendell Phillips delivered the eulogy at Brown's funeral during which he stated (Puleo 2012, 284):

> History will date Virginia emancipation from Harpers Ferry. True, the slave is still there. So, when the tempest uproots a pine on your hill, it looks green for months—a year or two. Still, it is timber, not a tree. John Brown has loosened the roots of the slave system; it only breathes—it does not live—hereafter.

While Lincoln may have remarked that the publication of *Uncle Tom's Cabin* helped bring about the Civil War, a more accurate observation would be that John Brown made war more likely.

CHAPTER 7

INDIVIDUALISM

No one has the right to place one human being in
a position of political power over another.
—Wendy McElroy

Southern individualism was not associated with an individual's sense of freedom or acceptance of experimentation. A person can assert his or her individuality through art, intellectualism, religion, scientific studies, or eccentricity. In the traditional Southern culture, however, individualism was not encouraged if it involved openly breaking with tradition (Cash 1941, 44 and 97). That is why most innovators and inventors lived in the North and not in the South. Secession was defined not as political change but as a return to the older founding fathers' values, including individualism and a traditional constitutional protection of slavery.

Southern religion was more monolithic than in the North. Religious beliefs were more varied in the North and characterized by numerous schisms and religious innovations. Northern religious beliefs were more likely to promote changes in society. By contrast, Southern religious beliefs stressed the individual. Instead of reforming society, Southerners believed reform should be based on changing individuals rather than institutions. There was also a greater belief in fatalism in that God intervened in local affairs to determine whether a battle would be lost or won.

The Southern cult of individualism (the term is better described as "egocentric individualism") focused on the freedom to be a powerful and aggressive white male (Beringer et al. 1986, 434). There were family loyalties and close friendships, but the cavalier's other loyalties were often to himself, his honor, his sense of independence, and his place in society. He generally evaluated others outside the boundaries of family and friends in terms of possible threats to his honor. In the context of the Civil War, considerations of personal freedom were often more important than supporting the immediate goals of the Confederacy. A major failure of Confederate commanders was an unwillingness to cooperate with their peers or superiors.

Southern individualism was also closely associated with masculinity and honor (Wyatt-Brown 1985, 149). Individualism encourages a white man to protect or augment his honor by being recognized as courageous and willing to defend his honor and reputation. Decades of promoting secession by emphasizing the values of freedom and political independence reinforced the already existing cultural value of personal individualism within a traditional framework.

Army life demands discipline and conformity, and military duty conflicts with one's sense of individual freedom (Rubin 2005, 50–51). It is a tribute to Southern culture that many Confederate soldiers were able to restrain much of their individuality and still support the war under very harsh conditions. Other Confederates were unable to conform to military demands and discipline and created problems, resulting in weaknesses for the Confederacy.

Southerners themselves recognized that the values of cavalier individualism weakened the war effort (Daniel 1868, 161–62):

> The character of the soldier himself … renders it difficult to secure that complete efficiency which

> marks the perfection of a disciplined army. The very reckless bravery which gives him his victorious elan is difficult to reconcile with strict discipline, the sleepless vigilance, which are indispensable to success in war.

Jefferson Davis similarly noted this lack of discipline when he summarized the failures of the founding members of the Confederacy (Davis 1994, 407):

> They all suffered in some degree from a drought of the one trait that Southern leaders most desperately needed before and during the war, moderation.

William Wing Loring was a brave Confederate officer who was wounded three times, had one arm amputated, and performed well in some instances during the Civil War. Loring was also overly concerned with his independence and his insistence to be able to act in an individual manner. He was one of the generals who refused to cooperate with two of his colleagues as well as with Robert E. Lee in Western Virginia and was partly responsible for the failure of the campaign. "Stonewall" Jackson later filed a court-martial against Loring. Loring also quarreled with John Letcher, the governor of Virginia.

These values encouraged Confederates to act independently of orders and to consider their own interests over the military's. Future Brigadier General John Buchanan Floyd, commander of the Army of Kanawha, refused to cooperate with his fellow commander, Henry A. Wise, because they had been prewar political competitors. They would not even camp together, thus dividing the Confederate forces. Loring would cooperate with neither man nor with Robert E. Lee when Lee was sent to command the three (Mitcham 2022, 191).

Sent to Mississippi by Robert E. Lee because of his quarrels as a member of the Army of Northern Virginia, Loring quarreled with his new superior, John C. Pemberton. Loring has been accused by many of hating Pemberton so much that he was willing for Pemberton to lose a battle so he could be promoted and replace Pemberton. The Battle of Champion Hill might have been won by the Confederates had Loring obeyed his orders or been willing to communicate with Pemberton (Mitcham 2022, 408–9).

Individualism and Disobedience

Line soldiers expressed their individualism in a number of ways that harmed the Confederacy. In a culture glorifying individualism, enlistees defined themselves as citizens who had volunteered to be soldiers while maintaining most of their rights as citizens. Orders that seemed irrational to enlistees were often disobeyed as infringements upon personal liberty. At times, soldiers would retaliate when their officers' issuing orders were defined as not honorable enough to legitimately order individuals. During the summer of 1862, an officer was so unpopular that sixty men deserted in one night because they refused to accept him as their commander. Most returned to their units when the disliked officer resigned and was replaced by someone more acceptable (Linderman 1987, 56).

Soldiers publicly ridiculed officers they did not respect and even fired into an officer's tent as a warning. There were enough rumors that some officers had been killed during battles by their own men to force officers to resign in fear or not allow part of their command to remain behind them during the battle (Linderman 1987, 52–53). The term for facing possible fire from enemy or friend was called being "between two fires."

One of Lee's major weaknesses as a commander was giving too much freedom to subordinates, many of whom were either incapable of following general orders or, equally likely, preferred to act according to their individual tendencies (Fuller 1957, 162). Specific orders might have been disobeyed or "interpreted" to better fit a subordinate's wish to act as he wished. This problem was more likely because Lee tended to be an inactive observer during battle. Even a strong admirer of Lee admitted Lee's inaction during the third day of the Battle of Gettysburg (Snow 1867, 103):

> During the whole time the firing continued he sent only one message, and received only one report. It was evidently his system to arrange the plan thoroughly with the three corps commanders, and then leave to them the duty of modifying and carrying it out to the best of their abilities.

Lee observed his battles, but he did not interfere in ongoing maneuvers when a battle began. Lee did notice events during battle and observed the behavior of his generals and men. Lee criticized those officers he thought had exposed themselves unnecessarily to enemy fire, and he praised those who had showed unusual bravery or expertise. Lee's passivity was most likely a valid practice. Communication through couriers on foot or on horses was slow and could be outdated or misunderstood in the excitement of battle. Constant messaging, which might be outdated, could only distract and confuse local commanders.

Lee was in a quandary. He could issue direct, specific orders that might be disobeyed or useless when battle conditions changed. He might also insult his generals who preferred independence of action. Lee could form his orders in a vague fashion, which might not lead to the specific behavior he preferred. The Gettysburg Battle might not have taken place had General Henry Heth and his division not entered the town of Gettysburg to confiscate shoes and other supplies even though he had been clearly ordered by Lee to avoid conflict, which he would not when he met a Union force.

Lee sent a telegram to Jefferson Davis indicating his anger at not being obeyed by General D. H. Hill, one of his more respected generals (Freeman 1957, 99):

> I gave Genl Hill Discretionary orders from Richmond to apportion his force to the strength of the Enemy and send what could be spared. *He declined to act and requested positive orders. I gave such orders as I could at this distance. Now he objects.* I cannot operate in this manner. I request you to cause such orders to be given him as your judgment dictates (emphasis added).

No officer wants to decrease the size of his command, and Hill was obviously no exception. However, Lee had issued his command twice and was forced to ask Jefferson Davis to support his authority. This reflected badly on Lee's strength of command and was humiliating. Lee's strategies often were based on complex tactics and a sense of timing known only to himself. Hill would not know why he was ordered to reduce his command, though it might have been crucial to do so. Lee was always asking for more troops and supplies, and Hill may have felt Lee's orders were not important and rationalized he had the liberty to disobey.

Lee also considered his staff and army as members of his extended family, and he called the soldiers of the Army of Northern Virginia his "sons." His staff and officers—some of whom were his actual sons and a nephew—were also members of his military "family." As a father figure, Lee would be expected to soften his criticisms. After all, Lee had joined the Confederacy in large part to protect his family.

The men refused to march in cadence. Each march resulted in large numbers of stragglers arriving to camp late or not being in place at the start of a battle. Such men also had little respect for military equipment they thought unnecessary at the time. Equipment would be mishandled, lost, discarded, or sold for food or alcohol. Men would stop whenever possible to plunder enemy bodies for equipment (especially shoes and overcoats) and food with the result in a loss of momentum and organization. While such actions have always been common in all wars, they disrupted battlefield coherence and weakened the momentum of attacks following a retreating enemy.

Individualism and Rejection of Hierarchy

A major reason for battle losses in the Army of Tennessee was a result of interpersonal conflicts among its officers. Negative behavior due to Southern individualism among officers occurred when Nathan Bedford Forrest warned his superior, Braxton Bragg, that he would kill him if he saw him again. Bragg, arrogant and always inept in personnel matters, had transferred Forrest to a unit commanded by Joseph Wheeler, a man Forrest disliked even though both were superior cavalry raiders. Upon learning about his transfer, Forrest may have said to Bragg (Murray and Wei-Hsieh 2015, 344):

> I have stood your meanness as long as I intend to. You have played the part of a damned scoundrel, and are a coward, and if you were any part of a man, I would slap your jaws and force you to resent it. You may as well not issue any more orders to me, for I will not obey them …

Braxton Bragg experienced hostility from many of his subordinates. With an acerbic temperament and high-performance expectations, Bragg managed to alienate most of his generals. The result was that his three corps commanders (James Longstreet,

Leonidas Polk, and Daniel H. Hill), among others, refused to cooperate or obey Bragg. Bragg believed that a large number of his subordinate officers were either inadequate or consistently refused to follow his orders—while his own actions were faultless. Such behavior violated military protocols, but the presence of individualism in Southern culture resulted in behaviors that weakened the military efficiency of the Confederacy.

After the Battle of Chickamauga had been won by the Confederate forces, James Longstreet did not bother to inform Bragg of his success (Hess 2016, 175). He claimed Bragg would have heard the cheers of his troops and realized the battle had been won! Under normal circumstances, a subordinate would have been glad to announce to his superior that a battle had been won.

Many of Bragg's other officers also refused to communicate with him whenever possible. These officers petitioned several times to have Bragg replaced as commander of the Army of Tennessee. In addition, commanders in the other departments comprising the western theater refused to recognize Bragg's authority to give them orders. The result was that there was no functional central authority over half of the Confederacy.

Bragg would have been more successful as a commander if his subordinates had followed his orders. The blame for the loss of roughly half of the Confederacy's land area can be largely attributed to the recalcitrance of officers refusing to obey orders or cooperate with their peers.

Individualism and the Refusal to Accept Military Discipline

Rejecting discipline does not necessarily indicate a lack of patriotism, a rejection of the aims of the Confederacy, or laziness. Yeoman farmer Samuel E. Burges was a South Carolinian who owned one enslaved person. An entry in his diary describes his rejection of military discipline and the maintenance of his citizen rights as he confronted his captain (Gienapp 2001, 237–38):

> Quarrel with Capt about breakfast. Said if I got none it would be my fault. Replied it would be his fault and if I could not get it in my place where I then was it would be his fault, that he never troubled himself to see that the men were properly provided. On inspection said my rifle was dirty. Replied it was clean, having cleaned it 3 days ago and not used it since. Gave me an hour to clean it in. replied I would think of it and laughed at him. Ordered Lieut to report me … Went off laughing at him.

Lee realized that the Confederate type of individualism weakened his army (Glatthaar 2008, 176). He complained that soldiers did not accept military discipline even though they fought well when they were commanded well and, as important, when they personally respected their leaders.

White male Southerners equated orders with being treated as slaves rather than as honorable individuals. In a slave-based society, orders are defined as insults to whites' sense of honor and self-worth. Maintaining one's manhood demanded the liberty to act as one wished rather than being compelled to do so (Glatthaar 2008, 176–77). An honorable man is expected to fulfill his duty as he defines it, but he would reject being forced to behave when ordered. Military orders are accepted when defined as necessary and appropriate or when given by those who are respected.

The lack of cooperation and obedience frustrated Lee during the Battle of Gettysburg. Generals rode their horses during the battle when Lee ordered them not to do so. A bombardment ordered for twenty minutes lasted two hours, and men were not moved into position at the time ordered (Tucker 2016, 79). One artillery unit retreated to a safer location, but its commander failed to inform his superior of the move.

Rank-and-file soldiers expressed their dislike of their superior officers. Brigadier General George H. Steuart was a strict disciplinarian and a martinet, especially in terms of hygiene. Steuart also had a practice of sneaking through the camp's perimeter to test the alertness of the sentries. He was once caught by an alert sentry and beaten. The sentry later claimed that he had not recognized the general! Later, Steuart's method of discipline and emphasis on health were accepted by this troops, and he became a respected commander. Steuart had been highly unpopular at the time of his beating.

Individualism and Lack of Organization

Joseph T. Glatthaar noted that a major weakness of the Confederacy leadership was an inability to coordinate. The Civil War involved too many new factors, such as the increased size of armies, increased amount of logistics needed, and more modern armaments, to be successfully fought in a more individualist manner. The Mexican-American War (1846–1848), when most Confederate generals gained their experience leading somewhat larger units, was fought with a force of sixteen thousand—roughly the size of Pickett's Charge during the Battle of Gettysburg. A semimodern war such as the Civil War required less individualism and more cooperation at all levels:

> Political and military leaders … needed to learn how to join with others to harness and employ their resources most efficiently in order to triumph in the war. (Glatthaar 1994, vii)

Most experienced antebellum officers had fought in the Mexican War, had been stationed in small forts on the frontier, and/or had experienced guerrilla warfare in the three Seminole Wars during 1816–1858.

Jefferson Davis was frustratingly familiar with this lack of cooperation at the higher levels because of personal conflicts and feelings of independence (individualism) among his generals. Even as late as July 1864, Davis pleaded with the generals in the Army of Tennessee to accept the transfer of command from Joseph E. Johnston to John Bell Hood, to ignore their mutual dislikes, and to promote the common good (the army had experienced bitter feuds and jealousies among the higher ranks since its beginning). Even the very patriotic Robert E. Lee refused to be sent by Davis to the western theater to protect the city of Vicksburg from the armies of Grant and Sherman. Lee believed he would not be able to end the internal conflicts among the generals of the Army of Tennessee and that they would not accept him as their commander. Lee also refused to leave the state of Virginia.

Major General Thomas Carmichael Hindman had just entered Missouri and was planning a campaign to take control of Missouri from the occupying Union forces. He was ordered to take his eleven thousand men to the east of the Mississippi River and help protect the city of Vicksburg from the Federals. Instead of immediately following orders, Hindman decided to fight one more battle and recover Missouri from the enemy before obeying his orders. Hindman and his forces met Union forces at Pine Grove on December 7, 1862. Hindman's First Corps of the Trans-Mississippi Army was forced to retreat, but each side suffered roughly the same number of casualties. The practical results of the Battle of Pine Grove, Arkansas, was the Union control of northwestern Arkansas, and the city of Vicksburg did not receive reinforcements. Vicksburg was lost to the Confederacy eight months later. The Confederacy might have protected Vicksburg and the surrounding area better had Hindman followed orders. On the other hand, many of Hindman's command might not have been willing to cross the Mississippi River and leave Arkansas and Missouri. Men in the trans-Mississippi armies were generally unwilling to leave their states (Eaton 1954, 201).

Another instance of Southern individualism resulting in a lack of cooperation among Confederate officers is the infamous "shad bake," hastening the surrender of the Army of Northern Virginia. On April 1, 1865, Generals George Pickett (the senior officer), Thomas Rosser, and Fitzhugh Lee (Robert E. Lee's nephew) left their Petersburg headquarters without informing their staff. They went to attend a shad bake (a Virginian tradition of an evening of broiling shad over an open fire). Meanwhile, their men were on short rations.

Lee had ordered the defense of the area "at all hazards," meaning its defense was critical. As senior officer, Pickett had convinced himself there would be no further Union attacks and was willing to travel three miles to enjoy a pleasant respite from the war—in spite of the fact that attacks had taken place the day before, and the three Confederate commanders were aware the enemy was nearby and aggressively active.

Union forces attacked the Confederate position during the generals' absence. There were woods between the Confederate position at Five Forks and the shad bake, and the errant officers could not hear the sounds of the battle (Patterson 2002, 136–37). The absence of the three highest-ranked officers prevented a coordination for the defense against the Union's attack. The general left in charge after the three generals left for the shad bake, George H. "Maryland Steuart" Steuart, lost three thousand of his own command of ten thousand.

The lack of the presence of the three highest-level officers and a previously high rate of desertions among the Confederate forces resulted in units of the Union Army of the Potomac breaking through the Confederate defenses and forcing Lee and his army soon after to abandon the Petersburg-Richmond entrenchments. Both Petersburg and Richmond were left defenseless, and the Confederate government began its evacuation of Richmond.

Lee's near-starving forces couldn't escape Grant's gradual encirclement and surrendered on April 9, eight days after retreating from the temporary safety of the Petersburg defenses. Grant's forces, aided by Sherman's approaching army, would have surrounded Petersburg and breached its thirty-five miles of fortifications eventually, but the shad bake fiasco hastened Lee's surrender, the capture of Jefferson Davis, and the surrender of the Confederacy.

The April 1, 1865, Battle of Five Forks ended with an estimate of more than five thousand casualties. Though seldom showing emotion when angry, Lee was later heard to ask an aide when he spied Pickett from afar: "Is that man still with the army?" The fact that Lee did not use Pickett's name was an insult as if Pickett had experienced a social death and was no longer a respected individual. Lee similarly described the Federal forces as "those people." Pickett was removed from his command a few days later (Heilder and Heilder 2000, 1519).

Pickett had earlier deserted his post a number of times. He rode fifteen miles during the late afternoon and evening to visit "Sallie" Corbett, one half his age, during the siege of Suffolk, Virginia, during April and May 1863. Pickett continued his long-distance courtship even when ordered not to do so (Walsh 2002, 335).

Individualism and Desertion

Always short of men, partly because of battle casualties, Lee complained of the large numbers of those absent from his army. Though he realized some would return, Lee could not count on the official numbers of soldiers present when they were needed.

Lee wrote to Jefferson Davis on July 25, 1863, to complain about his troop's individualism, but he never complained about their bravery (Dowdy and Manorin 1961, 563):

> Our people are so little liable to control that it is difficult to get them to follow any course not in accordance with their inclinations.

The above complaint indicates Lee was aware of his men's individualism and their resistance to military discipline. He was so worried about the rate of desertions in his army that he proposed harsh punishments for deserters (Dowdy and Manorin 1961, 563): "Nothing will redeem this great evil [i.e., desertions] which so much endangers our cause except the rigid enforcement of the death penalty in future cases of conviction."

The high respect for masculine individualism among Southerners also resulted in a dysfunctional tendency for many Confederate soldiers to permanently desert their military posts or temporarily desert to return home for limited periods of time (the military did not differentiate between being temporarily or permanently absent).

An estimated hundred thousand or more Confederates deserted, and 229 deserters were executed during the war. Manpower was too needed for deserters to be regularly given the death penalty, but at first, both Lee and Jackson were willing to establish the death penalty for desertion. Most punishments involved a stay in the camp's prison, being forced into an uncomfortable position, or wearing irons for a time. Some were shamed by wearing a sign saying "deserter" and paraded in front of his company. Desertions took place primarily while soldiers were in camp. While there were occasions when groups retreated during a battle—especially during a failed charge—and some men hid until there were no more dangers. Few were willing to desert when their comrades were experiencing fire. Nevertheless, battle reports of the number of those "missing" include those who had deserted.

While desertions occurred after a Confederate battle loss, they also took place after Confederate victories, suggesting that a minority of Rebel soldiers believed they had completed their share of the war and could go back to their families on a permanent or temporary basis. Another rationale for desertions was that those who volunteered at the beginning of the war had signed up for one year. The Confederacy's war department arbitrarily extended the enlistment period from one to three years. Those who had volunteered but did not bring with them a battle-quality musket also had their time of service extended. The few who could afford to bring an acceptable musket kept their shorter enlistment period for a while. Eventually, all enlistees were forced to remain in the military until the end of the war.

When he assumed the command of the Army of Northern Virginia, Lee discovered the tendency of the men under his command to leave the camp or army without permission for various periods of time, and the men devised ingenious ways of leaving camp. Most of the men in the army were Virginians, and some would leave camp or while on a march to visit nearby families for short periods of time, taking "French leave." To these men, they were not deserting; they were using their individual civilian rights as they saw fit. Foreigners called desertion the "American problem." Those who were severely wounded could be sent to their homes to recuperate and heal. These men could have refused to return, but most did return to rejoin their comrades.

Lee's reaction to the large numbers of absentees in his army was contradictory. Lee and "Stonewall" Jackson wanted deserters punished, including the use of firing squads. Both believed that strict obedience to military protocols was necessary for a well-functioning army. Lee also realized he needed every soldier he could retain. Lee wrote to Jefferson Davis on April 7, 1864, asking that a number of court-martialed deserters who had received death sentences be forgiven (Freeman 1957, 149):

> I would beg to call your Excellency's attention to the following cases, in which sentences of death have been passed and in which I, having suspended the execution of the sentences, have forwarded the proceedings with the recommendation that the sentences be remitted ... I am desirous of having the men returned to the army in time to take part in the approaching campaign.

A problem with deserters was that they often took their rifles with them. These armaments made the deserters capable of defending themselves from local enforcement officers and civilians as they stole food from farms along their path to their homes or places of safety. Private William A. Fletcher, who served under "Stonewall Jackson," recounts gathering chickens, corn, and fruit from Virginian farms in addition to stealing from merchants (Fletcher 1908) when stationed in camps. The editor of the *Richmond Enquirer* on August 22, 1862, wrote an editorial complaining that (Tatum 2000, x):

> We often hear persons say, "The Yankees cannot do us any more harm than our own soldiers have done."

According to the Southern honor code, one's loyalty was limited to self, family, and friends, but potentially dangerous strangers generally received little sympathy. Reaching their homes, these deserters would be protected by family members, neighbors, and fellow "absentees." Returning to one's family became increasingly common as war-weariness and inflation took their tolls.

Jefferson Davis resorted to issuing general amnesties several times during the war to pardon all absent men if they returned to their posts within twenty days of the publication in their states of the amnesty proclamations. Contrary to the intent of these amnesties, many soldiers interpreted these announcements as opportunities to leave camp, which would be forgiven when they returned! In the short term, the result was more rather than less temporary desertions. Lee complained to Davis (Freeman 1957, 122–23):

> The number of desertions from the army is so great and still continues to such an extent that unless some secession of them can be caused I fear success in the field will be seriously endangered … Night before last thirty went from one regiment and eighteen from another [a regiment officially numbered one thousand men but always contained fewer available for battle]. Great dissatisfaction is reported among the good men in the Army at the apparent impunity of deserters.

The problem of desertions and absenteeism became greater as men became war-weary, worried about the needs of their families, or both. When Union forces won their siege of Vicksburg, Grant offered parole to the captured 29,500 Confederates. Hundreds chose to reject parole to spend the rest of the war in Northern prisons. Among those who accepted parole, many deserted and returned to their homes rather than going to temporary Confederate military camps established for parolees. These men often deserted in groups and terrorized the areas they traveled through on their way home. Confederate General Pemberton ordered these deserters to be shot if they were caught riding the trains "on which they had swarmed to return home" (Bonekemper 2015, 232).

The above term "swarmed" shows that deserters were considered less than human since only animals swarmed. The quote above also indicates that officers realized that deserters wanted to return home where they would be both needed and protected. Family loyalty in these cases trumped loyalty to the Confederacy.

Grant recognized the allure of desertion among Confederates. During the ten-month siege of Petersburg, Union officers offered deserters food and train tickets home (if their homes were located in areas controlled by the Union and if they were willing to take the oath of allegiance to the Union).

The general American public as well as authorities defined desertion as a sign of cowardice and lack of patriotism. Union deserters were more likely to live outside their home states after the war than those veterans who did not desert. Even deserters who lived in their home states after the war were more likely to live in a different part of the state than where they were recruited (Costa and Kahn 2008, 175). We assume the same patterns among Confederate soldiers would be found, though the necessary data do not exist.

Individualism and the Citizen-Soldier Tradition

Southern patriotism conflicted with the well-established American tradition of the soldier-citizen. The belief was that any citizen benefiting from democratic government, in the words of George Washington, "owes … his personal services to the defense of it." This cultural element is the foundational rationale for militias and the concept of the volunteering citizen-soldier who returns home when no longer needed. The major rationale after independence was for militias to protect local communities from Indian marauders, outlaws and, in the South, potential slave insurrections.

In a society where personal and local loyalties prevailed, the military responsibility of citizens has traditionally been limited to protecting families, communities, or states. If sent to fight beyond the limits of their geographic or social loyalties, citizen-soldiers became mercenaries or professional soldiers instead of local defenders (Burk 2000, 156).

Soldiers refused to follow Lee into the states of Maryland and Pennsylvania during the Antietam and Gettysburg campaigns. The loyalties of these citizens-soldiers were in large part local rather than national, and personal feelings and familial values were considered more important than their military responsibilities, especially during the last part of the war. Lee believed he could have won the battle of Antietam if he had not lost roughly one-third of his command through temporary desertions and straggling (straggling could also be the first stage of desertion).

Some stragglers may have been too tired or shoeless to keep up, and others suffered from bad diets and related diseases. Others took the opportunity to desert at least for a while. The last issue constantly concerned Lee (Weitz 2005, 96). Some Virginians refused to leave the state of Virginia. They had volunteered to protect their homes and state from invading Yankees—but not to fight on Northern soil. Robert E. Lee can be similarly blamed for resisting being sent west to command the Army of Tennessee and protect the city of Vicksburg from Federal forces.

The Confederate Cavalry of Individualists

Cavalry officers became heroes in part because their exploits were dramatic and theatrical. Cavalry units were also consistently successful. They reflected the core values of Southern culture of courage, independent behavior, and knightly appearance and behavior.

The martial skills most respected by Southerners were found in the Confederate cavalry, which was consistently superior to the Union's during the first three years of the war. The Confederate cavalry attracted many of the most grandiose generals in the Confederacy because they were able to behave in independent and adventurous ways. The public admired these "theatrical generals" even when their behavior was more symbolic than effective. Mary Chesnut (Woodward 1981, 90) described how a cavalry trooper rode his horse through the barroom of a hotel and "scattered people and things right and left." A Confederate infantry captain who witnessed the event remarked, "He was intoxicated of course, but he was a splendid rider." Men on horseback were seen as knightly and unrestricted.

Cavalier-type behavior was admired no matter the context. Reflecting the same cavalier values, Earl Van Dorn was described as "sitting astride his horse like a knight, and looking every inch a soldier" (Carter 1999, 129). Van Dorn was a failure as an infantry commander, but he performed much better when leading cavalry troopers.

Troopers in the Confederate cavalry were expected to furnish their own horses. Riders were paid rental fees and remunerations if their horses were killed during battle. The result of this policy was that cavalry recruiters accepted only those who could afford to provide their own mounts and replacements. After the war began and horses became casualties, the government began to provide horses for its cavalry. An estimated one to three million horses died during the war. An estimated three thousand horses died during the Battle of Gettysburg.

Cavalry troopers returned to their homes to obtain new mounts if they could not capture mounts from the enemy, which they often did, or "liberate" horses from both Northern and Southern civilians. Rebel officers made a point of exposing themselves and their horses to enemy fire to show their bravery and be an example to their command. As a result, many officers lost their horses to enemy fire and were wounded or killed as well as their mounts. Officers could lose up to six horses during a battle.

The supply of quality horses was ample during the early years of the war because upper-class Southerners were expected to be good riders and had access to mounts. Many plantations had their own racetracks and stables, and horse racing and betting were popular (Faust 1982, 159). There was a higher number of horses in the North because Southern farmers were more likely to use mules than horses. Since riding horses was a major means of transportation, the North would be expected to contain more horses just because of its larger population.

Thoroughbreds were not always the best mounts for military purposes. The best cavalry mounts came from the Union's Upper Midwest rather than from the South. The most practical mounts for the Confederacy originated from border states, such as Kentucky, which were early controlled by Union forces. One of the more spectacular actions of the Confederacy cavalry was raiding Northern states and Union depots to steal horses and mules.

A disadvantage of the Confederate policy of not providing horses for its cavalry meant that up to half of its troops could be absent at any time while procuring new horses from their homes (Walsh 2002, 250). While this policy resulted in better-quality horses at first and a monetary saving for the military, this policy also decreased the number of riders available for duty. An exception to this general policy was adopted by Nathan Forrest. He promised any recruits that he would capture horses for them from Union forces, which he did successfully.

Individualism and Lack of Organizational Skills

The cultural value of individualism decreased the willingness of Southerners to cooperate with strangers. The result was a relative lack of the ability to manage large-scale organizations as compared to the North (Fuller 1957, 27). As an example, there were only two gunpowder mills in the South when war was declared. These factories serviced local customers and were small compared to those in the North. Plantations were large-scale complex organizations, but their overseers managed the daily responsibilities to allow plantation owners to avoid any managerial responsibilities. Planters tended to be more concerned with profit and maintaining their lifestyles than spending time with administrative minutia. Managing enslaved workers demanded different skills than when the labor force was free or under military discipline.

There were Southerners who could create and manage organizations, but there had been little encouragement or opportunity to do so before the Civil War. Southern culture did not encourage entrepreneurships, and its educational system did not prepare many students for occupational success. In contrast, there was more interest among Northern investors to support new ventures. Northern education offered more avenues for social and economic mobility (Clark 2001, 222).

Larger businesses and factories were more common in the North, but the largest organizations in the South were plantations. Most Southern factories and workshops catered to local markets. Northern factories were larger, and their markets were more extensive. These were supported by better and longer transportation systems, including the 524 miles of the Erie Canal and its lateral connections. The canal alone linked the coastal cities with the emerging Midwest.

There were exceptions to this general lack of organizational skills. Before the war, Zebulon York and a partner began with one plantation and eventually owned six plantations with 1,500 enslaved persons. Their plantations eventually produced 4,500 bales of cotton a year. After losing his plantations and enslaved laborers during the war, York owned a boardinghouse and managed six steamboats that transported supplies and passengers (Mitcham 2022, 727 and 729).

The city of Richmond, Virginia, contained a number of large-scale flour and cotton mills. The gem of Richmond's extensive industrial capability was the Tredegar Iron Works, one of the largest foundries in the United States, but there were complaints that many of its products were shoddy (Vandiver 1994, 112). The foundry was the only one in the Confederacy capable of producing heavy ordnance until 1863. In 1861, the foundry included eight hundred workers, including enslaved workers. More than a thousand cannons were manufactured by the Tredegar foundry during the war. The Tredegar Iron Works showed that enslaved workers could be used in nonagricultural tasks. By the end of the war, half of the Tredegar workers were enslaved workers.

The Industrial Revolution had not completely bypassed the South, but 90 percent of American factories in 1860 were located in the North. The Confederacy needed large amounts of military imports from Europe, and two-thirds of all arms used by the Confederacy were imported. Some arms were obtained on the battlefield or through raids on Union supply depots and supply wagons.

Scapegoating Others by Individualists' Faults

Scapegoating is the deflection of blame from oneself to other parties. Scapegoating blames innocent others for the presumed behavior of the accuser. The postwar Lost Cause movement was in large part directed by former Confederate Virginian generals wanting to shift the blame for losing the Civil War from themselves to others.

The combination of the values of individualism—or in extreme cases, narcissistic individualism—and honor results in a reluctance to admit a mistake to avoid being shamed for personal failures. Those who depend on others for the recognition of their honor are more likely to refuse to acknowledge their mistakes. The scapegoating individual rejects personal accountability and continues to feel infallible and free of errors. The practice in such situations is to blame others instead of admitting one is at fault or has failed because of one's weaknesses.

After the military reverses during 1863, newspaper editor John M. Daniel, in an editorial on July 21, 1863, blamed the larger plantation owners of the Deep South for the weaknesses of the Confederacy (Daniel 1868, 101):

> The want of tenacity of purpose and inflexibility of patriotism in the character of a class (i.e., the cotton planters) of southern people, is painfully conspicuous.

It was common for Confederates to blame fate, anonymous and identified others, God, and general conditions for their lack of military successes.

After the loss of the Battle of Gettysburg, Robert E. Lee told his retreating soldiers the failure of Pickett's Charge was his fault for encouraging them to return to the fight. He later shifted the blame of the charge's loss (Fuller 1957, 112): "If I had Stonewall Jackson at Gettysburg, I would have won a great victory." Lee was blaming the dead for the defeat of a charge he had ordered. In his official report, Lee later blamed the charge's loss on a lack of artillery ammunition. There is no mention that the Confederate artillery failed in its attempt to weaken the Union forces (Snow 1867, 104–5):

> Our troops succeeded in entering the advanced works of the enemy … but our artillery having expending its ammunition, the attacking columns became exposed to the heavy fire of the numerous batteries near the summit of the ridge … were compelled to relinquish their advantage and fall back.

A positive element of scapegoating is that self-images are maintained rather than questioned. Scapegoating allowed Confederates to assume they were superior to Yankees and that their cause for independence would eventually be successful in spite of numerous loses. The War Department's Robert Garlick Kean maintained his expectations of a final victory for independence, but he blamed the Confederacy's civilian and military leaders, including President Davis and Jeb Stuart. Lee was especially angry with General Samuel Cooper, adjutant general and inspector general and close friend of Davis. Kean remarked in his diary that (Younger 1985, 119):

> I have never actually despaired of the cause, priceless, holy as it is, but my faith in the adequacy of the men in whose hands we are, is daily weakened.

There is no mention of the Union's military skills as a reason for Confederacy failures.

Scapegoating and the Protection of Slavery

Comparisons of the 1850 and 1860 censuses indicated increasing Northern superiority in population and resources, as did numerous other publications, including the widely read *De Bow's Review* (1820–1884) and *The Farmers' Register.* For decades, the authors of the *Review* had encouraged Southerners to invest in industrialization. In addition to De Bow himself, writers for the *De Bow's Review* included well-known Southern nationalists Judah B. Benjamin ("the brain of the Confederacy"), James H. Hammond, and Edmund Ruffin III.

James D. B. De Bow (1820–1867) was founder, editor, and contributor of the most widely read Southern periodical in the antebellum South. De Bow was an ardent Southern nationalist and was proslavery. He advocated for the resumption of the international slave trade and promoted "the best practices for wringing profits from slaves." He encouraged the industrialization and agricultural improvements of the Southern economy and was the first head of the Louisiana Bureau of Statistics. Having been the head of the US Census Bureau during collection of the 1850 US census, De Bow was familiar with the material superiority of the North. De Bow also published *The Statistical View of the United States* in 1855, which was easily available in the South.

A problem with the *Review*'s readers was that they did not want to face any criticism of the South and/or slavery—even when it originated from would-be reformers. They were more interested in reading articles supporting their biases and making their plantations more profitable. Slave owners did not want to admit enslaved labor was inefficient compared to free labor or that the enslaved were unhappy and wanted to escape slavery. It was easier to rationalize why the enslaved continued their attempts to escape to the North and freedom without questioning the institution of slavery and the character of Black Americans.

An 1851 article in *De Bow's Review* attempted to explain why enslaved persons became fugitives. The author, physician Samuel A. Cartwright, suggested fugitives were suffering from *Drapetomania*, a "disease of the mind" peculiar to Black Americans. The causes of this disease were too much idleness and free time. Proposed cures were hard work and a beating with a leather strap (Pastoff and Wilson 1982, 27–43). This reasoning supported the scapegoating beliefs that harsh treatments by slave owners were not responsible for the desire of slaves for freedom or that slaves rationally wanted to be free.

Edmund Ruffin ("the father of soil science") was the editor of *The Farmers' Register,* which promoted agricultural productivity. Though the magazine contained defenses of slavery, the majority of articles dealt with the improvements of agriculture procedures. His proslavery works were more popular than his attempts to improve farmland. Ruffin was an absentee owner of several plantations and owned more than one hundred enslaved persons, and he wanted to increase the productivity of the South's farmland through more modern procedures.

Ruffin recommended crop rotation, letting the land stay fallow for several seasons, and using marl and manure to rejuvenate the soil. He also promoted experimenting with new farming and husbandry techniques. In the 1833 issue of the *Farmers' Register*, Ruffin recommended choosing the best treatment and species of sheep (Ruffin 1834, 182) for the highest return. In the same issue (133), Ruffin presented a table showing the improvements due to crop rotation of wheat and corn yields from reclaimed swampland. In six years, the wheat crop increased 46 percent, and the corn yield increased 14 percent. There was even a long and detailed article showing modern techniques of beekeeping.

Ruffin also reprinted material from other sources, especially England. He also encouraged amateur agriculturalists to closely observe and measure agricultural events. One such report probably less scientifically observed dealt with "STRANGE MODE OF CURING A VICIOUS HORSE" (Ruffin 1834, 766):

> I have seen vicious horses in Egypt cured of the habit of biting, by presenting to them, while in the act of doing so, a leg of mutton just taken from the fire: the pain which a horse feels in biting through the hot meat, causes it, after a few lessons, to abandon the vicious habit.

While the above item seems far-fetched, Ruffin published observed and recorded data that improved soil production and a wide variety of farming procedures.

De Bow, Ruffin, and other authors realized the Southern economy contained grave weaknesses, but they avoided the suggestion that these weaknesses were caused by the presence of slavery.

Southerners also tried to shift the blame for the existence of slavery. The British and Northerners who had shipped enslaved persons from Africa to the South several generations before were blamed for the introduction of slavery into colonial America. Southerners also pointed out that Northerners and their economy benefited from slavery. The "positive good" of slavery for the North was based on the use and the exportation of cotton, tobacco, sugar, and rice. Northerners also benefited from the sale of Northern-manufactured goods used by enslaved workers and the Southern population.

Most owners of enslaved persons seemed to feel that the enslaved were satisfied with their lot. Rice planter Robert F. W. Allston, who owned 590 enslaved persons at his death, believed in the frequent use of whippings to maintain a sense order and feigned satisfaction. He also punished any sign of threats to his authority—even though he considered himself the paternal patriarch to his family and enslaved workers. Allston even demanded that his enslaved workers behaved as if they were happy as well as obedient (Easterby 2004, 150):

> *I like to be kind to my people* [i.e., enslaved persons] but I *imperatively require* of them honesty, truth, diligence and *cheerfulness* in their work, whenever and whatever it is [emphasis added].

Allston does not mention that rice-growing demands, often working in waist-deep water, the construction of canals and levees, and stooping for hours to collect rice as well as suffering from malaria and other work-related diseases.

Scapegoating, Inflation, and Food Scarcity

Scapegoating was used in the reactions by Confederate War Department clerk John Beauchamp Jones to the inflationary trend (a rate of 9,000 percent by the end of the war) of Confederate money and the lack of food in local markets. Jones joined the War Department to witness and record the Civil War's progress. He was a fervent patriot and, while highly critical of Jefferson Davis and the way the war was conducted, never lost his dedication to the Confederacy itself.

Jones nevertheless managed to get his son a position in the government in order to exempt him from the draft and receive a dependable salary that was higher than the pay of ordinary soldiers. Jones was outraged when his son was placed in a militia and sent to defend the Richmond-Petersburg fortifications. In this instance, family loyalty conflicted with Jones's patriotism.

Jones's clerkship paid him a salary of $1,200 a year, and in addition, he received book royalties and rental income. While working for the War Department, his son was earning the same salary as his father—and the family was able to rent an enslaved women to perform housework. These combined incomes should have provided a very comfortable income for the Jones household, but inflation quickly decreased their combined buying power. As a government official, Jones was also able to use government resources for his own use. Jones hired a government shoemaker to make him a pair of boots at below-market price. The cobbler should have been working making boots for the troops.

In spite of his wish to record the progress of the war, Jones spent considerable time in his diary on his own affairs, especially his finances. He recorded in detail the increasing costs of consumer products. Jones blamed speculators for rising prices rather than the real reasons. The actual reasons included the reluctance of the planters to plant more food crops than cotton, the refusal to allow their property (including the enslaved) to be taxed at full value, the printing of worthless money by the government, the Confederacy's inadequate transportation systems, and the lack of organizational ability of those working in the Commissary Department.

Jones also blamed social marginals, anonymous government bureaucrats, and alleged greedy merchants (Jones 1866, 183):

> The speculators and extortioners seem to act in concert, and the government appears to be no match for them. It is not the scarcity of food which causes the high prices ... But it is an insatiable thirst for gain, which I fear the Almighty Justicer will rebuke in some signal manner, perhaps in the emancipation of the slaves ... I fear a nation of extortioners are unworthy of independence.

The above term "insatiable thirst for gain" had been used by Southerners during previous decades to describe Southern merchants and Yankees in general. Southern merchants were denounced with the derogative term "Yankee Southerner" since a "true" Southerner would never seek excessive profits. It is telling that Jones could think of no greater punishment from God than the end of slavery since Southerners defended white supremacy and slavery as established by God.

War Department clerk J. B. Jones also blamed the scarcity of food on speculators' greed, resulting in the possible punishment by God of the Confederacy as a whole. Individual greed became a national sin rather than the result of the Southern culture of individualism, lack of transportation, bad financial policies, or Union control of Confederate farmland.

Inflation, whatever its sources, was real, and most Southerners suffered and went hungry partly because wage earners, poor farmers, and those in the military lost large amounts of purchasing power. The war disrupted transportation systems, and many products, including salt and sugar, could no longer be sent where they were needed. Those who owned hogs or cattle could no longer preserve meat or tan hides without salt. Certain farming areas, such as central Georgia, South Carolina, the Shenandoah Valley, and other parts of Virginia, were devastated due to Union raids and the presence of marching armies and battlegrounds. The Federal naval blockade interrupted the vital intercoastal trade routes.

While prices in the Union doubled during the war, inflation in the Confederacy rose to such heights that the Confederate currency became worthless and was often rejected by merchants in exchange for their goods. The joke at that time was that a man could take a wheelbarrow of Confederate currency to the store and return with a wallet full of food. Barter became common. Many merchants accepted only Yankee greenbacks or specie.

One hundred Union dollars backed by gold was worth $120 in Confederacy currency on January 1, 1862; the same $100 in gold on April 10, 1865, had increased its worth to $5,500 in Confederate currency (Katcher 2003, 216 [the value of gold during the war varied in part according to which side won or lost a battle in addition to increasing inflation]). At the end of the war, prices became too high for many Confederate families to buy food when it was available.

Joseph Davis, the older brother and mentor of the president of the Confederacy, Jefferson Davis, continued to grow cotton and illegally hid his baled cotton instead of burning it when Union soldiers arrived in the area. Angered by Davis's lack of patriotism, outraged neighbors reported Joseph Davis's hidden two hundred bales (Levine 2013, 80), but he continued to grow cotton and hide his cotton bales. Davis's enslaved workers later showed Union forces where he had hidden his cotton bales, and they were confiscated and sent north.

Robert Toombs, a fervent secessionist, also continued to plant more than eight hundred acres of cotton when planters were being urged to increase their food crops and to grow less cotton. Toombs insisted he would use his land in any way he chose. The individualism (and monetary greed) of the Confederate elite resulted in being too independent to follow others' orders to consider the common good. The individualistic culture of the planters and their mindset of growing cotton rather than increased amounts of food crops inhibited adequate food production for the Confederacy.

Not all Southerners went hungry. Those with gold could always buy food for themselves. Fanny Young had six barrels of flour when the war ended (Rubin 2005, 118). Plantation owners could also feed themselves, their families, and their friends since they owned agricultural land and enslaved labor to grow food crops. The food planters grew was kept for themselves and relatives or sold to the highest bidders, often speculators.

Elite diarist Mary Chesnut attended a Christmas dinner on December 25, 1863, when many families were going hungry and soldiers were on short rations. The menu included oyster soup, boiled mutton, ham, boned turkey, wild ducks, partridges, plum pudding, sauterne, burgundy, sherry, and Madeira wines (Woodward et al. 1981, 515). Mary dined at home the next day and recorded in her diary, "Today my dinner was comparatively simple—oysters, ham, turkey, partridges, and a good wine." Mary was fortunate because a nearby plantation furnished her with adequate food.

David Williams (Williams: 2008, 68) summarizes this mindset:

> Planters and merchants both took the same self-interested path that had served them so well before the war, following the dollar wherever it led. But in so doing, they left the interests of the soldiers, their families, and ultimately the Confederacy itself far behind.

The cultural values supporting slavery and growing cotton became increasingly dysfunctional after 1862, but many planters refused to change their behavior even when it harmed the Confederacy, and they ignored the pleas of the central government. They had bought—generally on credit—expensive enslaved workers and trained them to farm cotton, and the growing and selling of food crops would not pay for their investments in land and slaves. They would not receive the respect by growing vegetables that they had growing cotton. Cotton—rather than wheat or corn—was "king."

Cultivating food crops demanded fewer man-hours to grow than cotton, and the shorter growing season for food crops would leave enslaved field workers idle if they did not continuously tend acreage devoted to cotton plants. At first, growing cotton was a rational decision since most Southerners believed the war would be short. The Union blockade of Confederate ports dramatically reduced the export of cotton until the warehouses were overflowing with cotton bales—and many bales were stored in the streets. During 1859–1860, the export of cotton reached three million bales. In 1863, the Confederacy exported fifty thousand bales (Foote and Hess 2021, 61).

In the planters' defense, growing, cleaning, baling, and preparing for the next year's crop of cotton involved more than a year of work (Current 1998, 156) since the selling of cotton often took place while the next crop was being prepared. Ceasing to process cotton for a short period would disrupt a plantation's work cycles because both corn and cotton are planted at the same time of the year. Planters needed to make a decision on what and how much to plant for the coming growing season since labor had to be allocated for either cotton or food crops. Cotton was a labor-intensive crop, and planters who planted more corn might not have enough labor to plant, hoe, or harvest the corn and cotton at the same time (Wetherington 2005, 16).

The cultivation of cotton depends on large amounts of labor, and a number of operations is needed to prepare cotton for the market. First, the soil was cleared of the last crop. Stalks had to be removed, crushed with clubs, or pulled out by hand. The soil then needed to be turned over by plows or hoes, and manure or other fertilizers had to be placed in the rows. This was done during February or March.

Cotton seeds are planted during April. The sprouts were thinned a month later. The fields are hoed four or five times, and the cotton plants bloom during June. Cotton bolls open during late July or early August, and picking starts in late August. The cotton is ginned to separate the seeds from the fiber and then baled. Bales are transported to seaports during September through January, dominating roads and cargo space in steamboats and railroad cars. It is at that time that planters begin to receive payment for their products less 20–30 percent charged for commissions, transportation, insurance, and other fees. They also paid off their other debts. Planters might warehouse their cotton bales to wait for higher prices. Timing the market properly is a planter's or his factor's major concern.

If their cotton crops did not cover the planters' total debts, the custom was to sell some of their enslaved workers. These workers always feared the end of the year since they or their family members might be sold to other owners to repay debts. During the 1850s, it was common for planters from states on the Atlantic coast to sell enslaved workers to planters who had migrated to the more fertile western states of Louisiana, Texas, and Arkansas. Enslaved workers were needed to work in the cotton and sugar plantations and were treated even more harshly. Western planters needed primarily male field workers, which resulted in the enslaved being torn from their familiar environment and separated from their families.

Blaming God and Sinners for National Failures

At the start of the war, white Southerners were enthusiastic Confederates, but there were exceptions. An estimated 10 percent of the Southern white population was strongly Unionist. An additional 40 percent of the total population was enslaved, and few of these supported the Confederacy. At least half of the Confederate population was Unionist to various degrees in their loyalties.

Patriotic Confederates assumed secession was supported by God because they were God's "chosen people." Two days after the fall of Fort Sumter, a woman claimed (Woodward et al. 1981, 48) "God is on our side. … Of course He hates Yankees." While relatively few Southerners were formally church members, most were religious to some degree. Their moral codes were embedded in religious themes.

This religiously based optimism continued until the war began to result in poverty, casualties, lost battles, and lost territory. Faith in God continued, and white Confederates added to their theology the insistence that battle losses were punishments for presumed Southern individuals' lack of faith instead of the prowess of Union forces or inadequate Confederate military leadership. Their cause remained just and sanctioned by God, but the "people" or other general categories of scapegoats were unworthy in God's eyes.

The response was to encourage individuals to become more moral—including avoiding the sin of pride—and increase their loyalty to the Confederacy. God and sinners became the scapegoats for the Confederacy's lack of success. Editor John M. Daniel clearly supported this theological position when he editorialized on July 1, 1863 (Daniel 1868, 88):

> Punishment of crime is a necessity of society, and, when communities are guilty, the same justice which is meted to individuals, is also fitting for them.

There is in addition an attitude that victory would occur after a medieval-like "trial by combat," and God would award victory to the more virtuous opponent. The cavalier mindset permeated Southern religious sentiments.

The pattern of blaming God for Confederate hardships because of the sins of individuals was a common response to adversity. Southern Christianity was primarily evangelical, which included the belief in a direct link between national destiny and personal behavior. God would not allow a nation to prosper unless its citizens conducted themselves in the properly moral fashion. Editor John M. Daniel remarked in his December 31, 1863, editorial (Daniel 1868, 156) that: "Theologians will tell us that the disasters of the closing year are the punishment of our sins." The biblical account of the destruction of Sodom and Gomorrah was understood as examples of divine retribution for the sins of individuals.

A lost battle was seen as punishment because individuals were sinful. A positive result of this belief is that a loss did not necessarily reduce morale among soldiers because a battle loss would not be their fault. God was punishing the Confederacy because of the sins of anonymous civilians. Lost battles and casualties encouraged frontline soldiers to take part in camp revivals and increased personal religiosity.

A national cause fails when an undetermined number of its citizens are sinful and guilty of the generic but vague sin of pride (Quigly 2014, 210). Pride is a major sin, but it was not focused on specific individuals because it is easier to transfer this vague sense of guilt onto others, including God. A guilt seen as collective avoids the necessity of pinpointing in detail the reason why God is angry and seeking a practical solution. A young girl in South Carolina reacted to the death of "Stonewall" Jackson by blaming God (Clinton 1995, 155):

> How terrible is the wrath of god [*sic*], our sins as a people has [*sic*} brought this [the death of Jackson] upon us and we should humble ourselves before him.

Some believed the "people" had depended too much on the prowess of "Stonewall" Jackson—an act of pride—instead of being grateful that God would eventually provide the ultimate victory.

Many white Confederates also believed God was testing the "chosen people" to see if they were worthy of His support. After numerous Confederate defeats during 1863, organizational genius Josiah Gorgias became less certain that God would allow the Confederacy to win its independence. Gorgias wrote in his diary (Vandiver 1994, 195):

> Can we believe in the justice of Providence, or must we conclude that we are after all wrong? Such visitations give me to great bitterness of heart and repining at His decrees. *It is apparent that we are not yet sufficiently tried* [emphasis added].

The concerns for humility and the sin of pride involved a social class element. The leaders of the Confederacy, the cavaliers, were expected to be proud, ready to defend their honor, and superior warriors. Members of the lower classes were blamed for being too proud rather than the elite. The elite were blaming others for their own errors.

Robert E. Lee was a model of religiosity, though his faith was more private than institutional. He brought his favorite dog to services, often slept through sermons, and criticized ministers when they were too conservative. As part of his elite standing, he attended Episcopal services, but he did not formally become an Episcopalian until he was forty-six years old. Lee prayed and read the Bible daily, and he attended church services as often as possible.

During the war, Lee encouraged church attendance of his command because he believed doing so would increase their morale. Lee's faith also had a fatalistic element in that winning or losing a battle or the war seemed to be based on God's will.

During 1861, Lee stated (Reid 2005, 32): "I fear it [i.e., secession] is now out of the powers of men, and in God alone must be our trust that a merciful Providence will not dash us from the height to which his smiles had raised us." He would do his best developing a campaign or battle plan and then assume the result would be determined by God.

Lee's faith had a moral character that was similar to the ideals of a Southern gentleman. His best-known prayer (which President Harry Truman recited by memory daily) was:

> Help me to be, to think, to act what is right because it is right; make me truthful, honest, and honorable in all things; make me intellectually honest for the sake of right and honor and without thought of reward to me.

Days of Humiliation and Fasting

President Jefferson Davis declared days of humiliation and fasting to purify the nation. He asked the public to (Rubin 2005, 84):

> Receive in humble thankfulness the lesson [i.e., battle losses] which He has taught in our recent reverses.

The same religious orientation that God would eventually give the Confederacy ultimate victory when all individuals became worthy of independence was reflected in Robert E. Lee's beliefs. Lee, on September 18, 1863, wrote to his wife (Lee 2007, 110):

> The enemy state that they have heard of a great reduction in our forces here, and are now going to drive us back to Richmond. I trust they will

> not succeed; *but our hope and our refuge is [sic] in our merciful Father in Heaven* ... [emphasis added]

The above quote reveals a central belief of both the Confederacy in general and Robert E. Lee in particular. When Jefferson Davis appointed August 21, 1863, as a national day of "fasting, humiliation, and prayer," Lee then issued a general order to his troops (Lee 2007, 110–06):

> A strict observance of the day is enjoined upon the officers and soldiers of this army ... Soldiers! *We have sinned against Almighty God*. We have forgotten His signal mercies, and have cultivated a revengeful, haughty, and boastful spirit. *We have not remembered that the defenders of a just cause should be pure in His eyes*; that our times are in his hands, and we have relied too much on our own arms for the achievement of our independence. God is our only refuge and our strength. Let us humble ourselves before Him. Let us confess our many sins, and beseech Him to give us a higher courage, a purer patriotism, and more determined will ... [emphasis added]

Lee was correct when he characterized the core of Southern cultural value as a "revengeful, haughty, and boastful spirit" because these cultural traits were central in the Southern code of honor. Being "haughty" and "boastful" were also central to the Southern definition of masculinity. The central cultural characteristic of Southern pride is reflected in Lee's claim (Pryor 2007, 235):

> I hope God will at last crown our efforts with success but the contest must be long & severe & the whole country has to go through much suffering. It

> is necessary we should be humbled & taught to be less boastful, less selfish & more devoted to right & justice to all the world.

The purpose of official days of fasting and humiliation was to seek God's favor and corresponding victories. A Rebel wrote his sister, "It is a notable fact that we have never yet met with disaster immediately after a fast day. Our arms have always been blessed with success" (Phillips 2007, 26).

After the battle of Second Manassas, Jefferson Davis declared a day of Thanksgiving to offer thanks for the victory (Varon 2019, 131), which Davis described as God's "vengeance of retributive justice." After the losses of Vicksburg and the Battle of Gettysburg, Davis called for a national day of fasting on August 21, 1863. Many members of the Army of Northern Virginia also took part in a religious revival. The above losses were seen as punishments for relying on themselves and General Lee instead of trusting God to provide victories (Phillips 2007, 27).

The religious fervor underpinning Confederate morale continued after the war ended. During March 1890, Dr. John Clerborne orated the paean presented below of the Army of Northern Virginia in spite of its failures and ultimate surrender. Bernard was unable to accept the fact that the Army of Northern Virginia had surrendered (Bernard 1892, 253):

> To me, as to every Southron, as to every soldier, as to every man and woman and child of the Confederacy, it [Lee's army] had been the embodiment of courage and fortitude and heroism. The cause for which it contended was the cause of liberty and truth and right. God would never suffer those brave battalions to go down, even before might, whose standards had been upheld for so many years by the arms of our heroes;

> those battle-flags could never trail in dust, which, consecrated and kissed by southern women, had been baptized in the blood of the truest and best of the earth. *The prayers of a million of Christian men and women, proving their faith by their works of self-abnegation and self-surrender, could not fail to have a hearing above, where the destiny of nations were [sic] ordained and determined* [emphasis added].

CHAPTER 8

LOCALISM

Home is the seminary of all other institutions.
—E. H. Chapin

Localism is defined as loyalty to a limited geographic area, custom, institution, tribe, clan, or government agency that is smaller than the largest level of identity, usually a nation. Local units include a region, state, county, town, or neighborhood. A person can prefer his or her local language, foods, religion, or government, civilian, and military units. In the antebellum South, there were strong preferences for the local loyalties of family, county, region, and state. By 1860, most major religious organizations—except the Roman Catholic Church, Quakers, and Mormonism—had separated into Northern and Southern sections.

A person's loyalties can conflict with one another, and their relative strengths of loyalty vary in time. Near the end of the Civil War, many Confederate soldiers decided that their family loyalties had become stronger than their military ties. Wives who had previously supported or agreed to their husbands and sons enlisting in the military began, during 1863, to increasingly plead that they were more needed at home.

Robert E. Lee cited his loyalty to his family and to the state of Virginia as motivators for resigning his position in the US military to join the Confederacy. Like many Southern antebellum military officers, Lee was pro-Union and anti-secession, but he immediately resigned his military position when his state seceded to enlist in Virginia's militia. Lee's rationale for not staying with the Union and becoming chief of its armies was that he was reluctant to "draw his sword against his state." Thomas A. Flagel noted (2010, 222): "The best and the worse that can be said of Lee is that he fought for Virginia first and last … Lee was not particularly loyal to the Confederacy either."

While we do not agree with the last part of the above quotation, Lee's loyalty to his local ties superseded his antebellum military oath to defend the nation from its enemies.

Lee's decision to join the Confederacy was difficult because a major value of Southerners, especially the elite and those who considered themselves to be gentlemen, was doing one's duty. For many, duty meant being loyal to one's family and one's state. Those who failed to respect their obligations to their duty were considered cowards and traitors. Following the dictates of duty could be difficult because a person is always faced with multiple loyalties, and they may conflict with one another. For many military men, following their states when they seceded conflicted with their filial and occupational values.

Lee was conflicted in that he could not follow his professional duties in the Union army, his familial demands, his loyalty to the United States, and the expectations of the state of Virginia. Lee's wife, Mary Lee, remarked how difficult was Lee's decision (Snow 1867, 38):

> My husband has wept tears of blood over this terrible war, but he must, as a man of honor and a Virginian, share the destiny of his state, which has solemnly pronounced for independence.

Lee was not the only Southerner to decide to support the Confederacy instead of the Union because of his local loyalties. Jubal A. Early was born in Virginia, graduated from West Point, and fought in the Mexican-American War. Early was strongly against secession until Lincoln called for troops after the Confederate capture of Fort Sumter. Similar to Lee, Early's rationale for joining his state rather than continuing his loyalty to the Union was based on local loyalties (Wynstra 2018, 6): "I at once recognized my duty to abide the decision of my native State, and defend her soil against invasion."

Old Army Brigadier General Joseph E. Johnston also reflected this local loyalty. When he resigned his commission to return to his home state and enlist in the Confederacy's military, Johnston stated: "I naturally determined to return to the State of which I was a native, join the people among whom I was born, and live with my kindred, and if necessary, fight in their defense." In Johnson's case, his loyalties were to state, friends, and family and to the Confederacy. Like many others, Wade Hampton III was also a Unionist until South Carolina seceded.

Loyalty and self-identification to one's state was common. John "the Gray Ghost" Mosby was a Virginian Unionist who was also antislavery. Like many others, Mosby accepted secession and joined the military as soon as Virginia seceded. Mosby declared, "She is out of the Union now. Virginia is my mother, God bless her! I can't fight against my mother, can I?"

Civil War scholars have often ignored the fact that individuals hold multiple cultural values. The defeat of the Confederacy was multicausal with cultural dimensions that were as important as Union superiority in population, manufacturing, and armaments. A Confederate soldier may have hated Yankees, but he also felt loyalty to his family, his county, his state, his army comrades, and the Confederacy—all at the same time—even though the relative intensity of each of these loyalties might vary over time. The enthusiasm of Confederate nationalism might encourage a person to enlist with his friends and neighbors, but it might decrease when he felt his family needed him more than his company, comrades, or the Confederacy.

States' Rights and Localism

Frank L. Owsley describes the reason for the Confederacy's loss of the war as "died of states' rights." In a similar vein, David J. Eicher (2006, 13) declares, "State's rights wounded the United States but destroyed the Confederacy." It is also possible to state that the belief in states' rights as a significant example of localism was a strength since this belief encouraged men to join the Confederate military to protect their states (and homes) from invasion.

The dogma of states' rights was associated with the priority of state over central government and the wish to dissociate from the North. By 1860, Southerners were concerned with protecting the institution of slavery and the political separation from the hated Federals. Few Northerners—including Lincoln—realized how disliked they were. A member of the Georgian committee to discuss on and vote on secession was reported on July 25, 1860, to challenge Georgians (Davis and Hendrick 2022, 8): "States Rights men of Georgia, will you sustain the abominable Federal government? Are freemen of the South slaves of the Federal government?"

Soon after the capture of Fort Sumter on April 13, 1861, an editorial in the *Atlanta Daily Intelligencer* indicated the ferocious hatred of now-Confederates toward Northerners (Davis and Hendrick 2022, 5): "We are determined not only to achieve our independence at whatever the cost, but we will teach these Northern Goths and Vandals a lesson, before this war is over, which they will never forget."

Many Southerners believed the Confederate states were sovereign over their central government. The Confederate Constitution consistently mentions the term "Confederate States of

America" more often than the term "Confederacy." Howell Cobb, the president of the Montgomery Convention, which established the new government and its Constitution, began his opening address with the statement (Carpenter 1990, 228): "We meet as representatives of sovereign and independent States." There were three attempts to include in the Confederate Constitution the right of states to secede from the Confederacy, but they were defeated. The issue of how limited were of the powers of the new government in relationship to the states was never settled.

An example of the power of localism within the rubric of states' rights was the fact that the Confederacy never established a Supreme Court. Each state had a supreme court to settle local legal issues, but the Confederacy itself had no such mechanism. The Confederate Constitution included a provision for a Supreme Court, but the dogma of state-level localism did not encourage its establishment. President Jefferson Davis relied on his own interpretations of the Confederate Constitution to settle state-Confederacy conflicts.

Positive Elements of the States' Rights Ideology

While the belief in state sovereignty made governing the Confederacy more difficult, the belief in localism was a positive force for the Confederacy because the recruitment of soldiers was embedded in local loyalties. Companies, ideally containing one hundred men, were recruited from one county or town. Regiments, containing ten or more companies, were formed by uniting companies recruited from the same state. Civilians, as a result, maintained strong ties to armies consisting of local troops. After recruitment, these local units were inducted into their state's militia system. After receiving minimal training and equipment, these units were inducted into the Confederate military and sent as a group to their posts. These men were allowed to elect their officers.

Enlistees wanted to join the same military units as their friends, neighbors, and even family members. Colonel William C. Oates led the Fifteenth Alabama Infantry Regiment in a series of attacks at Little Round Top during the Battle of Gettysburg. His brother John Oates was also a member of the Fifteenth and was killed during an attack. Though ill, John insisted on taking part in the attacks, and William was forced to leave his body when forced to retreat. Once enlisted, these men preferred to be led by those from their own communities. Men fought better and were less likely to desert when their comrades and officers were local in origin.

Desertion began in earnest when military units on the company and regimental levels were no longer locally homogeneous and nonlocal men replaced the locals who had died or been sent home because of their casualties. During the last stage of the war, desertions increased when many regiments had been reduced to three hundred to five hundred men or fewer, and these regiments had received nonlocal recruits. Some regiments from different localities were merged together.

Localism and Loyalty to Family

An important element of localism was the centrality placed on the family and the wish to defend one's family by enlisting in a local military unit. To many Southern males, a person's strongest ties were to his family, but personal honor, duty, and the excitement of war also led many men to enlist. This mindset—called *familism*—encouraged Southerners to enlist because they believed they were defending their new nation and their families from invasion by Yankees. Another reason for enlistment was the chance to become fully recognized as adult members by the enlistees' families and neighbors.

One local element leading to increased enlistment was the promise from leaders of county and state governments as well as local plantation owners that the recruits' families would be cared for and provided food supplies, salt, and even clothing if needed. Planters often reneged on their promises as food prices increased during shortages. State governors also found they could not afford to feed the soldiers' needy families as promised. Both Jefferson Davis and Robert E. Lee complained that pleadings of hardships in letters from homes encouraged desertion.

Negative Elements of the States' Rights Ideology

Ironically, localism could work to the advantage of the Union as well as to the Confederacy. During the last part of the war, Union officers, including William Tecumseh Sherman, offered Confederates who deserted or voluntarily surrendered and took an oath of allegiance to be fed and given permission and support to return home. This policy was successful in encouraging desertions during and after the siege of Atlanta (Thrasher 2021, 55). The major reason for desertion at the time was a longing to go home (Thrasher 2021, 6 and 45).

The political ideology of states' rights was only a part of a general mindset defining localism. The values of loyalty to local entities, such as family, county, and state, at times proved stronger than Confederate nationalism.

An estimated one-third to one-half of his troops did not follow when Robert E. Lee invaded Delaware in September 1862 to begin his Antietam campaign. Many felt they had enlisted to defend the Confederacy and their homes from Union invasion and refused to fight in Northern territory (Boatner 1998, 169).

A wife of one of Lee's men wrote her husband that leaving the Confederacy to invade the Union was unjust and against God's will (Guelzo 2013, 66). Desertions also occurred whenever an army marched near soldiers' homes, and many would leave the army to go home. Some returned after short visits, but a minority stayed permanently.

Governor Brown and North Carolina Governor Zebulon Vance believed the Confederacy's central government had limited rights vis-à-vis the states (Wesley 2001, 62). Based on this rationale, these governors kept military supplies from the Confederacy to provide for their own state militias. The government of North Carolina kept up to twenty thousand men from being drafted into the Confederate armies during 1864 when the shortage of troops had become critical. While many men in the ranks were barefoot, wore rags, and lacked blankets and overcoats during the winters, the state of North Carolina kept ninety-two thousand uniforms, blankets, and a supply of leather for footwear in its warehouses undistributed until after the end of the war.

Governor Vance insisted its local militias were needed to protect his state from Northern invasion—as did the governors of Georgia, Mississippi, Alabama, Virginia, South Carolina, and the Trans-Mississippi area (Roland 1960, 142–43). They each demanded that their state have Confederate troops stationed to protect the states' borders. The governors insisted that their states were vitally important, but the central government had different priorities. This strategy of distributing troops throughout the Confederacy was impossible given the large size of the Confederacy and the lack of resources and manpower. Many areas deemed secondary nevertheless contained Confederate troops. The Union command considered Florida and Texas minor theaters and were only half-heartedly invaded a number of times. The result is that these two states were the only ones whose capital cities were neither occupied nor destroyed. The troops in these two states could have been better used elsewhere.

Conflicts between Professional and Political Officers

The consequences of localism are illustrated in two often-detrimental practices conducted by both sides during the Civil War. The first practice was conflicts between professional officers and those who had not attended West Point or other military academies and military schools. The second consequence of localism involved the practice of selecting civilians for military positions based on local or state political importance. Many were first appointed as colonels of militia units after they had recruited enough volunteers to form a company or a regiment.

The first locally based conflict involved hostility between officers who had graduated from West Point and those who had not. In this case, localism involved loyalty to the West Point Academy. West Point graduate Jefferson Davis did not commission any officer who had not graduated from West Point until late in the war when there was a lack of officers due to casualties ("promotion by attrition" rather than based on expertise). Davis remained loyal to generals with whom he had formed friendships during his years as a West Point cadet. A number of these generals proved inadequate, but Davis refused to replace them with better officers. From his experience at West Point, Davis often considered rank more important than talent. It is surprising how many West Point graduates on both sides were military failures.

Many accused West Pointers of being cliquish and overly concerned with procedures and promotions. General T. R. R. Cobb, a successfully self-taught officer, was typical of those who did not admire West Pointers. He described West Pointers as (Fair 1971, 251):

> They are very sociable fellows … but never have I seen men who had so little appreciation of merit in others. Self-sufficiency and self-aggrandizement are their … controlling characteristics.

Localism also influenced promotion. Earl Van Dorn was refused a deserved promotion because he was a Mississippian rather than a Virginian. He failed to be promoted to chief of cavalry in the Virginia theater even though he had the seniority and experience. Instead, Virginian James Ewell Brown ("Jeb") Stuart, a personal favorite of Lee's, was awarded the position (Carter 1999, 38). Wade Hampton III, although praised and promoted by Lee, also felt he was being discriminated against because his command was made up primarily of volunteers from South Carolina. The officers of Lee's Army of Northern Virginia were primarily composed of Virginians (McMurry 1989, 90, 98).

An unfortunate situation existing on both sides of the Civil War was that promotion was often based on political ties and personal influence. Few officers at the beginning of their careers expected to be promoted unless they were supported by hometown politicians or politically powerful relatives.

Militias became local arenas for military titles as well as political and social recognition. Without any military experience, John Henry Hammond became a colonel after he raised two companies during South Carolina's nullification crisis during 1832–1833. His nomination to colonel was due to his popularity among the state's leaders and his pledge to donate one hundred bales of cotton to defray the militia's costs. Hammond later became a brigadier general because of his political importance and wealth. His uniform included forty-dollar golden epaulettes, golden shoulder straps, and a white plume on his hat.

Not all militias or their political colonels proved to be completely militarily inadequate. Two militia units from Virginia and Delaware rushed to the Harpers Ferry arsenal when John Brown and twenty-one followers attempted to initiate a slave insurrection on October 17, 1859. Quickly forcing Brown's supporters into one building, members of the two militias and armed local residents surrounded the building and trapped the invaders. Unorganized volunteer citizens were also willing to defend their community and rushed with their muskets to face Brown and his men. One of the civilian deaths was Fontaine Beckham, the mayor of the town.

The militia members and volunteers did not know what else to do after the invading group had been trapped. They began to drink, and some became inebriated (Reynolds 2006, 323). A company of ninety marines, led by Robert E. Lee and Jeb Stuart, arrived that night. The next day, the marines stormed the building and captured Brown and his remaining men. This event showed the usefulness of militias—but also their limitations.

The Confederate Badge of Courage

Another example of the strength of localism reflected in Confederate behavior is the way exceptional bravery was recognized. Before 1862, there was no way to recognize extreme valor or performance except by promotion. When promotion was impractical, an officer would be awarded a *brevet promotion.* This was a "paper title" awarded to an officer. A brevet promotion did not include the authority or pay of a formal promotion, but it included the prestige of holding a higher rank. A breveted officer could sign his name as Bvt. Colonel Lee.

At times, a brevet promotion signified a future promotion should a position become vacant. Some brevet awards were given posthumously. An officer could be awarded several honorary brevet titles. Robert E. Lee was awarded three brevet promotions during the Mexican-American War.

The Union's Medal of Honor was established in July 1862 by Abraham Lincoln "to be presented, in the name of Congress, to such noncommissioned officers and privates as shall have most distinguished themselves by their gallantry in action." The process for being awarded the medal began with recommendations by the candidate's commander, but Lincoln sometimes awarded the medal for political reasons. A board was later established to recommend applications and to cancel inappropriately awarded brevets, which made the process even more bureaucratic.

Soon after the establishment of the Union's Medal of Honor, Jefferson Davis also decided to award those who showed "courage and good conduct on the field of battle." The conditions for the award suggest that the candidate was expected to be a gentleman or a man of "good conduct." Southern values equated courage with being a gentleman or a cavalier.

By contrast to the Union, the Confederacy created a process steeped in localism. The Badge of Courage and a cash amount was to be awarded to one private or noncommissioned officer in every company after a victorious battle. The recipients were to be selected by the vote of the members of each company involved in the battle. Lack of metal and cash, as well as the disapproval of Robert E. Lee, made the distribution of physical awards impossible. Instead, a Confederate "Roll of Honor" was established.

Political Generals

Men were recruited on the local level by individuals given permission by state governors to raise companies of one hundred men each or regiments of one thousand men. Recruits were then transferred to the authority of the state government for deployment into the Confederacy's armies after being given uniforms, equipment, and limited training. By the end of their training period, these groups had received a modicum of drilling knowledge and experience in living in camps. While in the camp, men learned domestic skills previously performed by women, such as cooking their own food and washing and repairing their clothes.

The men who became political officers were already recognized as leaders in their communities. These local leaders recruited supporters, friends, and neighbors and encouraged them to volunteer as a group. Recruits were honored by their neighbors with parades, banquets, and balls. Local Ladies Clubs presented hand-sewn regimental flags, and politicians gave patriotic speeches of encouragement. During the Civil War, the formation and leadership of companies and regiments were very local affairs. It was only later that these political officers were tested in battle. Many failed and damaged the Confederate cause.

The case of Henry King Burgwyn Jr. is a typical example of the importance of civilian ties in receiving commissions during the first part of the war. Burgwyn Jr. was the son of a wealthy Virginian and a graduate of the Virginia Military Institute (Sword 1992, 80–81). Burgwyn (1841–1863) was a Virginian aristocrat with military training, yet he was afraid he might have to enlist as a private. Burgwyn had been a senior when his class was given early diplomas and ordered to report to the War Department at Richmond. Among his recommendations was a very favorable evaluation from former professor Thomas J. Jackson, soon to be given the nickname "Stonewall."

Burgwyn was eager to serve, but he also wanted to do so while holding the rank appropriate to his social station and cavalier self-image. Burgwyn complained to his father (Sword 1992, 80):

> Considerable dissatisfaction exists among us that they expect us to fight as privates through the war; or at all events commence it that way. We would thus be the only ones in the whole army who would be denied of the opportunity of distinguishing ourselves while having more military knowledge than any of the others … I would like to receive some letters of introduction to persons in Richmond [i.e., to get a commission].

Burgwyn reports in the quote above that he wanted to use the war as an opportunity to become "distinguished." Honor and being superior to others (the alpha complex) were important motivators to volunteer among upper-class men. The use above of the term "among us" suggests a group of men with similar high social statuses volunteered together. Burgwyn also assumes, rightly, that personal glory recognized by others could only be achieved by becoming an officer. He also stresses his superior social class position to other soldiers.

Burgwyn's (later called the "Boy Colonel") letters of recommendation and his family's social prestige resulted in his promotion to lieutenant colonel when he was nineteen years old in August 1861. His performance in two major battles was respectable, and he was promoted to colonel in August 1862. While leading a charge and carrying the company's flag during the Gettysburg campaign, twenty-one-year-old Burgwyn was mortally shot through both lungs. In this case, his appointment was the correct action, but he should not have been carrying the company's flag. Burgwyn was a typically rash but courageous cavalier. He was too eager to lead a charge and face danger to become "distinguished." He did not, as was common among cavaliers, consider the long-term consequences of his actions.

Wadc Hampton III was another success story of a person who used his wealth to begin a military career. Hampton became a superior cavalry officer even though he did not have any previous military experience. Not content with raising a company of one hundred recruits, Hampton volunteered to recruit a "legion" of one thousand men to include infantry, cavalry, and artillery units equipped at his expense. Hampton published a notice in the local newspaper that, in part, guaranteed the maintenance of the local nature of his legion (Cisco 2006, 58):

> The Legion is to serve wherever it may be ordered by the President [i.e., Jefferson Davis], and is to be on precisely the same footing, *except as to its peculiar organization* [i.e., to be kept intact], as the rest of the Provisional Army [emphasis added].

Hampton recruited and equipped "his" legion, and he was able to dictate that it would be kept together. This agreement illustrates both the scale of Hampton's influence and the importance of localism for recruitment. Hampton was later promoted, and he reluctantly gave up direct command of the legion. The members of the legion first enlisted for twelve months because Confederates expected a short war. Most reenlisted when their terms of service expired.

Localism and the Cordon Defense

T. Harry Williams (Donald 1996, 57) suggests that while the personalities and professional expertise of generals and civilian leaders are important factors in winning and losing battles, grand strategy is the result of cultural factors. Strategist Karl von Clausewitz (1997, 41, 109, and 311) wrote during the first part of the nineteenth century that nations fought in ways that resembled the cultures and social structures of their societies. On a more specific level, Frank E. Vandiver (1984, 3 and 21) stressed the importance of culture on the military ideologies and behaviors of leaders. The cordon strategy was the most comprehensive strategy of the Confederacy and was based on the cultural origins of Confederate decisions.

The major strategy guiding the Confederacy, the cordon strategy, involved protecting the Confederacy's borders. When border states were lost through Union invasion, civilian leaders and military officers were obsessed with regaining those areas. The cordon policy was a rational idea for a number of practical and cultural reasons. A major advantage of the strategy was that many leaders and communities had visible proof that the Confederacy was protecting them by stationing troops nearby. Distant losses would be easier to ignore when a population felt protected by

Confederate troops in the area. In this case, localism trumped Confederate nationalism.

Any loss of an area in the Confederacy's periphery diminished its ability to support the war, a fact recognized by Abraham Lincoln. Lincoln stated, "I hope to have God on my side, but I must have Kentucky." In a letter to a senator and close friend, Orville Browning, Lincoln was more specific about the importance of Kentucky for both sides:

> I think to lose Kentucky is nearly the same as to lose the whole game. Kentucky gone, we cannot hold Missouri, nor Maryland. These all against us, and the job on our hands is too large for us. We would as well consent to separation at once, including the surrender of this capitol.

Kentucky remained in the control of the Union, and 125,000 Kentuckians fought for the Union.

The cordon policy was based on the cultural value of localism because all areas of the Confederacy were considered equally important or even sacred. Armies and forts were to be located near the Confederacy's borders (Vandiver 1984, 16). When Union forces invaded the Confederacy, separate Rebel armies stationed near the threatened areas would combine, use their shorter interior lines to outnumber the invaders, and attack when doing so was to their advantage. The cavalry was expected to destroy the enemy's lines of communication and supplies.

A major element of Confederate foreign policy was to convince foreign governments that the Union was the aggressor (Guelzo 2013, 18). Davis even declared that the firing on Fort Sumter was forced upon the Confederacy by an aggressive Union! The cordon strategy was defensive because it showed foreign nations and the Union that the Confederacy had no aggressive geographic goals. This ignored the bombing of Fort Sumter and early attempts to extend the Confederacy into the southwest territories. Jefferson Davis also realized governmental representatives of foreign countries would be less likely to acknowledge the Confederacy as a valid nation if it could not defend its territory. This stance was important to British politicians (Jones 1961, 20).

Unannounced by Davis was that a nonaggressive stance did not include the four slave states staying in the Union. Southerners believed Delaware, Kentucky, Missouri, and Maryland rightly were part of the South and the Confederacy. Southerners were disappointed when Confederate armies entered Kentucky and Maryland and found the population refusing to welcome their "rescuers."

New military-related technology, such as the rifle, offered the defense an advantage over the defensive. The defensive policy reduces casualties, which would also reduce the Union's manpower advantage. The cordon strategy would hopefully gain time for the Union to became war-weary. The longer the war lasted, it was assumed, the more likely Europeans would also insist on an armistice to reestablish the cotton ("white gold") trade.

This defensive policy was Davis's first choice even though it conflicted with other major Southern cultural values. The Confederate public preferred a more aggressive policy and demanded that local communities be protected from Yankee invasion.

The cordon policy was adopted in part because the policy supported the more selfish value that local interests were paramount. The Confederacy could not successfully support the contradictory cultural demands of both localism and aggressive cavalier values.

The cordon defense demanded successful and coordinated responses, but the Confederate western theater was staffed by second-rate generals who refused to cooperate. The results were twofold. The Union's first victories and control of Confederate land areas took place in the west and on the Atlantic coast.

The cordon mindset was misguided in many ways. One weakness of this mindset was the continued attempts to recontrol areas lost to the Union. After losing the Battle of Atlanta and the surrender of Atlanta, Hood's Army of Tennessee remained functional in spite of numerous recent casualties. Hood's decision was not to continue to attack Sherman's forces but to march north to "liberate" Tennessee. After giving chase, Sherman decided to abandon Atlanta and begin his Savannah campaign to destroy the military and civilian resources of middle Georgia.

Hood could have turned around, followed Sherman, and harassed the Union forces. This tactic was a major concern of Sherman's since any pause in his march would have resulted in a loss of supplies and perhaps defeat. Instead, Hood decided that the border state of Tennessee was more important than Georgia. Hood also ignored the fact that a Union army was defending Tennessee.

At the time, the major responsibility of governments at all levels was to protect property. In the South, the protection of property included the protection of their ownership of enslaved persons. To the Southern elite, extensive landownership and owning enslaved persons were the basis of their wealth and prestige. Their major concern was protecting their local investments in land and enslaved persons. Slave owners believed, rightly so, that the presence of invading Union forces in the Confederacy would result in the liberation of the enslaved and their relocation beyond the owners' control.

The enslaved would also attempt to escape to nearby areas occupied by Federal forces. The presence of Union troops would also disrupt the plantations' growing cycle and the likelihood of the confiscation of baled cotton, livestock, and food supplies. The cordon defense protected the wealth of the elite and reinforced the illusion that local concerns would be an appropriate strategy for winning independence.

The elite expected their state representatives to protect their interests, and governors insisted that their states must be protected by stationing troops at the local levels. The Confederacy did not have the manpower to station troops throughout the new nation and still have enough soldiers to confront an invading Federal force. An associated problem of the cordon strategy was how to deal with the Confederate coastline of roughly 3,500 miles and 189 navigable rivers with many running from north to south.

While much of the coastline was not useable for amphibious operations—and was thereby safe from amphibious invasions—no one realized at first how easily forts could be captured and some seaports blockaded. The first successful invasions by the Union were areas on the Atlantic and Gulf coasts to provide bases for the Union's naval blockade of Confederate ports. Grant's first major victories consisted of the capture of the Tennessee Forts Donelson and Henry during February 1862 on the northern border of the Confederacy. These victories opened access to the Tennessee River and areas south. A little more than a year later, Union naval forces captured New Orleans and controlled the lower Mississippi River basin. On July 4, 1863, the Confederacy was split into two isolated areas after the surrender of Vicksburg.

The cordon defense's strategic emphasis on local defense diverted attention from one of the Confederacy's major advantages of a land mass of 770,400 square miles. One reason for the early British belief that the Confederacy enjoyed a high probability of gaining its independence was its large, almost continental, size. After all, colonial Americans had won the War of Independence in part because of the thirteen colonies' large territory. The cordon policy proved to be a failure for the Confederacy (Jones 1961, 20).

David Herbert Donald (1996, 50 and 57) suggests that a better Confederate strategy would have been to attack en masse where the enemy was weaker, unprepared, or inept. This strategy was successful on a number of battlefields, especially when Lee and "Stonewall" Jackson were involved. The Confederate cavalry could also have conducted multiple raids.

The cordon defense was successful a number of times. Using a railroad to transport troops during July 1861, General G. T. Beauregard was reinforced by Joseph E. Johnston's command, which had been stationed one hundred miles away. The two Rebel forces meet at Manassas, Virginia, and the result was a significant victory for the Confederate forces. The state of Virginia enjoyed the best railroad system in the Confederacy, was at its peak efficiency, and had not yet been damaged through war or overuse.

"Stonewall" Jackson's 1862 Valley Campaign was a successful use of internal lines to surprise and beat back four separate Union armies. Marching 646 miles in forty-eight days, Jackson's seventeen thousand men engaged three Union armies of fifty-two thousand men. However, few other commands could have continuously marched so far in such a short time. While Jackson's skills delayed Union armies from joining George B. McClellan's Peninsula Campaign, Jackson did not win any major battles or weaken the Yankees to any great extent. It might have been better to send Jackson north to threaten Union cities. The effort would have shocked the North's urban population and may have resulted in more practical consequences than Jackson's Valley Campaign.

Edmund Kirby Smith and His Texas "Empire"

An example of the weakness of the cordon strategy was the stationing of Edmund Kirby Smith during January 1863 as commander of the Trans-Mississippi Department, basically Texas, Arkansas, and part of Louisiana. The cordon culture-derived mindset dictated that as much land area as possible be kept from the enemy. A better strategy would have been to relocate Smith's forces to an eastern location before the Mississippi River became controlled by the Union and before the crossing of Confederate troops and supplies became impossible. Even before the fall of Vicksburg, Kirby's forces became useless because of interarmy conflicts, lack of logistics, and the lack of Confederate patriotism in parts of Texas.

Smith was unable to send troops to support Vicksburg before its capture on July 4, 1863, (Grimley and Simpson 2001, 41) and Smith's command of thirty thousand continued its isolation. Kirby's "Smithdom" became even more irrelevant to the war effort after the fall of Vicksburg. Clement Eaton summarized the sad condition of the "Smithdom" as (Eaton 1977, 195):

> Kirby Smith ... found unusual problems, such as marauding Indians, jayhawkers, and criminals, notably William C. Quantrill, leading guerrilla bands who masqueraded as Confederate soldiers but were completely lawless. Other problems were mutiny, officers quarrelling with and shooting each other in duels, and planters protesting against the government interfering with their profits from the illegal sale of cotton—it was certainly not a Confederate paradise, and far from the romantic legend of the Confederate soldiers.

Other problems Smith faced included bands of marauding deserters, Confederate refugees and their enslaved persons, low or nonexistent pay for soldiers, inadequate food supplies, no promotion of his officers, lack of shoes and other equipment, lack of funds, and conflicts with the governors of Texas and Arkansas.

Kirby organized armament factories and negotiated with foreign nations to sell cotton in exchange for supplies. He was able to export cotton by buying cotton at twelve cents a pound to sell at forty-eight cents a pound. He even promoted officers. Doing so was a responsibility limited to the Confederate congress and the War Department, and the promotions were not officially recognized.

Planters in cooperation with Yankee speculators would buy cotton in the interior of Texas for three cents a pound to be sold at the border for fifty to sixty cents a pound. This conflicted with Smith's attempts to confiscate cotton for the Confederacy in part because Governor Pendleton Murrah of Texas refused to cooperate (Eaton 1977, 192).

There were Union attempts to control Texas after the fall of Vicksburg, but Grant and Sherman focused their efforts elsewhere. The Red River Campaign took place in the Trans-Mississippi Department during spring 1864 to close the ports of Mobile and Shreveport and confiscate an estimated one hundred thousand bales of cotton from the plantations along the Red River. These bales were to be sold to Northern speculators and Union officers for their own profit. The expedition, led by an inept Nathaniel P. Banks, was a failure, and the area was ignored for the rest of the war.

Grant and Sherman had little interest in invading Texas after the capture of Vicksburg. They turned their attention to where Lee was located in Virginia and Atlanta, Georgia, Chattanooga, Tennessee, and possibly Mobile, Mississippi.

The strategy adopted by Grant was for Union armies to cooperate to destroy the two major Confederate armies and their military-related industries and sources of supplies, including food. Capturing territory was now a secondary goal. Even the central city Atlanta, Georgia, was abandoned after its military industries were destroyed. By this time, the Union had also adopted a "hard war" strategy to attack the civilian economic sector and lower civilian morale.

Localism and the Lack of a Unified Command

President Davis separated the Confederacy into independent military theaters. He believed that each commander of the departments should be independent of the others. Davis also assumed the commanders would cooperate when each saw the necessity (Jones 1961, 128). Davis ignored the strong mindset of West Point graduate officers of valuing rank and independence. Few wanted to be subordinate to the others if doing so meant a loss of independence and alpha dominance.

When the secretary of war, George Randolph, ordered the commander of the Trans-Mississippi Department (Arkansas, western Louisiana, and Texas) to move units east to help protect Vicksburg before Grant's forces besieged the city, Davis vetoed the plan and ordered all forces to stay in their allotted areas (Keegan 2009, 205). In this instance, Davis's mindset was local. The commanders of the Trans-Mississippi Department also insisted on the independence to issue their own orders.

The local mindsets of Davis and Lee can be contrasted to Grant's grand strategy. When Grant became commander in chief, he immediately established the principle of coordination of all Union armies in time and space. Grant wanted all Union armies to attack Confederate forces at the same time and to continue their offensives without the usual pauses between battles and campaigns.

While Grant's plan was not completely successful because of inept corps commanders, Grant and Sherman forced the two largest Confederate armies on the defensive (Foote 2016, 5). The separated Confederate forces could not combine to threaten Sherman or Grant. The Confederate forces were being destroyed bit by bit. The Army of Northern Virginia was penned in at Petersburg, and Atlanta and Savannah had been captured. The Confederate Army of Tennessee was weakened and had retreated from Georgia and would be destroyed later as an effective fighting force. The Confederacy seldom achieved the coordination of military commands achieved by the Union.

Localism and Desertion

There was no doubt among Confederates that a major reason for the loss of the war and battles was the large number of deserters. Many thought the loss of Vicksburg was caused by a high rate of desertion rather than by a lack of cooperation among commanders. Lee believed his failures at the battles of Antietam and Gettysburg were due to the same cause. Deserters were also blamed for the defeats that led to the loss of the vital state of Tennessee.

Desertions were also blamed for the fall of Atlanta (Martin 2003, 256). Confederate cavaliers and Southerners in general tended to blame others for their mistakes. Even a private mused (Martin 2003, 256) during April 1865, "And who was the cause of it [i.e., the loss of the war]. Skulkers, Cowards, extortioners and Deserters not the Yankees." In the same manner, Colonel W. H. Stewart accused deserters as being "the assassins of the Confederate States." Desertions, largely based on the central values of family, amoral familism, and localism must be considered significant cultural causes of Confederate weakness.

Members of the Texas Brigade, part of the Army of Northern Virginia, were among the most unruly and independent of Confederate soldiers (Louisianans would be a close second.) They were infamous for stealing food, such as hogs and chicken, from local Southerners. Only an officer who understood their subculture could successfully control Texans. Almost all the members of the Texas Brigade marching through Richmond decided to temporarily desert and enjoy a rest. When an officer tried to prevent the action, their commander, John Bell Hood, told the officer (Patterson 2002, 116), "Let 'em go, General, let 'em go … you'll get them back in time for the next battle." Hood understood the culture of westerners. He also ignored their practice of confiscating food supplies from Southern citizens. A common rationalization for killing a farmer's hog for food was that the hog in question was a "Yankee hog" and had refused to surrender.

War-weariness was a factor for desertion along with a lack of good nutrition, footwear, and warm clothing, constant marching, and not being able to keep up with their stronger brethren. "Stonewall" Jackson's strategy was to surprise the enemy using fast-paced marches. Jackson probably lost up to one-third of his men through desertions since not all could maintain the grueling marches (Weirtz 2005, 95).

Familism and Desertion

The most important factor encouraging desertion was the belief that one's family needed a father or husband more than the Confederacy did. These deserters were neither cowards nor inexperienced soldiers. Many of these temporary or permanent deserters were members of seasoned elite military units. These citizen-soldiers went home when they thought they were no longer needed after a battle or between campaigns. More properly called absentees, these men were absent without leave (AWOL), but they expected to return to their units. These men were generally considered deserters by their field officers and could be court-martialed and punished for their absence.

The value of familism over military demands was more common among poorer enlistees who could no longer support their families. A private's monthly pay of eleven Confederate dollars during the first part of the war was inadequate even before inflation rendered this amount almost worthless. A laborer could earn roughly thirty dollars a month, even though this amount could barely support a family. Creating more anxiety, soldiers from areas controlled by Union forces became isolated from their families.

Confederate government agents were allowed to seize food products and pay as little as half current market prices. At times, payment was made in script that needed to be redeemed at a distant government office—if currency was available. Food collectors were often stationed at the entrances of cities to catch farmers bringing food to sell and taxing farmers by confiscating part of their wares. This practice resulted in food shortages since farmers refused to approach cities to sell their produce.

As harmful to poorer families, the tax-in-kind impressment law, enacted during April 1863, allowed agents to legally seize 10 percent of a family's food supply. These losses were significant since many subsistence-level farms were producing at lower prewar levels since the adult male family members were serving in the military or had become casualties.

With poorer families suffering from lack of food and deprivations caused by deserters, outlaws, passing armies from both sides, and government impressment of food, forage, mules, and horses, it was no wonder enlistees began to believe their families needed them more than the Confederacy did.

The result of these deprivations and actual hunger encouraged poorer enlistees to consider deserting and returning home. Joseph T. Glatthaar (2011, 16–17), in his sample of members of the Army of Northern Virginia, found that 52 percent of deserters were from those Glatthaar defined as belonging to the lower classes. The majority of these deserters were those who were both poor and married with wives and children. Those loyal to their families may have maintained their allegiance to the Confederacy but decided for family over nationalism.

The seven thousand Texans who joined the Texas Brigade, part of the Army of Northern Virginia, were unable to travel a thousand miles to visit their families. While these men did not lose faith in the Confederacy's ultimate victory over the Union, their rate of desertion (6 percent), though low, was primarily the result of wanting to be with their families (Ural 2017, 238).

Desertion and Amoral Familism

Edward C. Banfield (1958) presented a concept related to localism and desertion by posing the conflict between family and nonfamily called *amoral familism*. In essence, a person owes loyalty to his or her family members and to no other institutions or individuals defined as outsiders. A man is expected to support his family members and promote only their advantage.

By the same token, a family member owes few or no obligations to nonfamily outsiders or institutions; anyone outside the extended family and circle of trusted friends was considered a threat. Such societies often brought nonmembers into the families through special ceremonies, such as making neighbors godfathers or godmothers or honorary cousins, uncles, and aunts. A common practice among these inner-directed societies was for members to marry either within tribes or extended families. Marrying cousins was acceptable. Another common practice wherever amoral familism is practiced (i.e., most agricultural societies and rural subcultures) is to name a child after a family member, in-law, or close friend.

This feeling of mistrust of outsiders in isolated Southern areas was augmented during 1863 and 1864. Many states during this time enacted laws stating that anyone not reporting deserters would be punished with fines and/or imprisonment. The state of Texas, for example, passed a law punishing anyone giving aid to deserters—even food or shelter—up to five years of hard labor (Lonn 1928, 105). Obviously, these laws forced Southern families to protect their members who had deserted and become suspicious of local law officials and neighbors who might become paid informers. The fact that government officials and military groups could "impress" food and equipment further increased the distrust of strangers.

Soldiers often gave nicknames to their officers that reflected a fictional personal or family relationship. Robert E. Lee was given a number of family-based nicknames. Lee was called "Marse" Robert. The term "marse" is slang for "master" of a family and is a term denoting respect and affection. Lee's other familial nicknames included "Uncle Robert" and "Bobby Lee."

Strangers and outsiders are defined in the amoral familism complex as potential dangers and as persons to whom no loyalty is offered or expected. An example of amoral familism was the conduct of deserters who did not go home. Those who would not or could not reach their homes banded together into quasi-family groups to hide in mountainous or other isolated areas to form lawless bands. These bands would then terrorize communities as their members stole supplies and then returned to their hideouts (Weitz 2005, 112).

Desertion and Family Suffering

The combination of the suffering of families and the danger to them from deserters-turned-outlaws was a strong motivation for desertion. Historian Ella Lonn (2028, 12–13) summarized this causation:

> The men felt that their services in the army were useless and that their families required their attention, especially when their homes lay hopelessly within the Federal line. Furthermore, many a man felt himself literally forced to desert in order to defend his family from outlaws ... Appeals and laments from these same families did not fail to reveal their sufferings.

Ella Lonn continues by describing the rationale for Edward Cooper's desertion. In his defense, during his court-martial for desertion, Cooper showed the court an iconic letter sent to him by his wife. Mary Cooper wrote:

> I have always been proud of you, and since your connection with the Confederate Army, I have been prouder of you than before … Edward, unless you come home, we must die. Last night, I was aroused by little Eddie's crying … [H]e said, "O mama! I am so hungry." And Lucy, Edward, your darling Lucy; she never complains, but she is growing thinner and thinner every day. And before God, Edward, unless you come home, we must die.

Edward Cooper was sentenced to death, but he was pardoned by Robert E. Lee. Edward returned to his unit and was later killed in action (Gienapp 2001, 216). Mary's letter indicates a continuing strong loyalty to the Confederacy, but her familial concerns became paramount when her family lacked food.

Pursuit by Confederate units of deserters was often negligible. It made little sense to temporarily lose more men by sending them to chase after deserters. In desperation, the Confederacy offered citizen bounty hunters a reward of twenty dollars for each man brought in. This policy of using bounty hunters to return deserters strengthened the distrust of strangers.

Letters from home after 1862 increasingly began to beg men to return home. Wives reminded their husbands of their duty to protect their families, especially children, as did Mary Cooper. These letters were so effective in lowering soldiers' morale and increasing desertion that Jefferson Davis during 1863 announced amnesty for all deserters who returned to their units. He pleaded with women to send their husbands back to their posts (Martin 2003, 212):

> I conjure my countrywomen—mothers, wives, sisters, and daughters of the Confederacy—to use

> their all powerful influence in aid of this call [i.e., amnesty], to add one crowning sacrifice … and take care that none who owe service … shall be sheltered at home.

Davis's use of the term "sheltered" indicates he realized family members hid and protected family members who had deserted.

Localism of Southern Railroad Lines

A negative consequence of localism in the South was the lack of standardization of railroad gauges and generally short rail lines that served local interests. The Southern West Maryland Railroad was only twenty miles long. In contrast, the Northern Baltimore and Ohio Railroad was sixty miles long and had several trunk lines (Brown 2021, 71).

Rails in one state or town might not be the same gauge (there were six different gauges used in the United States) as those in the next state or community. The result was increased localism since different companies could not use a competitor's line. Rail lines generally had one track, resulting in limited service.

The South had few integrated marketing systems. The relatively few nonsubsistence farmers, aside from wealthier plantation owners, relied on local markets to sell their produce and products and buy supplies. They often used river transportation for longer distances when possible. The longer rail lines were generally used by cotton producers. They could send their baled cotton directly to cities where their agents sent the bales to seaports to be warehoused, tested for quality, sold, and sent to New York to be exported (Vandiver 1947, 64). Wealthier farmers and planters also used longer railroad lines for other agricultural products such as rice, wheat, corn, and hay to sell in larger urban centers. Cotton (white gold) was the most common and most profitable product transported by railroads.

Railroads in the South profited more from carrying freight than people (Black 1998, 37), making cotton and other large-scale crops "kings" to railroad owners and stockholders. Southern railroads were also funded by the states by offering bonds, thus increasing the probability that political and elite interests were primary motivators on where to build railroads. Many rail lines lost their main civilian function during the Civil War when the Union blockade closed most Southern seaports, and cotton could no longer be exported (Foote and Hess 2021, 56).

This aspect of localism was economically advantageous to planters, but it became a disadvantage when the Confederacy needed more centralized systems of transportation to meet its military demands. The Confederacy's rail system was so localized that the Union's military railroad unit built two thousand miles of rail for its own use in the Confederacy to facilitate the delivery of supplies and troops (Stahr 2017, 174).

Southern state governments did support the building of railroads as part of expanding their states' economies. The Western & Atlantic Railroad was owned by the state of Georgia. The railroad was established in 1836 and linked the two important cities of Atlanta and Chattanooga, a distance of 138 miles. Atlanta became an important economic and railroad center. Economic development in Georgia was in large part made possible by the fact that the emerging middle classes in a number of Georgia cities did not depend on the elite plantation owners (DeCredico 1990, xiv). The Southern economy during the first half of the 1850s was not as static as usually recognized.

The dysfunctional effects of the local nature of Southern railroads during the Civil War were experienced when James Longstreet led his corps from Virginia to Georgia in 1863 to support Braxton Bragg's army. The distance was nine hundred miles and consisted of a dozen changes of railroad lines, necessitating the loading and unloading of men and supplies at each of these stages (Keegan 2009, 222). The effort was successful and showed the railroads' potential for shifting troops to distant areas where they were most needed. Generally, the Confederacy failed to organize its rail system efficiently (Clark 2001, chapter 3 and page 218).

Christopher Gabe (2020, 40) noted that while the Confederacy was given large discounts for the use of railroads, they were also given second-rate service. Civilian cargo, especially cotton, continued to be given the most attention because such traffic remained more profitable. Railroad owners were willing to give the Confederacy a 50 percent discount to move equipment and supplies as well as charging two cents per man per mile, but they still expected to gain profits.

Dividends remained high throughout most of the war, and railroad owners continued paying their capital investment loans since most owners had borrowed from their state governments to begin construction. Most holders of railroad stocks and bonds were planters whose political influence included demanding profits from their investments.

Federal officials realized early in the war the importance of controlling the railroads for the benefit of the war effort. The US Military Railroads (USMRR) commission under the War Department was given compulsory power over the Northern railroads. The head of the USMRR, Daniel McCullum, was a pioneer in railroad organization. He was commissioned as a colonel and was later promoted to brigadier general. McCullum enjoyed both expertise and the right to give orders.

By contrast, the first nominal head of the Confederate railroads was a politician and held the inadequate military rank of major. He could advise but not order. His successor was more successful but primarily used his personality to coordinate military traffic.

Southern rail lines were generally of low quality compared to Northern lines, in part because the Confederacy lacked skilled repair personnel. Some rail lines still used rails called "strap and stringer" or "flatbar" that quickly wore out. "Strap and stringer" construction consisted of wooden rails covered with a thin band of iron (Foote and Hess 2021, 56).

Though the method was uncomfortable for passengers, and heavy loads quickly destroyed the rail, "strap and stringer" rails could be repaired with untrained (i.e., enslaved) labor, and wood was easily available. The Confederacy eventually was not able to repair its higher-quality lines because the Union blockade made the importation of iron rails almost impossible. Investors in ships that could avoid the Union blockade did not want to waste space and weight on low-profit freight, such as rails, in comparison to more profitable luxury goods.

A Complex Case of Localism

An estimated seven thousand Texans served in the Texas Brigade, which was part of Lee's Army of Northern Virginia. During the beginning of the war, Jefferson Davis urged Texans to remain in Texas to protect Texans from attacks by Apache and Comanche. However, many Texans believed the best chance to fight Yankees was in the eastern theater. Texans did not want to miss the opportunity of taking part in a battle before the war ended. These men insisted on staying together by forming the Texas Brigade. The Texas Brigade became a very cohesive military unit and maintained its local ties with their friends and families more than one thousand miles away.

The Brigade (also known as Hood's Texas Brigade) was used by Lee as a shock troop unit similar to the Stonewall Brigade and was sent where it was most needed. The Texas Brigade contained ten companies. Two companies originated from Georgia and Arkansas, and Texans were members of the other eight companies. The Brigade was given the best equipment available, including Enfield rifles; 20 percent died of disease, and an additional 62 percent died of battle wounds, making the Brigade's mortality casualty rate 82 percent. These figures do not include those who were wounded and survived. The Brigade was especially effective during the Battle of Sharpsburg (Antietam) by closing a gap in the Confederate lines and, outnumbered, forcing the retreat of two attacking Union corps. The Brigade experienced a casualty rate of 64 percent wounded or killed in the battle.

Members of the Texas Brigade kept in touch with their families and also formed a tightly knit unit within the Brigade. Because they considered themselves citizen-soldiers, members of the Texas Brigade insisted on selecting their own officers. Officers who were not accepted by the Brigade were harassed until they insisted on being transferred elsewhere.

The distinctly local nature of the Brigade was maintained in a number of other ways. The dead were buried together and apart from other Confederates. The men's families united to send provisions and supplies until it became impossible to do so. Counties supported the soldiers by providing their families with materials to produce uniforms and other clothing. Texas citizens as a whole provided finances to construct and maintain the Texas Hospital in Richmond, Virginia, for "their" soldiers (Ural 2017, 244 and 246).

The ties formed earlier and in Virginia were maintained after the war when the survivors returned to Texas. Former members of the Brigade supported one another on economic and political issues. Though they lost much during the war, Brigade veterans improved their economic conditions between 1860 and 1870 better than nonmember Texans did (Ural 2017, 230). The state, communities, and former Brigade members also continued to provide supplies and support to the Brigade's widows and former members in need.

The Texas Brigade represented a small proportion of military-age Texans serving in the Confederate military. Most (82 percent) military-age Texans chose to stay in Texas by joining the state militia (Jewett 2002, 116 and 239). Militia members, in contrast to members of Virginia's Brigade, believed they could better protect their families, their economic well-being, and Texas by remaining in Texas. Similar to members of the Brigade, the members of the Texas militias supported the Confederacy and were overrepresented in being members of households that owned enslaved persons. Both groups were likely to be wealthier than average in their home counties (Jewett 2002, 117).

CHAPTER 9

THE CULTURE OF VIOLENCE AND AGGRESSION

We mourn the loss of our gallant dead in every conflict, yet our gratitude to Almighty God for his mercies rises higher each day. To him and the valor of our troops a nation's gratitude is due.

—Robert E. Lee

Jefferson Davis was typical of those who characterized Southern culture as warlike. He expressed this view to William Howard Russell, a British correspondent (Russell 1863, 173–4):

> In Europe ... they laugh at us because of our fondness for military titles and display. All your travelers in the country [i.e., the South] have commented on the number of generals and majors all over the states. But the fact is, we are a military people, and these signs of the fact were ignored. We are not less military because we have had no great standing armies. But perhaps we are the only people in the world where gentlemen go to a military academy who do not intend to follow the profession of arms.

A consequence of Southern aggression was the preference for aggression in battle rather than using defensive tactics. Confederates attacked first in eight out of the twelve largest battles of the war. The Confederates experienced ninety-seven thousand casualties while the Union suffered seventy-seven thousand (McWhiney 2002, 126). Confederate victories, some resulting in no appreciable advantage, were often costly in terms of deaths and wounds that the Confederacy could not afford.

Jefferson Davis was correct when he claimed that sons of the elite ("gentlemen") attended military academies without expecting to become professional soldiers. Most of the graduates of the South's premier military institution, the Virginia Military Institute, did not enroll in the military. Instead, they resigned their commissions to take civilian occupations or rely on their (or their wives') plantations for incomes. However, they did join the military when Virginia seceded. Even before the war began, cadets took temporary leave to help train raw recruits when Thomas Jackson asked for cadets to volunteer as drill teachers.

VMI cadets later took part in a battle. Ranging in age from fifteen to twenty-five years old, VMI cadets were asked to form a battalion of four companies of infantry and one artillery unit when Union Major General Franz Sigel invaded the Shenandoah Valley. A battle to stop Sigel's forces was expected near the town of New Market. The VMI student body of 257 marched eighty miles in four days from Lexington City, Virginia, to New Market, Virginia. The Battle of New Market took place on May 15, 1864. A gap in the Confederate line developed during the battle, and the cadet corps was ordered to the front. Those cadets who had been ordered to guard the supply wagons disobeyed and joined their fellow cadets at the front. The cadets received casualties from Union artillery while taking part in a charge that forced the Union soldiers to retreat.

The Confederates experienced 588 casualties, and the retreating Federals lost 744. The disparity in casualties and the Union retreat resulted in a clear victory for the Confederates (Bierle 2019, 135).

The VMI corps experienced the death of ten members (3.9 percent). Forty-seven cadets were wounded for a total rate of deaths and casualties of 22 percent (Bierle 2019, 157). The cadets, mostly teens, had performed honorably in their first battle.

Jefferson Davis had been an aggressive youth and young adult. He once tried to shoot another boy and later had arguments with at least eight persons leading to near-duels, including Judah Benjamin (Davis 1996, 3).

Davis attended West Point and served with distinction in the Mexican-American War. He received a wound that pained him throughout his life, but it gave him gravitas and respect as a wounded veteran. After secession, Davis hoped to be appointed commander in chief of the Confederate armies. Selected as president, Davis nevertheless became an active head of the Confederate military and served as his own secretary of war. Several of his four secretaries of war resigned because Davis insisted on making major and minor decisions about the war. Davis once remarked that with Lee on one flank and himself on the other, they could beat any Union army.

William Howard Russell offered a similar evaluation of the Southern fondness for war (Russell 1863, 189):

> There is a bucolic ferocity about these Southern people which will stand them good stead in the shock of battle.

Their enemies respected the tenacity and courage of Confederate soldiers, but this attraction to violence resulted in dysfunctional behaviors, including frequent interpersonal quarrels and lack of cooperation among officers. The guiding image of these would-be cavaliers was a lone knight personally defeating a number of opponents.

An illustrative example of the prevalence of Southern violence among all social classes and ages is found in an interpersonal conflict taking place during the first day of the Battle of Gettysburg.

Fifteen-year-old John Cabell Early was a volunteer aide on the staff of his uncle, Major General Jubal Anderson Early. Young Early found two stretcher-bearers who were avoiding going to the front to retrieve the wounded, and he told them to go at once to where the battle was taking place. Words were exchanged, and the two slackers challenged John to a fight.

John dismounted, took off his jacket, and was ready to brawl. From an elite family, John assumed he was qualified in spite of his age to order others to fulfill their duty (Guelzo 2013, 199). An officer passed by and cursed the three to go about their official businesses. Aggression would easily turn from fighting the enemy to interpersonal verbal or physical attacks.

Aggression for its own sake and pleasure was at times more important than fighting the enemy. During the Battle of the Wilderness in 1864, a Rebel about to be captured challenged a Yankee to a wrestling match. The challenge was accepted, and the Rebel won by gouging his opponent. Everyone watching was amused.

Many incidents of aggression involved groups rather than individuals because one element of honor was the readiness to support friends when involved in a fight. Thomas Carmichael Hindman responded to a challenge when he called a former colleague a "mulatto" because Dorsey Rice had changed his political affiliation. Hindman considered the change of political membership of his former friend a personal insult. Hindman (known later as the Confederate "Lion of the west") asked his friend Patrick Cleburne (later called the "Stonewall of the west") to help him confront Rice, Rice's brother-in-law, and a friend. Kin and friends were expected to protect one another.

Rice and his allies faced Hindman and Cleburne in the main street of the small town of Helena, Arkansas. Instead of apologizing and ending the issue, Hindman—aggressive both as a civilian and as a future general—continued to insult Dorsey Rice. In response, Rice drew and fired his revolver, wounding Hindman in the arm and chest. Cleburne was also wounded in the chest. Cleburne then fatally wounded Rice's brother-in-law. Cleburne suffered for years from his wound. A bullet had passed through a lung and lodged near his spine (Symonds 1997, 40–41).

After successful careers as a Confederate general, a politician, and an attorney, Hindman was assassinated on September 28, 1868. An assassin shot through Hindman's office window and fatally hit Hindman. Neither the motive nor the guilty party was discovered. Though a conservative Democrat, Hindman had advocated during an 1868 local election campaign that Black Americans be allowed to vote and join white conservatives against Republicans. He also encouraged Confederate veterans to take the oath of allegiance so they could vote against Republicans.

Mob violence was common in the South as early as the colonial era. Robert E. Lee's father, "Lighthorse" Harry Lee, was a famous cavalry leader and a friend of George Washington. After the Revolutionary War, Harry Lee became a member of the minority Federalist political party. A mob of Democratic Republicans attacked the publisher of a Federalist newspaper. Harry Lee and a dozen supporters took refuge in the newspaper building to protect the editor and the printing press. The group surrendered to the local sheriff to avoid bloodshed. The mob then broke into the jail, took the Federalists outside, and severely beat and tortured their captives for three hours. After beating Lee, the members of the mob poured melted wax into his eyes in an attempt to blind him. Harry never fully recovered and later died of his injuries.

In defense of Southern aggression, this cultural trait also provided the necessary courage to face extreme dangers in battle. Many battle casualties during the Civil War took place with opponents facing each other at eighty to one hundred yards or less (the same kill zone of the British longbow that was used so effectively during the Battle of Crecy in 1346). Soldiers' courage also enabled the infantry to withstand murderous artillery fire as they advanced toward an enemy.

The Romance of War

A significant element of Southern culture was the romanticism and glorification of aggression, war, and battle. Cavaliers viewed war as a glorious adventure that could prove their bravery and self-worth. General Nathan Bedford Forrest used the following phrase to encourage those who were considering joining his cavalry unit during 1862 (Wills 1992, 71): "Come on, boys, if you want a heap of fun and to kill some Yankees."

Confederates also considered participation in battles more important than nonmartial activities and occupations. Generals refused to release artisans in their commands when they were needed elsewhere. A shoemaker or blacksmith would have been more useful to the Confederacy by working his trade than by serving in an army. Robert E. Lee ceaselessly complained of a shortage of troops and was very reluctant to release any troops in his command. Lee refused to transfer mechanics to repair and maintain the Confederate railroad system (Younger 1985, 47). Ironically, Lee also complained about the lack of adequate railroad transportation.

Joseph Reid Anderson founded the Tredegar Iron Works and developed it into the South's largest foundry. He was a superb manager, and the Works produced military ordnance, such as locomotives and cannons. In spite of his managerial skills, Brigadier General Anderson joined the military at the beginning of the war (Clark 2001, 224–5). Though he returned to the Works a year later, after being wounded, his skills would have been better used during the first year of the war at his foundry. There was less glory among Confederates in managing munitions factories than in being an artillery general.

An element of the Southern acceptance of violence is the assumption that a man should be brave and fearless. He should be willing to avenge insults and attack his enemies however defined. Being known as fearless was a key element of manliness.

A fear of untested troops was that they might show their comrades they were afraid. Company members might suspect their colleagues were also afraid, but no one was expected to admit his fear. Civil War enlistees wondered whether battle would prove them to be courageous or not. The more modern custom is for soldiers to admit fear before combat, and courage is now defined as being afraid but overcoming this fear by behaving bravely. During the Civil War, no one was expected to admit to or show fear.

Aggression and Masculinity

Secessionist Lucius Quintus Cincinnatus Lamar explained the reason for the start of the Civil War as the Northerners' avoidance of duels and physical violence because they were lacking in masculine courage. Lamar believed regional differences could have been solved through personal duels in the classic medieval manner as described in Walter Scott's *Ivanhoe.* "We are men, not women," Lamar declared, and "men" solve their conflicts through personal violence (Wyatt-Brown 1986, 27–28).

Lamar also reduced the cause of the Civil War to Charles Sumner's lack of challenging Preston Brooks to a duel after he had been caned by Brooks. Political and personal disagreements, to Lamar, were tests of manhood and were better solved by violence at the personal level as he thought was done in antiquity. Scholar Bertram Wyatt-Brown held beliefs that were similar to Lamar (Wyatt-Brown 2007, 5): "It was the threat of honor lost, no less than slavery, that led them to secession."

To be recognized as honorable, a man was expected to violently defend his honor. Many Southerners believed aggressive masculinity was a central characteristic of honorable men. Many volunteers viewed the experience of having taken part in a battle ("seeing the elephant") as a rite of passage from dependent child to independent manhood. "I have acted the part of a man," said a cavalry trooper from Virginia after taking part in a battle (McPherson 1997, 26).

A soldier from Kentucky who left his university to join the Confederate military wrote his father: "[Your] boy who left you six or seven years ago a mere child has now has now grown to manhood" (Murrell 2002, 365). The writer was declaring himself a man, not because of his education or age but because of his war experiences, which allowed him to declare himself independent from his father's authority because war had made him a "man."

Young white males from the elite social class were expected to defend their honor, which resulted in disobedient acts against teachers who were considered to belong to a lower class. An adolescent boy shot and killed his younger brother's teacher for daring to whip his younger brother. The older brother was acquitted because his defense was that he was defending his family's honor (Wyatt-Brown 2007, 162). Homicide was generally excused or lightly punished in the South when the act was based on a defense of honor.

Robert Potter is a typical example of the Southern acceptance of violence when honor was involved. Potter was jailed for castrating two ministers whom he thought had committed adultery with his wife. A congressman of the US House of Representative when he committed his crime, Potter was expelled, served a six-month sentence, and paid a thousand-dollar fine. Potter was later reelected to the North Carolina state legislature (Freeman 2018, 70). Castration was not specifically illegal at the time in North Carolina, and a year later, the Potter's Act was enacted, making castration ("potterizing") illegal.

Potter was again expelled from the North Carolina State Legislature during 1835 for either cheating at cards or threatening another player with a gun and a knife. Potter died in 1842, a victim of the Regulator-Moderator War in northeast Texas. Potter was a member of the Moderators and was ambushed and killed by members of the Regulators. Both parties were responsible for numerous killings in their attempts to control the area's politics. A county in Texas, Potter County, was named in his honor during 1876 in part because Potter had been a signer of the Texas Declaration of Independence in 1836.

After the Civil War, Mary Chesnut mentioned this Confederate tendency for personal disputes, often over minor events, weakening Confederate solidarity (Woodward 1981, 659): "We crippled ourselves—blew ourselves up by intestine strife."

The Culture of Defeat

Violence was so central to Confederate culture that its consequences were often less important than the act of violence itself. Whether a battle was lost or won was almost irrelevant as long as the related violence was conducted with heroic and "gallant" behavior. John Lewis was a member of Pickett's Charge during the Battle of Gettysburg. He described his participation in the charge in his 1905 memoir. From a perspective of more than forty years, Lewis recorded only the heroic actions of his and his comrades' heroism and nothing of the consequences of the battle itself (Lewis 2016, 61). Lewis neither believed that the battle had been lost nor that Lee retreated, but he noted how the army experienced "a great loss" [i.e., fatalities] of participants. He describes the Army of Northern Virginia as "checked."

John Lewis summarized the results of the battle only in terms of heroism rather than a loss and a retreat (Lewis 2016, 60):

> While the Army of Northern Virginia was for the time checked, it had shown to the world of what stuff it was made; and in the three days' fighting it had shown to the world a gallantry that would go down the ages and grow in brightness as time rolls on.

Lewis's comments show the cavalier's concern for a reputation for bravery and honor. His last comment above stresses the "gallantry" and "brightness" of courage rather than whether this courage was effective. The bravery of Union soldiers was ignored.

The successes of the enemy tended to be ignored by cavaliers. Lewis concluded, "Lee's command moved back to Virginia, checked but not a defeated army." The heroic elements of the battle were remembered more than their consequences. It is important that Lewis mentioned that the men's behavior showed "the world" how gallant the participants' heroism was. Heroic behavior must be witnessed by others; otherwise, heroism becomes irrelevant.

A similar refusal to accept defeat at the Battle of Gettysburg was declared by newspaper editor John M. Daniel in a July 15, 1863, editorial (Daniel 1868, 97):

> So far as the fighting went, all that the Federal army did was to prevent its own annihilation. *The Confederates were repulsed, but cannot, at present, with justice or candor be said to have suffered defeat* [emphasis added]. We were not entirely victorious at Gettysburg, and the South is impatient at the contradiction to its usual fortune. Southern men of constitutional despondence are unduly depressed ... We are not worse off than before it began, nor is the North a whit stronger.

The Code Duello

Dueling formed a central attribute of Southern and Confederate culture. The different forms of dueling and the frequent ambushes and assassinations indicate the wide practice of violence, but most formal duels ended in mutual apologies before a shot was fired (Greenberg 1985, 23).

Dueling involved a number of elements that reflected the Southern sense of honor and the importance of rank and social class. Duels, called "affairs of honor," allowed participants to defend their honor in a ritualistic, potentially violent, and individualistic manner. Duelists showed their bravery as well as their superiority in very public spectacles. Participating in duels also indicated the participants were masculine. After studying the history of duels, Georgian, historian, and mayor of Savannah, Georgia Thomas Gamble Jr. (Gamble 1923, 111) claimed dueling made duelists "virile" and achieve "high manhoods."

Gamble ignored the many forms of duels taking place during the 1800s. The Richardson and Jones families maintained a long-lasting feud. St. John Richardson Liddell was expelled from West Point for bad conduct and low grades. He was promoted to general during the war but afterward quarreled with his superiors. Liddell shot and killed two members of the Jones family. Liddell was arrested, tried for murder, and found not guilty due to his defense of justifiable homicide.

On February 14, 1870, patriarch Charles Jones and two sons mortally shot Liddell seven times. On February 27, a mob of an estimated thirty men caught Charles Jones and one son and mortally shot them in return (Mitcham 2022, 398). Deaths from formal duels were rare compared to other forms of homicidal violence.

Southern culture promoted a mindset that political differences—or any disagreement—threatened an opponent's honor and demanded a violent response. Losing a vote or being criticized for defending slavery was seen as a blow to a proslavery politician's honor and a threat to his social standing. There could be no compromise under such circumstances. The Republican Party's policy of prohibiting the extension of slavery demanded a violent response from insulted Southerners. A compromise would be understood as a surrender of honor and a lack of masculine courage (Greenberg 1985, 139–43).

A central aspect of defending one's honor is that the code duello allowed for public shaming. If a gentleman refused to accept a duel, his opponent was allowed to post an announcement of his cowardice in public places. Someone who lost a duel and survived was respected because he had shown the public a willingness to defend his honor.

Dueling during the 1850s was closely associated with attacks on slavery. Used to having unlimited control over enslaved persons, slave owners did not peacefully accept opposition from others since violence was a common form of controlling the enslaved (Franklin 2002, 44).

Duels were also safety valves for more aggressive behavior since duels provided mechanisms to honorably avoid violence. A man could apologize for presumably insulting behavior after agreeing to a duel. Having shown his manly courage by accepting a challenge, the involved seconds could convince the challenged party to apologize without being shamed. An important function of seconds in duels was to defuse the situation in an acceptable, honorable manner. By contrast, refusing a challenge to duel meant shame and possible ostracism or "social death" (McWhiney 1988, 156). Those who refused challenges to duel would suffer "the stigma of cowardice" (Gamble 1923, 225). According to Southern culture, a man who was unwilling to defend his honor was no better than a coward or an enslaved person. He was also no longer defined as masculine.

Dueling per se was not as important as how it was conducted. There were different social class expectations for how conflicts should take place. Cavaliers were expected to use gentlemen's weapons when dueling, which generally meant the use of revolvers. A "Code of Honor" was published in Baltimore in 1847 (Gamble 1923, 223):

> Should both parties be gentlemen, recognizing the propriety of the duel, they may not have recourse to

> fisticuffs or cudgels, which, though as obvious and mode of determining difficulties, is one properly at a discount among men of honor.

Duels forced participants to face one another in the manner of knights. Duels also emphasized the cultural element of individualism since duelists fought alone. McWhiney and Jamieson (1982) noted the propensity of Southerners for frontal attacks even after experience should have taught them this tactic resulted in large numbers of casualties. To some extent, battles were duels in the cavalier mindset. This attitude helps explain why Confederate officers personally led their men in battle. Many felt their honor demanded they place themselves ahead of their troops when facing danger.

Kenneth S. Greenberg (1996, 74) noted that while issues of honor were the cause of duels, dueling also showed others the duelists did not fear death. Most duelists did not expect to kill their opponents—even though deaths and serious wounds happened often enough to make duels dangerous. Dueling cavaliers expected to show the public they could face possible death without flinching. Many who were challenged might not have wanted to accept but did so to avoid being seen as "unmanly" cowards, thereby losing influence in their communities (Eaton 1949, 452).

North Carolinian historian Clement Eaton believed the possibility of being challenged increased Southerners' good manners. Even Northerners opposed to slavery found Southerners to be charming and well-mannered unless insulted. Benjamin F. Perry, a South Carolina newspaper editor who had killed a rival editor in a duel, defended the Southern code duello (Eaton 1949, 452): "When a man knows that he is to be held accountable for his want of courtesy, he is not so apt to indulge in abuse [of others]. In this way dueling produces a greater courtesy in a society and a higher refinement.

There is no way to prove that the threat of being challenged to duels made men more courteous. Duels often occurred because one party felt insulted when that was not the case. There is also the possibility that an insult was made to show others the speaker was brave and honorable. In addition, many Southerners believed that political differences were legitimate reasons to issue challenges to duel or to murder political foes. A hired assassin shot at and missed Cassius Clay during a political rally.

Cassius Marcellus Clay—who always wore one or two bowie knives across his chest and carried two pistols in a bag—announced he would kill anyone who threatened him. This threat, however, did not deter a number of Clay's political opponents from attempting to assassinate or personally murder him. When he learned James C. Sprigg would attack him after Clay gave a speech denouncing slavery, Clay approached Sprigg—who was waiting in ambush as was his custom—and began to beat him with his fists. Friends of Sprigg led him to safety when it became clear he was thoroughly outmatched (Clay 1886, 78–79).

Another incident involving an ambush, a street brawl, and an outnumbered Cassius Clay took place when professional assassin Samuel L. Brown attacked Clay and hit him with a club. Brown was a well-known brawler who was reputed to have fought "forty fights, and never lost a battle." Clay drew his bowie knife but was seized from behind by Brown's friends and dragged backward about fifteen feet (Richardson 1976, 35). Clay was hit with hickory sticks and chairs while being held by Brown's supporters. Brown drew his pistol and yelled to his friends, "Clear the way, and let me kill the damned rascal."

Clay managed to break free, rushed Brown, and was shot in the breast (his knife's chest scabbard stopped the bullet). He slashed Brown's skull in several places and left a three-inch cut, almost cut off an ear, slit his nose, cut out an eye, and wounded Brown in several other places (Clay 1886, 83–85). The bowie knife was a formidable weapon when used by an expert! Later, Brown's son and Clay became friends and political partners.

Someone who felt he had been insulted could seek revenge without demanding a duel. On May 7, 1863, physician Dr. Peters fatally shot Confederate General Earl Van Dorn in the head for allegedly having an affair with his wife. Van Dorn was a reputed philanderer, and his murderer was exonerated as justified (Vandiver 1999, 246). Van Dorn's death was on the whole a blessing for the Confederacy. Jefferson Davis wrote to his brother that Van Dorn's earlier retreat from northern Mississippi was "one of those blunders which it is difficult to compensate for."

Some duels had their absurd elements. When the Confederate capital was located in Montgomery, Alabama, two men dueled each other with derringer pistols. After firing and missing, the men began to beat each other's heads with their pistol butts until both became unconscious (Davis 1994, 288). Duels could also devolve into brawls not conducted according to formal rules. At times, a murder would be excused because the murderer had an acceptable reason for his act.

Extreme bravery during a duel could be shown by refusing to shoot one's opponent. An admittedly rare practice was to allow an opponent to shoot first. The other would then refuse to fire or would fire in the air. The opponents were expected to reconcile because bravery had been shown by both opponents.

The Southern cultural propensity toward violence was found among all social classes. An experience of Nathan Bedford Forrest illustrates how non-elites sometimes fought duels. Forrest's uncle was threatened in the town's square by three family members and a friend who had been former business partners of the uncle. Forrest tried to calm matters by saying that a fight of four against one was unfair.

In response, one of the four drew a pistol, fired at Forrest, and wounded him. The other three assailants also drew and fired their pistols, killing the uncle. Forrest drew his two-barreled pistol and wounded two of the attackers, leaving him facing the last two opponents. Not liking the odds, a bystander (probably a poor white man) handed Forrest his own bowie knife. The attackers then fled (Wyeth 1989, 15–16).

The townspeople so respected Forrest's courage that they elected him constable and the county's coroner (Wills 1992, 23). Forrest fought two major duels during his first three years living in the town.

In 1842, Abraham Lincoln had anonymously ridiculed a political opponent, James Shields, in a series of newspaper editorials called "letters" as a "smelly, foolish liar." When Shields discovered that Lincoln was the author, he challenged Lincoln to a duel. As the challenged party, Lincoln chose swords on the basis that his longer arms would give him an advantage. Lincoln was six foot four, and Shields was five foot nine. The fashion of using swords as dueling weapons was anachronistic and had been replaced by the use of firearms, generally revolvers.

Lincoln did not believe in dueling, but he realized his political career would be over should he not accept the challenge. Fortunately, Lincoln, encouraged by friends who intervened on the day of the duel, reconsidered and apologized, making the impending duel unnecessary. Lincoln and his challenger afterward became friends (Davis 2014).

William Lowndes Yancey, who was always armed, killed his wife's uncle in a street brawl because a political statement was defined as an insult to Yancey's sense of honor. Yancey served several months in jail and was then pardoned. Yancey faced near-bankruptcy from a feud between his plantation's overseer and a neighbor's overseer. The latter poisoned Yancey's enslaved workers. Two died, and the rest could not work for months. The result was a lack of income for the year, and Yancey was forced to sell most of his enslaved workers to pay his debts.

Robert E. Lee, for practical reasons, was against dueling. Lee could not have a functioning coterie of officers if they solved their numerous personal conflicts of honor through duels. A newspaper had praised A. P. Hill's action during the 1862 Seven Days Battle, but his superior, James Longstreet, thought he had been slighted. The two exchanged a series of bitter letters until Longstreet placed Hill under arrest (McPherson 2007, 161). Hill then challenged Longstreet to a duel, but their commander, Robert E. Lee, transferred Hill and his division to Thomas "Stonewall" Jackson's corps.

Hill and Jackson frequently quarreled, and Hill was arrested by Jackson a number of times. Jackson expected complete obedience from his subordinates and once charged him with eight counts of dereliction of duty (Lee ignored their antagonism). Their feud continued, but Hill performed well while he served under Jackson.

Lee tried to defuse numerous interpersonal conflicts among his officers by transferring one party. He also ignored demands for court-martials until passions had cooled.

The Cultural Meaning of the Bowie Knife

The bowie knife became a significant symbol of bravery and aggressiveness during the 1850s and 1860s in addition to swords, revolvers, walking canes, and bayonets. Perhaps first made in 1830 by Rezin Bowie for his brother James "Jim" Bowie, the bowie knife was first used by Jim after he had recuperated from a gunshot wound from Norris Wright. Members of rival groups, the two met again to continue their feud in a duel known as the Sandbar Fight. Bowie discharged his pistols and drew his knife. Wright shot Bowie, hitting a lung, drew his sword cane, and wounded Bowie in the sternum where the blade stuck. Bowie then stabbed Wright through the heart, killing him, and wounded another attacker (Phillips 2018, 27–28).

The bowie knife—with its ten-inch blade and its variations such as the Arkansas toothpick and D-Guard bowie—became weapons of choice in the South and West. (The musician David Robert Jones

[1947–2016] adopted the surname "Bowie" in honor of Jim Bowie and his representation in the movie *The Alamo*.) The wearing of a bowie knife in a boot or belt with the handle exposed indicated the carrier was ready to fight and kill an opponent. Belt knives became both weapons and fashionable items for those wishing to publicly pose as dangerous.

It was common for soldiers preparing to leave home to pose for photographs for their families. Many photographs show soldiers with bowie knives in their hands, but most probably did not carry them into the field. Photographs of a man with a rifle and a bowie knife showed he was brave and willing to fight.

With typical frontier humor, a bowie knife was to be "long enough to use as a sword, sharp enough to use as a razor, wide enough to use as a paddle, and heavy enough to use as a hatchet" (Krick 2007, 34). This weapon, weighing at least six pounds, was too heavy to carry during a long march and would soon be discarded or sold along with any other unnecessary objects. (Generally, Rebels carried half the weight of equipment than did Union rank-and-files did). At close quarters, combatants would be more likely to use their muskets as clubs or handy rocks.

Bowie knives were popular during the early part of the war when the supply of muskets was too few to be issued to all Confederate volunteers, but the knife's weight caused carriers to discard them after several long marches (Griffith 2001, 93). Bowie knives were more popular among Rebels than Yankees (Steplyk 2018, 93).

The knife's lack of military effectiveness was illustrated in a newspaper report on August 13, 1861 (Griffith 2001, 27): "The Tiger Rifles … charged with Bowie knives at Manassas. But 26 out of 83 rank and file survive."

The use of a bowie knife during a debate in the Arkansas House during 1837 is best described by historian Joanne Freeman (2018, 5):

> When a representative insulted the Speaker during debate, the Speaker stepped down from his platform, bowie knife in hand, and killed him. Expelled and tried for murder, he was acquitted for excusable homicide and reelected, only to pull his knife on *another* legislator during debate, though this time the sound of colleagues' cocking pistols stopped him cold.

The Master of the Bowie Knife

Kentuckian abolitionist Cassius Marcellus Clay became a proponent of the bowie knife, fought numerous duels and street brawls, and wrote a pamphlet on how to fight with a bowie knife. Carrying one or two bowie knives at all times, Clay had two bowie knives made for him: one for formal affairs and one for daily use. Born in Kentucky and an early member of the Republican Party, Clay, an abolitionist, liberated his slaves and became a founder of the Republic Party in Kentucky. After serving in the Mexican-American War and the Civil War, Clay was appointed ambassador to Russia.

Though performing well as ambassador—and being partly responsible for Russia's support of the Union and later the purchase of Alaska—Clay was challenged to duels by members of the Russian nobility for his excessive flirting with their wives. Clay always chose as a weapon the bowie knife, which was rejected by his challengers. Two Russians decided to trick Clay into challenging one of the two, thereby allowing the Russian to choose the weapon. A would-be duelist approached Clay while dining out and slapped him with a glove. Clay immediately reacted by hitting the offender with his fist, breaking his nose, and sending him crashing into another table. He then sat down and calmly continued his meal while his attackers retreated (Richardson 1976, 101).

Clay fought a number of duels, but most were more street brawls than formal duels based on the code duello. Two days before his wedding to Mary Jane Warfield, a former suitor sent a letter to Clay's future mother-in-law, falsely denouncing Clay as unrefined and lacking in character (Ellison 2005, 35). After being shown the insulting letter, Clay and a friend sought out the author, Dr. John P. Declarey. They met on a street, and Clay demanded an apology. When Declarey refused, Clay began to beat him with a hickory stick. Spectators attempted to stop the beating, but they were stopped when Clay's friend threatened them with a revolver (Richardson 1976, 29).

Clay and Declarey twice scheduled a formal duel. Declarey then announced he would whip Clay with a cowhide. This was a whip that was commonly used to punish enslaved males and females. This serious insult could not be ignored. After his honeymoon, Clay searched for Declarey, and they met at the latter's hotel. Instead of confronting Clay, Declarey retreated to his room and later committed suicide.

Clay was involved in another brawl that was based on political issues. In 1849, Clay gave a political speech a mile from his plantation. Feeling safe so close to his home, he had neglected to bring his two pistols with him. During a debate, proslavery candidate Cyrus Turner charged that Clay was lying and struck him. Clay drew his bowie knife but was quickly surrounded by forty men supporting Cyrus (Richardson 1976, 69). He was struck with clubs on his back, kidneys, and pelvis and was stabbed in a lung. Finally reaching his opponent, Clay pushed his bowie knife to the hilt into Turner's body, resulting in a fatal wound. Almost losing consciousness due to loss of blood, Clay's son handed him a pistol while a Turner supporter tried to shoot Cassius Clay in the head, but his revolver failed to fire, and the brawl ended. Clay suffered from occasional pain in his pelvis and spine for the rest of his life (Richardson 1976, 71).

Militancy and Military Titles

Southerners enjoyed receiving military titles. An advantage of supporting and becoming a member of a local militia group was being elected as an officer. The ranks (and titles) gave holders higher status and more prestige in civilian society.

An attraction to receiving military titles is that they are permanent: once a colonel, always a colonel (Wyatt-Brown 1986, 146). A common joke of the period was that if a coach overturned in the South, out would tumble four generals, three colonels, and two captains. A number of Southern white males without any military experience were given "colonel" or "captain" titles by friends to show their respect. Others assumed military titles on their own.

In order to encourage those with previous military ranks to join the Confederacy, officers in the Old Army were offered one higher rank than their previous position—even though many did not deserve a promotion. Promotion and better assignments were offered to those who were wealthy and had the support of politicians and senior officers.

Jefferson Davis continued the practice of promoting his friends and refusing promotions to those he disliked. Davis promoted friends with little military expertise to the rank of general (McWhiney 1973, 93). Samuel Cooper was one of six officers to be promoted to full general at the start of the war. He was sixty-four years old in 1861 and had held a desk job in the prewar army for twenty-three years. Cooper turned out to be an inactive and inefficient adjutant and inspector general.

These dysfunctional practices were necessary because of the need for officers, and promotions of talented persons occurred rapidly. Nathan Forrest was promoted from a private to a general in one year. Forty former members of the Old Army who had been captains or above before secession became generals in 1861 (McWhiney 1973, 92–93).

The South and Military Education

The South contained military-oriented academies and military schools of excellent quality, including Virginia Military Institute, the Citadel, Georgia Military Institute, and the North Carolina Military Academy. Some of the most talented generals in the Civil War taught in Southern military academies, including Thomas J. "Stonewall" Jackson, Pierre G. T. Beauregard, and William Tecumseh Sherman. It was common for West Point cadets who were knowledgeable in a topic to teach at West Point after graduation.

Ninety-six military schools and military academies were founded in the South during 1827–1860—compared to fifteen in the North in spite of the latter's larger population and greater wealth (Wagner et al. 2002, 369). There were a number of reasons for this Southern increase in military-oriented educational institutions. There was already an established respect for military activities. The presence of enslaved persons fed the fear that "servile insurrections" were possible. There was a need for more whites trained in military procedures to prevent and combat slave rebellions.

Southerners glorified the military, and military discipline was often the only respected way to educate and discipline the young sons of planters. There is no question the Confederacy enjoyed a larger cadre of well-trained officers at the start of the war than the Union did. Southerners were also overrepresented at West Point, and a larger percentage than Northerners became military careerists (Hartje 1967, 16). Planters' sons had few honorable career choices except plantation ownership, medicine, law, politics, or the military. Robert E. Lee's mother could not afford to send him to an elite university, and she did not own a plantation for him to inherit. Lee was sent to West Point because of its free tuition and as preparation for a respectable military career. Lee did not become a slaveholder until he married a wealthy distant cousin.

Not all these academies were academically rigorous, but all taught the fundamentals of military practice, such as training troops to march. Cadets also learned the fundamentals of organizing men into a functioning army. The Citadel (then called the South Carolina Military Academy) was established in 1842 to provide trained personnel for slave patrols, defend against slave insurrections, and expose the sons of the elite to military discipline.

Unlike the West Point curriculum, Southern military academies did not offer practical courses. West Point was primarily an engineering university—and the only one in the nation. Later engineering companies were established and staffed by West Point graduates. Robert E. Lee spent most of his prewar career directing engineering projects. He built forts and redirected the Mississippi, making St. Louis a major port.

Military academies provided manpower or boy power—most cadets were in their teens—when the adult pool of recruits was exhausted. On March 6, 1865, cadets from the Florida Military and Collegiate Institute took part in the Battle of Natural Bridge. The Rebels experienced twenty-six casualties and the Union forces experienced 148.

Established in 1839 as an alternative to the United States Military Academy at West Point, New York, the Virginia Military Institute offered a military-inspired education. Similar to West Point, VMI's curriculum stressed a strict academic and military-style regimen to develop a first-class cadre of future officers. There was an emphasis on teaching cadets the practice of attention to detail and the necessity of cooperation. These attributes were often lacking among the Southern elite.

VMI students were also taught to persevere in any task until completed. A criticism of Southerners by reformers was that Southerners were more attracted to an easy life than to finishing onerous tasks.

VMI first-year students were called "rats," an insult Southerners would not normally accept. The school owned unique cannons for artillery practice. The small cannons were pulled to various locations by the "rats" rather than by horses. This practice reinforced the notion that dealing with war-related activities and the military were not demeaning even for sons of the elite. A bonus for VMI students was their professor of artillery, Thomas Jackson. Though a failure as a classroom teacher, Jackson was an efficient and enthusiastic teacher when teaching the practice of artillery science in the field.

"Rats" were also taught to focus on problems during chaotic conditions. The hazing of "rats" also taught them to rely on and cooperate with fellow "rats." They also learned that war was more than parades and impressive uniforms, but many cavalry officers and others ignored this lesson.

Battle Aggression

Associated with a propensity for violence in Southern culture is a corresponding preference for aggressive military behavior. Attacking the enemy was more popular with troops than fighting in trenches or behind fortifications (Tanner 2001, 144–45). Both Robert E. Lee and Stonewall Jackson knew how to use the aggression among their commands with great success. They believed surprise, attacking the enemy at its weakest point, and rapid maneuvers were tactics that promised the best chances for victory.

Such beliefs were common among officers on both sides. Veterans of the Mexican-American War (1846–1848) had learned that frontal attacks brought the best results, including personal fame and brevets. This aggressive action often proved dysfunctional during the Civil War. Ignored was that Mexican fortifications were poorly constructed and more easily overcome than Civil War fortifications (Hagerman 1988, 15). The ill-trained Mexican soldiers used traditional nonrifled muskets.

A major element of the West Point curriculum was teaching cadets to be "gentlemen." Doing so included the expectation of maintaining one's honor as well as being courageous. Included in this mindset was avoiding being evaluated as timid during combat or when exposed to enemy gunfire.

As important, military technology had changed since 1848. The introduction of rifled muskets and artillery as well as the use of quickly made fortifications gave defenders an advantage over attackers. Veterans of the Mexican-American War found it difficult to change their battle tactics. The cultural habit of using partly outmoded aggressive battle tactics continued to be preferred. Ordering charges and marches involved military units that were much smaller than during the Civil War. Successfully ordering movements and charges were tactics that were easier to coordinate during the Mexican-American War than during the Civil War.

Charging with fixed bayonets, though heroic, was no longer as successful during 1861–1865 because rifles were loaded and fired more quickly than unrifled muskets. Charging units were now more often badly damaged by the defenders' fire. Even when Confederates made successful frontal attacks, the victor experienced high levels of casualties. At the Battle of Shiloh, the Eighteenth Louisiana lost almost half (41 percent) of its members during a charge. The Eleventh Louisiana attacked the same fortified position a number of times and lost 90 percent of the involved 550 members. Some of the casualties were stragglers, counted as missing, or wounded, and some may have later returned to their unit, but the company nevertheless suffered a terrific high level of losses (McWhiney 1969, 237).

During the first day of the Battle of Gettysburg, the Twenty-Sixth North Carolina Infantry lost 588 men during a charge for a total of 73 percent casualties. Their leader, the well-respected and aggressive Henry King Burgwyn, also died that day (Tucker 2016, 40). Many second-rate officers were promoted because of the high casualty rate of their superior officers. Two Union corps were similarly mauled during the first two days of the Battle of Gettysburg. These high casualties may have encouraged Lee to continue the battle on the third day.

The Battle of Griswoldville

A tragic example of the Confederate propensity toward aggressive military tactics occurred during the Battle of Griswoldville in Georgia. The town of Griswoldville had already been partially destroyed during Sherman's March to Savannah. Union Brigadier General Charles C. Walcutt believed an attack on Sherman's supply wagons might occur near the town, and he fortified the high ground. General Pleasant J. Philips—a heavy drinker who had been ordered not to attack but to only observe—decided to attack Walcutt's position. It was as if he could not imagine any other tactic than attacking—even when ordered not to do so. Waiting and observing were activities that cavaliers too often rejected.

Most of Philip's force was made up of militia members who were either too young or too old to be part of a regular army. Other members were local men who had been forced to join Philip's command. The Federal veterans had fortified their position with dirt and fence rails, and an artillery unit had been positioned at the breastworks.

Unknown to Philips and his officers, most of the soldiers facing his command were armed with Spencer repeating rifles that held seven cartridges per magazine. Carriers of Spencer rifles were usually issued ten magazines, resulting in seventy rapid-shot rounds. The Spencer used a lighter round than the more common Enfield and Springfield rifled muskets and was neither as accurate nor as effective at long ranges. However, the Spencer provided deadly rapid fire at close ranges.

Infantry seldom received much firing instruction, and a high volume of fire was a significant way to inflict casualties on an approaching enemy. It was said that it took a man's weight of lead to kill a man. At the Battle of Chickamauga, the 535 members of the Twenty-First Ohio were armed with Colt revolving rifles. The group fired 43,550 rounds in five hours. Repeating and breach-loading rifles gave fortified defenders a great advantage.

The Battle of Griswoldville did not last long. Reportedly drunk, Philips ordered repulsed charge after charge. The ill-trained Confederates fired too high, and the Federals experienced light casualties. The Federals expended their ammunition during a charge, and the drummer boys were sent for more cartridges (Davis 1980, 53–57). The defenders received their ammunition after the next charge had already begun, but they were able to begin to fire with deadly effect when the Rebels were fifty yards away. The battle finally ended with perhaps five hundred Confederate fatalities. Most of the casualties were boys, some barely in their teens, and older men. Among the fatalities were a fourteen-year-old boy, his father, two brothers, and an uncle (Davis 1980, 56). Localism and familism remained a factor in enlistment throughout the war.

The Confederates continued to believe that the only proper tactic was an aggressive charge. In defense of this cultural trait of aggressiveness, there were many times during the Civil War when an attack was the only acceptable alternative to fighting the enemy. A retreat or avoidance of battle would be considered a shameful act, and the Confederate public demanded victories of their generals. The Confederates were almost always fighting on their own land, and they wanted to destroy the invaders or chase them away from their nation.

Lee won the first two days of the Battle of Gettysburg. He could have declared the end of a victorious raid and returned to his base in Virginia. He had shown the Union and Europe that the Confederacy could invade the Union and threaten its major cities. Lee wanted a complete victory over the Army of the Potomac, and he refused to end the campaign before a total victory had been achieved. His ultimate goal when he fought was the total destruction of the armies he faced. Lee considered a battle partly a failure if the enemy was able to retreat in an organized manner.

Lee insisted on a frontal attack against a fortified enemy with artillery located on higher ground nearly a mile from where his troops would begin an attack. His favorite general, James Longstreet, had pleaded with Lee not to attack the fortified line and to adopt either a flanking movement or a return to Virginia. Flanking tactics had been very successful for Lee in the past. In defense of Lee, a flanking movement had been planned using Stuart's cavalry. The attempt failed at East Cavalry Field when George Armstrong Custer's unit defeated Stuart's maneuver. The battle's end may have changed to Lee's advantage if Stuart had been able to reach Meade's flank and attack his rear. This significant skirmish again showed that the Union cavalry had become as good or better than its Confederate counterpart.

Lee's aggression during the Battle of Gettysburg may also have been the result of Lee's impatience. Lee realized the Confederacy could not exchange casualties with the Union any further. The longer the war lasted, the worse conditions were becoming for the Rebels. Lee realized the Confederacy needed a major battle victory as soon as possible. With the Union's advantages in manpower and industrial capacity, Lee realized the longer the war lasted, the chances increased that the Confederacy would lose the war. A victory at Gettysburg might dishearten the Union population, encourage those demanding peace at any price, and encourage foreign recognition. It was worth it to Lee to gamble on a frontal attack. Though Pickett's Charge failed, the charge almost succeeded.

The Aggression of John Bell Hood

John Bell Hood was one of the most aggressive generals in the Confederacy ("too much lion's heart, but a wooden head"). Hood's qualities were limited to generally leading frontal charges—Hood did suggest less aggressive tactics a number of times when he was a subordinate—and he was also an inadequate leader of an army and a bad strategist. Hood was much more successful as a division commander than as a commander of an army.

Hood led the consistently aggressive and effective Hood's Texas Brigade and ordered successful charges. A frontal attack, along with Hampton's South Carolina Legion at Turkey Hill, was a significant contribution to the Confederate victory during the Battle of Gaines' Mill, Virginia. Lee, with Hood and Wade Hampton III, won a decisive victory, but the Confederacy lost a greater proportion of men than the Union did. Praised by both Lee and Jackson, Hood was promoted to major general and became a Confederate hero. Like many others, Hood was promoted beyond his qualifications.

Joseph Johnston had led the Army of Tennessee in an eighty-mile retreat from Dalton, Georgia, to the outskirts of Atlanta. Jefferson Davis decided a more aggressive general was needed, and Hood was appointed commander of the Army of Tennessee in spite of Lee's disapproval. Hood's orders from Davis were to save Atlanta and attack Sherman's army and hopefully destroy it.

Given orders to be aggressive, Hood organized three days of attacks. The first day's charge cost Hood's army five thousand casualties. The second day's charge resulted in a loss of eight thousand men. The third charge cost five thousand casualties. There were no advantages gained by these charges. Total losses were roughly twenty thousand for the Confederacy and almost eight thousand for the Union, and Atlanta was occupied by Sherman's forces (Sword 1992, 55–56). Hood's cavalier tactics lost Atlanta and weakened his army.

In spite of these experiences, Hood continued his preference for attacking, and the Army of Tennessee was later destroyed as a fighting force by ordering repeating charges.

The Kentucky Fiasco

When the Southern states began the process of secession, government officials of the slave state of Kentucky announced the state would remain neutral. This was a decision that could not last, but it is understandable in terms of the acceptance of the theory of states' rights. The population of Kentucky was divided in terms of its loyalties. The first reaction was to declare independence from both the Union and the Confederacy and become a neutral party.

In April 1861, Abraham Lincoln announced that he would respect Kentucky's neutrality, but he realized that it was vital that Kentucky remain in the Union. Lincoln believed that Kentucky was the key to the control of the Mississippi and Ohio Rivers. The state was also a major source of foodstuffs, mules, and horses. Impatient Kentuckians who wanted to enlist moved north or south to join volunteer units outside the state's borders since both sides had established enlisting camps.

Both Presidents Davis and Lincoln ordered their respective generals and military units to respect Kentucky's neutrality and not cross its borders. Ever patient, Lincoln ignored the fact that Northerners were selling supplies and armaments to Confederate loyalists in Kentucky because he dared not give Kentuckians an excuse to join the Confederacy.

Leonidas Polk, commander of the nearby Confederate forces, decided Union forces were on the verge of invading Kentucky. He responded by violating the truce and entering Kentucky to occupy Columbus. Pro-Confederacy Governor Magoffin resigned and was replaced by a pro-Union governor who formally led his state into the Union. At a minimum, Kentucky became the Union's path to Tennessee. Its agricultural bounty served the Union and not the Confederacy. Kentucky became an irreplaceable loss for the Confederacy because Polk would not remain idle when personal glory beckoned. Lincoln could be pragmatic and patient, but Polk could only be aggressive.

By the end of 1861, Union forces occupied most of the state of Kentucky and had established a pro-Union state government. The Confederacy also established a provisional secession government in the southwestern corner of the state. Because of Polk's cavalier aggressiveness and impatience, Kentucky was admitted as a Confederate state, but its status was symbolic. The slave states remaining in the Union contained majorities of Unionists, but Confederates continued to believe they "belonged" to them.

AFTERWORD

There is no better example of the contrasting cultures of the Union and the Confederacy than the scene of Robert E. Lee's surrender of the Army of Northern Virginia to Ulysses S. Grant and the Army of the Potomac at the home of Wilmer McLean, near Appomattox, Virginia, on April 9, 1865.

Lee was dressed in his formal uniform and carried his ceremonial sword. Accompanied by his aide-de-camp, Lee arrived at around one o'clock. Grant arrived half an hour later. He had been inspecting his troops in anticipation of attacking Lee's forces the next day. Grant could not reach his wagon train to change uniforms and was wearing his usual private's blouse and rumpled trousers stuffed in muddy boots. Lee, six feet tall, always dignified in posture, and a member of one of the South's elite families, faced a five-foot-eight, ill-dressed Grant, whose father was a tanner (McPherson 1988, 849).

Lee had adopted an aristocratic traditional war strategy that involved sophisticated maneuvers. Grant was more practical and was likely to approach the enemy and order continued attacks. His battle tactics were also more diverse and adaptive to the situation than Lee's. Grant's victories included the capture of two strategic forts and the city of Vicksburg. Grant captured three Confederate armies, but Lee was never able to do the same. Grant also had a more national view of the war and was able to coordinate Union armies for a single campaign; Lee was local in his perspective and was more concerned with protecting the state of Virginia.

Grant was a member of a society that was prosperous and able to support a semimodern war and still feed and employ an expanding population. During the war, the North was able to double its exports of grain while the Confederate public and its armies experienced hunger and near-starvation. Grant's Army of the Potomac was well fed and supplied while Lee's army was on short rations—and many were barefoot.

The Union was able to adapt and enroll roughly two hundred thousand African Americans and additional immigrants while Southern culture could not. Union members were more cooperative and had better organization skills. The Union was better able to achieve its diplomatic and economic goals while the Confederacy failed to do so.

More important, Northern culture was more realistic, flexible, and able to modernize while the Confederate culture was based on a mythical, medieval cavalier-related foundation. Its dysfunctional elements made defeat more likely. Thinking themselves superior to others and independent cavaliers, Confederate leaders involved themselves in internal conflicts and quarreled with their colleagues almost as much as they fought with the enemy.

The cavalier elites were often more loyal to their own interests than to the Confederacy or to the needs of the general population. Confederate culture, dominated by a self-involved elite concerned with the continuation of slavery over anything else, could not adapt to the North's more rational and effective culture. It has been said that if Jefferson Davis and Abraham Lincoln had exchanged positions, the Confederacy might have won. We believe that the cultural weaknesses of the Confederacy would have been too much for even Lincoln to succeed. Confederate culture had its heroic elements, but it was indeed a culture of defeat.

BIBLIOGRAPHY

Adams, Henry (1999) *The Education of Henry Adams: An Autobiography.* New York: Random House, Inc.

Adams, Michael C. C. (1978) *Our Masters the Rebels: A Speculation on Union Military Failure in the East 1861–1865.* Cambridge, Massachusetts: Harvard University Press.

Anderson, John Q. (ed.) (1995) *Brokenburn: The Journal of Kate Stone, 1861–1868.* Baton Rouge: Louisiana State University Press.

Ayers, Edward L. (2003) *In the Presence of Mine Enemies: The Civil War in the Heart of America 1859–1863.* New York: W. W. Norton & Company.

——— (2017) *The Thin Light of Freedom: The Civil War and Emancipation in the Heart of America.* New York: W. W. Norton & Company.

Banfield, Edward C. (1958) *Moral Basis of a Backward Society.* New York: Free Press.

Beadle, Irwin P. (2019) *Beadle's Dime Book of Practical Etiquette for Ladies and Gentlemen. Being a Guide to True Gentility and Good-Breeding, and a Complete Directory to the Usages and Observances of Society.* Conneaut Lake, Connecticut: Good Press.

Beringer, Richard E., Herman Hattaway, Archer Jones, and William N. Still Jr. (1986) *Why the South lost the Civil War.* Athens, Georgia: University of Georgia Press.

Berlin, IRA (2003) *Generations of Captivity: A History of African American Slaves.* Cambridge: Harvard University Press.

Bernard, George S. (ed.) (1892) *War Talks of Confederate Veterans.* Petersburg, Virginia: Fenn & Owen.

Berry II, Stephen W. (2003) *All that Makes a Man: Love and Ambition in the Civil War South*. New York: Oxford University Press.

Bielski, Mark F. (2021) *A Mortal Blow to the Confederacy: The Fall of New Orleans, 1862*. El Dorado Hills, California: Savas Beatie LLC.

Bierle, Sarah Kay (2019) *Call Out the Cadets. The Battle of New Market May 15, 1864*. El Dorado Hills, California: Savas Beatie LLC.

Black III, Robert C. (1998) *The Railroads of the Confederacy*. Chapel Hill: The University of North Carolina Press.

Blair, William (1998) *Virginia's Private War: Feeding Body and Soul in the Confederacy*. New York: Oxford University Press.

Blight, David W. (2018) *Frederick Douglass: Prophet of Freedom*. New York: Simon & Schuster.

Boatner III, Mark Mayo (1988) *The Civil War Dictionary*. New York: Vintage Books.

Bolton, Charles C. (1994) *Poor Whites of the Antebellum South: Tenants and Laborers in Central North Carolina and Northern Mississippi*. Durham, North Carolina: Duke University Press.

Bonekemper III, Edward H. (2015) *The Myth of the Lost Cause: Why the South Fought and Why the North Won*. Washington, DC: Regnery History.

Borcke, Heros von, and Justus Scheibert (1976) *The Great Cavalry Battle of Brandy Station, 9 June 1863*. Winston-Salem, North Carolina: Palaemon Press Ltd.

Boritt, Gabor S. (ed.) (1992) *Why the Confederacy Lost*. New York: Oxford University Press.

Bowers, Claude G. (1920) *The Tragic Era: The Revolution after Lincoln*. Cambridge: The Riverside Press.

Bradley Francis B. C. (1921) *The Story as Told to the Writer by James Magee of Marblehead, Seaman on the Kearsarge*. Bellevue, Washington: Big Byte Kooks.

Brands, H. W. (2020) *The Zealot and the Emancipator: John Brown, Abraham Lincoln, and the Struggle for American Freedom*. New York: Doubleday.

Briggs, Ward W., Jr. (ed.) (1998) *Soldier and Scholar: Basil Lanneau Gildersteeve and the Civil War.* Charlottesville: University Press of Virginia.

Brown, Kent Masterson (2021) *Meade at Gettysburg. A Study in Command.* Chapel Hill: The University of North Carolina Press.

Burk, James (2000) "The Citizen Soldier and Democratic Societies: A Comparative Analysis of America's Revolutionary and Civil Wars," *Citizenship Studies* 4 (2): 149–63.

Butler, Clayton Jonah (2021) "Union Troopers with a Southern Twang," *Civil War Times*, 60 (June): 38–45.

Carmichael, Peter S. (1995) *Lee's Young Artillerist.* Charlottesville: University Press of Virginia.

Carpenter, Jesse T. (1990) *The South as a Conscious Minority, 1789–1861.* Columbia: University of South Carolina Press.

Carter, Arthur B. (1999) *The Tarnished Cavalier: Major General Earl Van Dorn, CSA.* Knoxville: The University of Tennessee Press.

Cash, W. J. (1991) *The Mind of the South.* New York: Vintage Books.

Chater, Kathleen (2020) *Henry Brown: From Slavery to Show Business.* Jefferson, North Carolina: McFarland & Company.

Churchill, Sir Winston S. (1985) *The American Civil War.* New York: The Fairfax Press.

Cisco, Walter Brian (2006) *Wade Hampton: Confederate Warrior, Conservative Statesman.* Washington, DC: Potomac Books, Inc.

Clark, John E. Jr. (2001) *Railroads in the Civil War: The Impact of Management on Victory and Defeat.* Baton Rouge: Louisiana State University Press.

Clausewitz, Carl von (1997) *On War.* Ware, England: Wordsworth Editions Limited.

Clay, Cassius Marcellus (1886) *The Life of Cassius Marcellus Clay: Memoirs, Writings, and Speeches Showing His Conduct in the Overthrow of American Slavery, the Salvation of the Union, and the Restoration of the Autonomy of the States.* Cincinnati: J. Fletcher Brennan & Co. Republished by Andesite Press 2015.

Clinton, Catherine (1995) *Tara Revisited: Women, War, & the Plantation Legend.* New York: Abbeville Press.

Colaiaco, James A. (2006) *Frederick Douglass and the Fourth of July.* New York: Palgrave Macmillan.

Collins, Robert (1862) "Essay on the Management of Slaves," *De Bow's Review* 32 (January and February): 154–57.

Commanger, Henry Steele (ed.) Revised and expanded by Erik Bruun (2000), *Living History of the Civil War. The History of the War Between the States in Documents, Essays, Letters, and Poems.* New York: Tess Press.

Cordon, Lesley J. (1998) *General George E. Pickett in Life and Legend.* Chapel Hill: The University of North Carolina Press.

Costa, Dora L., and Matthew E. Kahn (2008) *Heroes & Cowards: The Social Face of War.* Princeton: Princeton University Press.

Cronk, Lee (1999) *That Complex Whole: Culture and the Evolution of Human Behavior.* Boulder, Colorado: Westview Press.

Current, Richard Nelson, editor-in-chief (1998) *The Confederacy.* Selections from the four-volume original. New York: Simon & Schuster Macmillan.

Daniel, Frederick S. (1868) *The Richmond Examiner During the War; or, The Writings of John M. Daniel.* New York: Printed by the author. Reprinted by London: Forgotten Books 2018.

Daniel, Larry J. (1991) *Soldiering in the Army of Tennessee. A Portrait of Life in a Confederate Army.* Chapel Hill: The University of North Carolina Press.

Davis, Burke (1980) *Sherman's March*. New York: Random House.

Davis, Julia (2014) "The Time Abe Lincoln and a Rival Almost Dueled," Mental Floss. September 18.

Davis, Stephen (2019) "Give Us Hood!" *America's Civil War.* 32 (September): 18–26.

——— and Bill Hendrick (2022) *The Atlanta Daily Intelligence Covers the Civil War.* Knoxville: The University of Tennessee Press.

Davis, William C. (2002) *A History of the Confederate States of America.* New York: The Free Press.

——— (1994) *A Government of Our Own: The Making of the Confederacy.* New York: The Free Press.

——— (1996) *The Cause Lost: Myths and Realities of the Confederacy.* Lawrence: University Press of Kansas.

DeCredico, Mary A. (1990) *Patriotism for Profit: Georgia's Urban Entrepreneurs and the Confederate War Effort.* Chapel Hill: The University of North Carolina Press.

Delbanco, Andrew (2018) *The War before the War: Fugitive Slaves and the Struggle for America's Soul from the Revolution to the Civil War.* New York: Penguin Press.

Dew, Charles B. (2016) *Apostles of Disunion: Southern Secession Commissioners and the Causes of the Civil War.* Charlottesville: University Press of Virginia.

Diemer, Andrew K. (2022) *Vigilance: The Life of William Still, Father of the Underground Railroad.* New York: Alfred A. Knopf.

Donald, David Herbert (ed.) (1996) *Why the North Won the Civil War.* New York: Touchstone.

——— (2009) *Charles Sumner and the Coming of the Civil War.* Naperville, Illinois: Sourcebooks, Inc.

Dowdy, Clifford and Louis H. Manarin (eds.) (1961) *The Wartime Papers of R. E. Lee.* Lebanon, Indiana: Da Capo Press.

Douglass, Frederick (2014) *Narrative of the Life of Frederick Douglass, An American Slave.* New York: Penguin Books. Edited and with an introduction by I. Dworkin.

Easterby, J. H. (ed.) (2004) *The South Carolina Rice Plantation as Revealed in the Papers of Robert F. W. Allston.* Columbia: University of South Carolina Press.

Eaton, Clement (1949) *A History of the Old South.* New York: The Macmillan Company.

——— (1954) *A History of the Southern Confederacy.* New York: The Free Press.

——— (1963) *The Growth of Southern Civilization, 1790–1860.* New York: Harper Torchbooks.

——— (1977) *Jefferson Davis.* New York: The Free Press.

Editors of Time-Life Books (1998) *Arms and Equipment of the Union.* Alexandria, Virginia: Time Life Books.

Eicher, David J. (2006) *Dixie Betrayed: How the South Really Lost the War.* New York: Little, Brown and Company.

Ellison, Betty Boles (2005) *A Man Seen But Once: Cassius Marcellus Clay.* Bloomington, Indiana: AuthorHouse.

Ethier, Eric (2008) "I Declare My Unmitigated Hatred to Yankee Rule," *America's Civil War,* 21 (November): 23.

Fair, Charles (1971) *From the Jaws of Victory.* New York: Simon and Schuster.

Faust, Drew Gilpin (ed.) (1981) *The Ideology of Slavery: Proslavery Thought in the Antebellum South, 1830–1860.* Baton Rouge: Louisiana State University Press.

——— (1982) *James Henry Hammond and the Old South: A Design for Mastery.* Baton Rouge: Louisiana State University Press.

Fawcett, Bill (ed.) (2011) *How to Lose the Civil War.* New York: Harper.

Ferapontov, Maxim (ed.) (2017) *Kearsarge vs. Alabama: Personal Accounts and Official Reports: A View of the Fight from a Rebel Standpoint.* Bellevue, Washington: Big Byte Books.

Fitzhugh, George (1858) "Origin of Civilization—What is Property?—Which is the Best Slave Race," *De Bow's Review* 25 (December): 653–54.

Fischer, David Hackett (1989) *Albion's Seed: Four British Folkways in America.* New York: Oxford University Press.

Flagel, Thomas R. (2010) *The History Buff's Guide to the Civil War.* Naperville, Illinois.

Fletcher, William A. (1908) *Rebel Private: Front and Rear. Memoirs of a Confederate Soldier.* Beaumont, Texas: Greer Press, Republished in 1977 by New York: Meridian.

Foote, Lorien (2010) *The Gentlemen and the Roughs: Violence, Honor, and Manhood in the Union Army.* New York: New York University Press.

——— (2016) *The Yankee Plague. Escaped Union Prisoners and the Collapse of the Confederacy*. Chapel Hill: The University of North Carolina Press.

——— (2021) *Rites of Retaliation: Civilization, Soldiers, and Campaigns in the American War*. Chapel Hill: The University of North Carolina Press.

——— and Earl J. Hess (eds.) (2021) *The Oxford Handbook of the American Civil War*. New York: Oxford University Press.

Foote, Shelby (1958) *The Civil War: A Narrative. Fort Sumter to Perryville*. New York: Random House.

Franklin, John Hope (2002) *The Militant South 1800–1861*. Urbana: University of Illinois Press.

Freeman, Douglas Southall (ed.) (1957) *Lee's Dispatches: Unpublished Letters of General Robert E. Lee, C.S.A. to Jefferson Davis and the War Department of the Confederate States of America 1862–65*. Baton Rouge: Louisiana State University Press. Includes additional dispatches by Grady McWhiney.

Freeman, Joanne B. (2018) *The Field of Blood: Violence in Congress and the Road to Civil War*. New York: Farrar, Straus and Giroux.

Fuller, J. F. C. (1957) *Grant & Lee: A Study in Personality and Generalship*. New York: MJF Books.

Gallagher, Gary W. (ed.) (1989) *Fighting for the Confederacy: The Personal Recollections of General Edward Porter Alexander*. Chapel Hill: The University of North Carolina Press.

Gamble, Thomas (1923) *Savannah Duels and Duelists, 1733–1877*. Savannah, Georgia: Review Publishing & Printing Company.

Gasparin, Count Agénor de (1862) *The Uprising of a Great People: The United States in 1861*. New York: Charles Scribner.

Gildersleeve, Basil Lanneau (1915) *The Creed of the Old South: 1865–1915*. Reprinted October 18 2021.

Gienapp, William E. (ed.) (2001) *The Civil War and Reconstruction: A Documentary Collection*. New York: W. W. Norton & Company.

Glatthaar, Joseph T. (1994) *Partners in Command: The Relationships between Leaders in the Civil War*. New York: The Free Press.

——— (2008) *General Lee's Army: From Victory to Defeat.* New York: Free Press.

——— (2011) *Soldiering in the Army of Northern Virginia: A Statistical Portrait of the Troops Who Served under Robert E. Lee.* Chapel Hill: The University of North Carolina Press.

Gragg, Rod (2013) *The Illustrated Gettysburg Reader: An Eyewitness History of the Civil War's Greatest Battle.* Washington, DC: Regnery History.

Grant, Alfred (2000) *The American Civil War and the British Press.* Jefferson, North Carolina: McFarland & Company, Inc.

Greenberg, Kenneth S. (1985) *Masters and Statesmen: The Political Culture of American Slavery.* Baltimore: The Johns Hopkins University Press.

——— (1996) *Honor & Slavery: Lies, Duels, Noses, Masks, Dressing as a Woman, Gifts, Strangers, Humanitarianism, Death, Slave Rebellions, the Pro-Slavery Argument, Baseball, Hunting, and Gambling in the Old South.* Princeton, NJ: Princeton University Press.

Grimley, Mark, and Brooks D. Simpson (eds.) (2001) *The Collapse of the Confederacy.* Lincoln: University of Nebraska Press.

Guelzo, Allen C. (2018) "The Decision," *The Civil War Monitor* 8 (Summer): 30–38, ff.

——— (2013) *Gettysburg: The Last Invasion.* New York: Alfred A. Knopf.

——— (2021) *Robert E. Lee: A Life.* New York: Alfred A. Knopf.

Hagerman, Edward (1988) *The American Civil War and the Origins of Modern Warfare: Ideas, Organization, and Field Command.* Bloomington: Indiana University Press.

Hammond, James H. (1866) *Selections from the Letters and Speeches of the Hon. James. H. Hammond of South Carolina.* Reprinted by South Yarra, Victoria, Australia: Leopold Classic Library 2021.

Hansen, Harry (2002) *The Civil War: A History.* New York: Signet Classics.

Hardesty, Steven (2016) *Confederate Origins of Union Victory: Culture & Decisions in War. An Argument*. Saratoga, Florida: Steven's & Marlin Publishing, LLC.

Hartje, Robert G. (1967) *Van Dorn: The Life and Times of a Confederate General*. Tennessee: Vanderbilt University Press.

Hattaway, Herman, and Archer Jones (1991) *How the North Won: A Military History of the Civil War*. Urbana: University of Illinois Press.

Hébert, Keith S. (2021) *Cornerstone of the Confederacy: Alexander Stephens and the Speech that Defined the Lost Cause*. Knoxville: The University of Tennessee Press.

Helper, Hinton Rowan (1859) *The Impending Crisis of the South: How to Meet It*. New York: A.B. Burdick, Publisher. (Kindle edition).

Hess, Earl J. (2008) *The Rifle Musket in Civil War Combat: Reality and Myth*. Lawrence, Kansas: University Press of Kansas.

——— (2016) *Braxton Bragg: The Most Hated Man of the Confederacy*. Chapel Hill: University of North Carolina Press.

Holzer, Harold (ed.) (2011) *Hearts Touched by Fire: The Best of Battles and Leaders of the Civil War*. New York: The Modern Library.

Horton, R. G. (1866) *A Youth's History of the Great Civil War in the United States, from 1861 to 1865*. New York: Van Evrie, Horton & Co.

Hubbard, Charles M. (1998) *The Burden of Confederate Diplomacy*. Knoxville: The University of Tennessee Press.

Hummel, Jeffrey (1996) *Emancipating Slaves, Enslaving Free Men*. Chicago: Open Court.

Hundley, D. R. (1860) *Social Relations in Our Southern States*. New York: Henry B. Price. Reprinted by Andesite Press 2017.

Hurt, R. Douglas (2015) *Agriculture and the Confederacy: Policy, Productivity, and Power in the Civil War South*. Chapel Hill: The University of North Carolina Press.

Johnson, Clint (1997) *Civil War Blunders*. Winston Salem: John F. Blair, Publisher.

Johnson, Michael P., and James L. Roark (1984) *Black Masters: A Free Family of Color in the Old South*. New York: W. W. Norton & Company.

Jones, Archer (1961) *Confederate Strategy from Shiloh to Vicksburg*. Baton Rouge: Louisiana State University Press.

Jones, John R. (1866) *A Rebel War Clerk's Diary at the Confederate State* Capital, volume II. Philadelphia: J. B. Lippincott & Co. Reprinted by Time Life Books, Inc., Alexandria, Virginia 1982.

Katcher, Philip (2003) *Brassey's Almanac: The American Civil War*. London: Brassey's.

Keegan, John (2009) *The American Civil War: A Military History*. New York: Alfred A. Knopf.

Kreiser, Lawrence A., Jr., and Ray B. Browne (eds.) (2011) *Voices of Civil War America: Contemporary Accounts of Daily Life*. Santa Barbara, CA: ABC-CLIO, LLC.

Krick, Robert K. (2007) "Naked, Knife-wielding Rebels at Fredericksburg?" *America's Civil War*, 19 (January): 28–35.

Lee, Captain Robert E. (ed.) (2007) *Recollections and Letters of Robert E. Lee*. New York: Dover Publications.

Levine, Bruce (1992) *Half Slave and Half Free: The Roots of Civil War*. New York: Hill and Wang.

——— (2013) *The Fall of the House of Dixie: The Civil War and the Social Revolution that Transformed the South*. New York: Random House.

Lewis, John H. (2016) *A Rebel in Pickett's Charge at Gettysburg*. Columbia, SC: Big Byte Books.

Linderman, Gerald F. (1987) *Embattled Courage: The Experience of Combat in the American Civil War*. New York: The Free Press.

Long, E. B. (1971) *The Civil War Day by Day: An Almanack, 1861–1865*. New York: Da Capo Press.

Lonn, Ella (1928) *Desertion During the Civil War*. Gloucester: Peter Smith. Reprinted by Big Byte Books 2016.

Lowe, Harriet Beecher (1852) *Uncle Tom's Cabin or Life Among the Lowly.* Reprinted by Coppell, Texas: Black and White Publications 2015.

Lowry, Thomas P., MD (1994) *The Story the Soldiers Wouldn't Tell: Sex in the Civil War.* Mechanicsburg: PA: Stackpole Books.

Luraghi, Raimondo (1978) *The Rise and Fall of the Plantation South.* New York: New Viewpoints.

Maddox, Jack P. Jr. (1974) *The Reconstruction of Edward A. Pollard.* Chapel Hill: The University of North Carolina Press.

Martin, Bessie (2003) *A Rich Man's War, A Poor Man's Fight.* Tuscaloosa: The University of Alabama Press.

Marvel, William (1996) *The Alabama and the Kearsarge: The Sailor's Civil War.* Chapel Hill: The University of North Carolina Press.

Matteson, John (2021) *A Place Worse than Hell: How the Civil War Battle of Fredericksburg Changed a Nation.* New York: W. W. Norton & Company.

McMillan, Tom (2021) *Armistead and Hancock: Behind the Gettysburg Legend of True Friends at the Turning Point of the Civil War.* Guilford, Connecticut: Stackpole Books.

McMurry, Richard M. (1989) *Two Great Armies: An Essay in Confederate Military History.* Chapel Hill: The University of North Carolina Press.

McPherson, James M. (1988) *Battle Cry of Freedom: The Civil War Era.* New York: Oxford University Press.

——— (1995) *What They Fought For, 1861–1865.* New York: Anchor Books.

——— (1997) *For Cause and Comrades: Why Men Fought in the Civil War.* New York: Oxford University Press.

——— (2007) *This Mighty Scourge: Perspectives on the Civil War.* New York: Oxford University Press.

——— (2014) *Embattled Rebel. Jefferson Davis as Commander in Chief.* New York: Penguin Press.

McWhiney, Grady (1969) *Braxton Bragg and Confederate Defeat, vol. I.* Tuscaloosa: The University of Alabama Press.

——— (1973) *Southerners and Other Americans.* New York: Basic Books, Inc., Publishers.

——— (1988) *Cracker Culture: Celtic Ways in the Old South.* Tuscaloosa: The University of Alabama Press.

——— (2002) *Confederate Crackers and Cavaliers.* Abilene, Texas: McWhiney Foundation Press.

——— and Perry D. Jamieson (1982) *Attack and Die: Civil War Military Tactics and the Southern Heritage.* Tuscaloosa: The University of Alabama Press.

Mitcham, Samuel W., Jr. (2022) *The Encyclopedia of Confederate Generals: The Definitive Guide to the 426 Leaders of the South's War Effort.* Washington, DC: Regnery History.

Mitchell, Jeffery, and Charles River Editors (2018) *The Grey Ghost of the Confederacy: The Life and Legacy of John Mosby.* Ann Arbor: Charles River Editors.

Murray, Williamson, and Wie-Siang Hsieh (2015) *A Savage War: A Military History of the Civil War.* Princeton: Princeton University Press.

Murrell, Amy E. (2002) "Union Father, Rebel Son: Families and the Question of Civil War Loyalty: 258–91 in Joan E. Cashin (editor), *The War You and Me: Civilians in the American Civil War.* Princeton, NJ: Princeton University Press.

National Park Service (1992) "The Galvanized Yankees," *Museum Gazette,* April, 1–4.

Nisbett, Richard E., and Dov Cohen (1996) *Culture of Honor: The Psychology of Violence in the South.* Boulder, Colorado: Westview Press.

Neal, Diane, and Thomas W. Kremm (1997) *The Lion of the South: General Thomas C. Hindman.* Macon, Georgia: Mercer University Press.

Nofi, Albert A. (1995) *A Civil War Treasury: Being a Miscellany of Arms & Artillery, Facts & Figures, Legends & Lore, Muses & Minstrels, & Personalities & People.* New York: Da Capo Press.

Olmsted, Frederick Law (2017) *A Journey in the Seaboard Slave States*. Columbia, South Carolina: Acadia Press.

Ownby, Ted (1990) *Subduing Satan: Religion, Recreation, & Manhood in the Rural South, 1865–1920*. Chapel Hill: The University of North Carolina Press.

Owsley, Frank Lawrence (1959) *King Cotton Diplomacy: Foreign Relations of the Confederate States of America*. Chicago: The University of Chicago Press. Revised by Harriet Chapelle Ousley.

Paskoff, Paul F., and Daniel J. Wilson (eds.) (1982) *The Cause of the South: Selections from De Bow's Review, 1846–1867*. Baton Rouge: Louisiana State University Press.

Patterson, Gerald A. (2002) *Rebels from West Point*. Mechanicsburg PA: Stackpole Books.

Pease, William H., and Jane H. Pease (1991) *The Web of Progress: Private Values and Public Styles in Boston and Charleston, 1828–1843*. Athens: The University of Georgia Press.

Phifer, Cameron (1967) "Mother, I Do Not Hate to Die," *American Heritage* 18 (February): 32–33, 108–11.

Phillips, Jason (2007) *Diehard Rebels: The Confederate Culture of Invincibility*. Athens, Georgia: The University of Georgia Press.

——— (2018) *Looming Civil War: How Nineteenth-Century Americans Imagined the Future*. New York: Oxford University Press.

Pierson, Parke (2009) "Parcel Post to Freedom," *America's Civil War* 22 (May): 25.

Pollard, Edward A. (1866) *Southern History of the Civil War, volumes 1 and 2*. New York: C. B. Richardson, New York. Reprinted by New York: The Fairfax Press, n.d.

——— (1869) *Life of Jefferson Davis with a Secret History of the Southern Confederacy*. Philadelphia: National Publishing Company. Reprinted by Bedford. Massachusetts: Applewood Books 2008.

——— (1866) *The Lost Cause*. New York: Gramercy Books. Reprinted by New York: Gramercy Books 1994.

Potter, David M. (1976) *The Impending Crisis 1848–1861*. New York: Harper & Row, Publishers.

Pryor, Elizabeth Brown (2007) *Reading the Man: A Portrait of Robert E. Lee through His Private Letters*. New York: Viking.

Puleo, Stephen (2012) *The Caning: The Assault that Drove America to Civil War*. Yardley, Pennsylvania: First Westholme Publishing, LLC.

Quigley, Paul (2012) *Shifting Grounds: Nationalism and the American South, 1848–1865*. New York: Oxford University Press.

Rable, George C. (2015) *Damn Yankees! Demonization & Defiance in the Confederate South*. Baton Rouge: Louisiana State University Press.

Redfield, Horace V. (1800) *Homicide: North and South Being a Comparative View of Crime Against the Person in Several Parts of the United States*. Philadelphia, PA: J. B. Lippincott & Co.

Reid, Brian Holden (2005) *Robert E. Lee: Icon for a Nation*. London: Weidenfeld & Nicolson.

Reynolds, Davis S. (2006) *John Brown, Abolitionist: The Man Who Killed Slavery, Sparked the Civil War, and Seeded Civil Rights*. New York: Vintage Books.

——— (2011) *Mightier than the Sword: Uncle Tom's Cabin and the Battle for America*. New York: W. W. Norton & Company.

Richardson, H. Edward (2076) *Cassius Marcellus Clay: Firebrand of Freedom*. Lexington: University Press of Kentucky.

Riesman, David, with Nathan Glazer and Reuel Denny (2001) *The Lonely Crowd: A Study of the Changing American Character*. New Haven: Yale University Press.

Roe, Mervin (ed.) (1912) *Speeches & Letters of Abraham Lincoln, 1832–1865*. New York: E. P. Dutton & Co.

Roland, Charles P. (1960) *The Confederacy*. Chicago: The University of Chicago Press.

——— (1995) *Reflections on Lee: A Historian's Assessment*. Baton Rouge: Louisiana State University Press.

Rosenthal, Caitlin (2018) *Accounting for Slavery: Masters and Management*. Cambridge: Harvard University Press.

Rubin, Anne Sarah (2005) *A Shattered Nation: The Rise and Fall of the Confederacy, 1861–1868*. Chapel Hill, North Carolina: The University of North Carolina Press.

Ruffin, Edmund (1834) *The Farmers' Register, 1834: A Monthly Publication Devoted to the Improvement of the Practice and Support of the Interests of Agriculture*. Shellbanks, Virginia: Shellbanks Press. Reprinted by Forgotten Books.

Russell, William Howard (n.d.) *The Civil War in America*. Boston: Gardner A. Fuller.

——— (1863) *My Diary North and South*. Boston: T. O. H. P. Burnham.

Salzman, Jack, editor-in-chief (1993) *The African-American Experience: Selections from the Five-Volume Macmillan Encyclopedia of African-American Culture and History*. New York: Macmillan Library Reference USA.

Schivelbusch, Wolfgang (2003) *The Culture of Defeat: On National Trauma, Mourning, and Recovery*. New York: Metropolitan Books.

Selcer, Richard (2020) "Blood Feud," *America's Civil War* 33 (March): 50–55.

Sheehan-Dean, Aaron (2018) *The Calculus of Violence: How Americans Fought the Civil War*. Cambridge, Massachusetts: Harvard University Press.

Sherman, William Tecumseh (2021) *The Complete Memoirs of General W. T. Sherman*. Coppell, Texas: Charles River Editions.

Smith, E. D. (1979) *Battle for Burma*. New York: Holmes & Meier Publishers, Inc.

Snow, William P. Captain (1867). *Lee and His Generals: Profiles of Robert E. Lee and Seventeen Other Generals of the Confederacy*. Reprinted by New York: Gramercy Books, 1996.

Sorrel, G. Moxley (2019) *Recollections of a Confederate Staff Officer*. San Bernardino, California: no publisher listed.

Stahr, Walter (2017) *Stanton: Lincoln's War Secretary*. New York: Simon & Schuster.

Stampp, Kenneth M. (1980) *The Imperiled Union: Essays on the Background of the Civil War.* New York: Oxford University Press.

———(ed.) (1991) *The Causes of the Civil War.* New York: Touchstone.

Starobin, Paul (2017) *Madness Rules the Hour: Charleston, 1860, and the Mania for War.* New York: PublicAffairs.

Steplyk, Jonathan M. (2018) *Fighting Means Killing: Civil War Soldiers and the Nature of Combat.* Lawrence, Kansas: University Press of Kansas.

Stout, Harry S. (2006) *Upon the Altar of the Nation: A Moral History of the Civil War.* New York: Viking.

Stowe, Harriet Beecher (1853) *A Key to Uncle Tom's Cabin. Presenting the Original Facts and Documents Upon Which the Story Is Founded.* Boston: John P. Hewett and Co. Reprinted by Mineola, New York: Dover Publications 2015.

Sword, Wiley (1992) *Last Hurrah: Spring Hill, Franklin, and Nashville.* New York: Open Road.

——— (1999) *Southern Invincibility: A History of the Confederate Heart.* New York: St. Martin's Press.

Snyder, Ann E. (1893) *The Civil War from a Southern Stand-Point.* Nashville: Publishing House of the M. E. Church, South.

Sydnor, Charles Sackett (1965) *Slavery in Mississippi.* Gloucester, Mass.: Peter Smith.

Symonds, Craig L. (1997) *Stonewall of the West: Patrick Cleburne and the Civil War.* Lawrence, Kansas: University Press of Kansas.

Tanner, Robert C. (2001) *Retreat to Victory? Confederate Strategy Reconsidered.* Willington: Scholarly Resources.

Tate, Allan (1998) *Jefferson Davis: His Rise and Fall.* Nashville: J. S. Sanders & Company.

Tatum, Georgia Lee (2000) *Disloyalty in the Confederacy.* Lincoln, Nebraska: University of Nebraska Press.

Taylor, John M. (1994) *Confederate Raider: Raphael Semmes of the* Alabama. Washington: Brassey's, Inc.

Thomas, William G. (2021) *The Iron Way: Railroads, the Civil War, and the Making of America.* New Haven: Yale University Press.

Thrasher, Christopher (2021) *Suffering in the Army of Tennessee: A Social History of the Confederate Army of the Heartland from the Battles for Atlanta to the Retreat from Nashville.* Knoxville: The University of Tennessee Press.

Tocqueville, Alexis de (2017) *Democracy in America, Volumes I and II.* Mineola, New York: Dover Publications, Inc. Translated by Henry Reeve and edited by Francis Bowen.

Toll, Ian W. (2020) *Twilight of the Gods: War in the Western Pacific, 1944–1945.* W. W. Norton & Company.

Tucker, Glenn (1983) *High Tide at Gettysburg: The Campaign in Pennsylvania.* Dayton: Morningside Bookstop.

Tucker, Phillip Thomas (2016) *Pickett's Charge: A New Look at Gettysburg's Attack.* New York: Skyhorse Publishing.

Twain, Mark (1883) *Life on the Mississippi.* Boston: James Osgood and Company. Reprinted by Seawolf Press 2019.

US Bureau of the Census (1960) *Historical Statistics of the United States, Colonial Times to 1937.* Washington, DC.

Vandiver, Frank E. (ed.) (1947) *Confederate Blockade Running Through Bermuda, 1861–1865: Letters and Cargo Manifests.* Austin: The University of Texas Press.

——— (1984) *Rebel Brass: The Confederate Command System.* Baton Rouge: Louisiana State University Press.

——— (1987) *Their Tattered Flags: The Epic of the Confederacy.* College Station: Texas A&M University Press.

——— (1994) *Plowshares into Swords: Josiah Gorgas and Confederate Ordinance.* College Station, Texas: Texas A&M University Press.

——— (1999) *1001 Things You Should Know About the Civil War.* New York: Doubleday.

Varon, Elizabeth R. (2019) *Armies of Deliverance: A New History of the Civil War.* New York: Oxford University Press.

Wagner, Margaret E., Gary W. Gallagher, and Paul Finkelman (eds.) (2002) *Civil War Desk Reference.* New York: Simon & Schuster.

Walsh, George (2002) *Damage Them All You Can: Robert E. Lee's Army of Northern Virginia*. New York: A Tom Doherty Associates Book.

Watson, Ritchie Devon, Jr. (1985) *The Cavalier in Virginia Fiction*. Baton Rouge: Louisiana State University Press.

Weigley, Russell F. (2000) *A Great Civil War: A Military and Political History, 1861–1865*. Bloomington: Indiana University Press.

Weitz, Mark A. (2005) *More Damning than Slaughter: Desertion in the Confederate Army*. Lincoln: University of Nebraska Press.

Wesley, Charles H. (2001) *The Collapse of the Confederacy*. Columbia, South Carolina: University of South Carolina Press.

Wetherington, Mark V. (2005) *Folk's Fight: The Civil War and Reconstruction in Piney Woods, Georgia*. Chapel Hill: the University of North Carolina Press.

Williams, David (2008) *Bitterly Divided: The South's Inner Civil War*. New York: The New Press.

Wills, Brian Steel (1992) *A Battle from the Start: The Life of Nathan Bedford Forrest*. New York: HarperCollins.

Wilson, Clyde N. (1990) *North Carolina Cavalier: The Life and Mind of James Johnston Pettigrew*. Athens: The University of Georgia Press.

Wittenberg, Eric J., and Daniel T. Davis (2016) *Out Flew the Sabers: The Battle of Brandy Station, June 9, 1863*. El Dorado Hills, California: Savas Beatie LLC.

Woodward, C. Vann, Sally Bland Metts, Barbara G. Carpenter, and Katherine W. Herbert (eds.) (1981) *Mary Chesnut's War*. Binghamton, New York: Vail-Ballou Press.

Woodworth, Steven E. (1990) *Jefferson Davis and His Generals: The Failure of Confederate Command in the West*. Lawrence: University Press of Kansas.

——— (2000) *Cultures in Conflict. The American Civil War*. Westport, CT: Greenwood Press.

Wyatt-Brown, Bertram (1985) *Yankee Saints and Southern Sinners*. Baton Rouge: Louisiana State University Press.

——— (1986) *Honor and Violence in the Old South*. New York: Oxford University Press.

——— (2001) *The Shaping of Southern Culture: Honor, Grace, and War, 1760s–1880s*. Chapel Hill: The University of North Carolina Press.

——— (2007) *Southern Honor: Ethics and Behavior in the Old South*. New York: Oxford University Press.

Wyeth, John Allan (1989) *That Devil Forrest: Life of General Nathan Bedford Forrest*. Baton Rouge: Louisiana State University Press.

Wynstra, Robert J. (2018) *At the Forefront of Lee's Invasion: Retribution, Plunder, and Clashing Cultures on Richard S. Ewell's Road to Gettysburg*. Kent, Ohio: The Kent State University Press.

Young, James C. (1929) *Marse Robert: Knight of the Confederacy*. New York: Rae Henkle, Inc.

Younger, Edward (ed.) (1985) *Inside the Confederate Government: The Diary of Robert Garlick Hill Kean*. Baton Rouge: Louisiana State University Press.

———. ([illegible]) *Honor and Violence in the Old South*. New York: Oxford University Press.

———. (2001) *The Shaping of Southern Culture: Honor, Grace, and War, 1760s–1880s*. Chapel Hill: The University of North Carolina Press.

———. 20[illegible] *Southern Honor: Ethics and Behavior in the Old South*. New York: Oxford University Press.

Wyeth, John Allan. (1989) *That Devil Forrest: Life of General Nathan Bedford Forrest*. Baton Rouge: Louisiana State University Press.

Wynstra, Robert J. (201[illegible]) *At the Forefront of Lee's Invasion: Retribution, Plunder, and Clashing Cultures on Richard S. Ewell's Road to Gettysburg*. Kent, Ohio: The Kent State University Press.

[illegible]

Younger, Edward, ed. ([illegible]) *Inside the Confederate Government: The Diary of Robert Garlick Hill Kean*. Baton Rouge: Louisiana State University Press.

INDEX

A

abolitionist movement, 12, 39, 60, 61, 74, 142–143, 159, 162–163, 165, 168, 176, 179, 182, 278. *See also* Adams, Henry; Butler, Benjamin F.; Clay, Cassius Marcellus; Douglass, Frederick; Lincoln, Abraham; McKim, James Miller

Adams, Henry, 10–11, 12, 13, 100

aggression
- battle aggression, 283–284
- culture of, 260–290
- of John Bell Hood, 287–288
- and masculinity, 266–268

alcohol, consequences of drinking, 23

Aldrich, Alfred P., 67–68

Allston, Robert F. W., 211

alpha complex, 62–84, 237

alpha diplomacy, negative outcomes of, 80

amoral familism, 251–252

Anderson, Joseph Reid, 265

Anderson, Robert, 154

"An Appeal to the Border States in Behalf of Compensated Emancipation" (Lincoln), 44

Arkansas toothpick, 276

Armistead, Lewis Addison, 100, 155–156

Army of Northern Virginia (Confederacy), 11, 14, 20–21, 45, 55, 155, 187, 189, 198, 223–224, 234, 247, 248, 250, 257, 291

Army of Tennessee (Confederacy), 21, 152, 190, 191, 194, 202, 242, 247, 288

Army of the Cumberland (Union), 152

Army of the Kanawha (Confederacy), 186

Army of the Potomac (Union), 22, 122, 125, 195–196, 291

Army of Vicksburg (Union), 21

athleticism, as more important to Southerners than learning, 90–92

Atlanta Daily Intelligencer, editorial on hatred of now-Confederates toward Northerners, 228

B

Badge of Courage (Confederacy), 235–236
Banfield, Edward C., 251
battle aggression, 283–284
Battle of Atlanta, 242
Battle of Champion Hill, 187
Battle of Chickamauga, 152, 191, 285
Battle of Crecy, 264
Battle of Five Forks, 196
Battle of Gaines' Mill, Virginia, 288
Battle of Gettysburg, 87, 110, 112, 113, 115, 125–126, 136, 155–156, 188, 192–193, 230, 262–263, 268, 269, 284
Battle of Griswoldville, 285–287
Battle of Nashville, 152
Battle of Natural Bridge, 282
Battle of New Market, 261
Battle of Pine Grove, 194
Battle of Pittsburgh Landing, 75
Battle of Shiloh, 8, 75, 284
Battle of the Wilderness, 263
battles. *See also specific battles*
  as decisive events, 17
  as discrete events, 17
  reasons for Confederate battle losses, 62
  refusal to admit losses in, 75
Baylor, George Wythe, 140–141
Beadle's Dime Book of Practical Etiquette for Ladies and Gentleman: Being a Guide to True Gentility and Good Breeding, 129–130
Beauregard, Pierre G. T., 27, 75, 139, 150, 244, 281
Beckham, Fontaine, 235
Benjamin, Judah B., 97, 151, 208, 262
Bonaparte, Napoleon, 70–71
Boston, Massachusetts, subcultural values of as compared to Charleston, South Carolina, 28–30
Bowie, James "Jim," 276–277
bowie knife
  cultural meaning of, 276–278
  master of, 278–279
Bragg, Braxton, xi, 21, 97, 190–191, 255
bravery, importance of for cavalier status, 92
brevet promotion, 235
Brooks, Preston S., 143–146, 266
Brown, Fred, 180
Brown, Henry "Box," 169–171
Brown, John, 158, 178–183, 234
Brown, Joseph E., 74, 232
Brown, Samuel L., 273–274
Buck, Pearl, ix
Burges, Samuel E., 191–192
Burgwyn, Henry King, Jr., "Boy Colonel," 237–238, 284
Burlingame, Anson, 145
Burns, Anthony, 165–166
Butler, Andrew, 144
Butler, Benjamin F., 137–139, 167

C

Caesar, Julius, 158
Carruthers, Alexander, 86
Cartwright, Samuel A., 209
Cash, J. W., 10, 13
cavalier ideal, emergence of, 89
cavalier individualism, 185–186

cavaliers
aggressive courage of, 102–103
consequence of cavalier self-image, 102–104
defined, 85
feelings of inferiority among, 78–80
impact of culture of, 292
love of gambling by, 114–116
mindset of, 85–126
negative example of, 106
Southerners as self-defined cavaliers, 147
types of, 93–106. *See also* Italian cavalier; Spanish cavalier
use of term, 86
The Cavaliers of Virginia, or The Recluse of Jamestown: An Historical Romance of the Old Dominion (Carruthers), 86
Cervantes, Miguel de, 99
Chapin, E. H., 225
Charleston-Hamburg rail line, 29–30
Chesnut, Mary, 36, 86, 88, 203, 215, 268
Churchill, Winston, 44–45, 64
the Citadel, 281
citizen-soldier tradition, individualism and, 201–202
Clay, Cassius Marcellus, 176, 273–274, 278–279
Cleburne, Patrick "Stonewall of the west," 263–264
Clerborne, John, 223
Cobb, Howell, 229
Cobb, T. R. R., 233
code duello, 269–276
"Code of Honor," for dueling, 271–272
Collins, Robert, 37–38
Colt, Samuel A. H., 67
Colt revolving rifles, 285
Committee of Five, and Declaration of Independence, 56
conditional Confederates, 5–7
Confederacy. *See also* Rebels; *specific individuals*; *specific units*
casualties of, 261
conditional Confederates, 5–7
as culture of defeat, 292
as dying of lack of cooperation, 153
galvanized Confederates, 7–8
officers' perks, 6
reenlistment of, 6
as separated into independent military theaters, 246–247
slave-based culture of, 33–61
surrender of, 196
Confederate Congress, conscription bill, 6
Confederate Constitution, 36–37, 229
Confederate prisoners, as joining Union military units, 7
Cooke, Philip St. George, 152
Cooper, Edward, 252–253
Cooper, Mary, 253
Cooper, Samuel, 208, 280
Cooper, Stanley, 150
Corbett, "Sallie," 196
cordon defense/cordon strategy, localism and, 239–244
"Cornerstone Speech" (Stephens), 40–43

cotton, cultivation of, 216–217
cotton boycott (1861–1862), 82–84
"Cotton is King" policy, 80, 81
"Crime Against Kansas" (Sumner), 143
criticism, Southern rejection of, 147
CSS *Alabama*, 118–119, 120
Cuba, the South's fantasy about colonization of, 49
culture. *See also* subcultures
of aggression, 260–290
of cavaliers. *See* cavaliers
changes in, 1–2
of defeat, 268–269
defined, 1
gentleman culture. *See* gentleman
ideal and real ones, 25–27
slave-based culture of the Confederacy, 33–61
of violence, 22–24, 260–290
and war, 16–18
of West Point, 11
Curtis, George Washington Parke, 38
Custer, George Armstrong, 287

D

Daniel, John M., 207, 218, 219, 269
Davis, Charles, 139
Davis, Jefferson
as aggressive youth and young adult, 262
as announcing amnesty for deserters, 253–254
annual salary of, xi
as appointing inappropriate representatives in diplomatic efforts, 80
appointment of Hood as commander of Army of Tennessee, 288
appointments of generals by, 150, 151
as attending West Point, 262
as awarding Badge of Courage, 236
brother and mentor of, 214
capture of, 196
as characterizing Southern culture as warlike, 260
on claiming that sons of elite attended military academies without expecting to become professional soldiers, 261
as considering rank more important than talent, 233
and cordon defense, 241
as declaring day of Thanksgiving, 223
as declaring days of humiliation and fasting, 221–224
education of, 129
familiarity of with lack of cooperation at higher levels, 194
father of as migrating from Kentucky, 52
on Fort Sumter, 240–241
friendships of with Northerners, 72–73
and gentleman culture, 25

as issuing general amnesties, 200
on lack of discipline in Confederacy, 186
Lee's anger with, 189
Lee's courtesy to, 133–135, 136
Lee's letter to asking forgiveness of death sentences for deserters, 198–199
Lee's letter to on desertions, 200
Lee's letter to on troop's individualism, 197
order to Pemberton, 110
Pollard as critical of, 92
on promotions, 280
quarrel with Stephens, 153
as realizing Southerners needed quick victories, 85
as respecting Kentucky's neutrality, 289
as separating Confederacy into independent military theaters, 246
as serving with distinction in Mexican-American War, 262
on slavery giving Southern whites an alpha-like superior position in society, 64
on Southerners as glorifying war and the warrior spirit, 102
as Spanish cavalier, 94, 96–97
Stephens as critical of, 40
as thinking England and France would intervene to the South's benefit, 81
as urging Texans to remain in Texas, 257
on Van Dorn's retreat from northern Mississippi, 274
Davis, Joseph, 214
Davis, Samuel, 129, 139–140
day of Thanksgiving, as declared by Davis, 223
days of humiliation and fasting, as declared by Davis, 221–224
De Bow, James D. B., 130–131, 175, 208–209, 210
De Bow's Review
article on comparison of quality of Union soldiers to Confederates, 73
on enslaved persons becoming fugitives, 209
Fitzhugh article, 64–65
on Northern superiority, 208
Turner article, 42
debts, repudiation of, 51–52
Declaration of Independent (July 4, 1776), by Second Continental Congress, 56–57
Declarations of Independence (18611), in Southern state legislative assemblies, 56, 57
Declarey, John P., 279
defeat, culture of, 268–269
Democratic Republicans, 264
desertion
American public's definition of, 201
and amoral familism, 251–252

familism and, 249–250
and family suffering, 252–254
individualism and, 196–201
localism and, 248–249
numbers of, 230, 231–232
Dew, Charles B., 59
Dew, Thomas R., 34
D-Guard bowie, 276
Dickens, Charles, 90
disobedience, individualism and, 187–190
District of Columbia Emancipation Act, 44
Don Quixote (Cervantes), 99
Donald, David Herbert, 243
Douglass, Frederick, 43, 48, 158–163, 172
Drapetomania, 209
dueling, 269–276

E

Early, John Cabell, 263
Early, Jubal A., 155, 227
East Cavalry Field engagement, 87
Eaton, Clement, 245, 272
Edmondston, Ann Devereux, 42
egocentric individualism, 185
Eicher, David J., 16, 228
Eighteenth Louisiana (Confederacy), 284
Eleventh Louisiana (Confederacy), 284
Ellison, William, as formerly enslaved Spanish cavalier, 97–98
Emancipation Proclamation, 44
Enfield rifles, 257
enslaved cotton-based economy, disadvantages of, 49–52
Evening Post, poem about Brooks, 146
Ewell, Richard Stoddert, 136
The Examiner, on Battle of Gettysburg, 113

F

failure
blaming God and sinners for national failures, 217–221
cavalier denial of, 93
familism
and desertion, 249–250
desertion and amoral familism, 251–252
family, loyalty to, localism and, 230–231
family suffering, desertion and, 252–254
The Farmers' Register
editor of, 209–210
on Northern superiority, 208
farming population, in the South, 30–32
Farragut, David, 137
Faulkner, William, 1
Fifteenth Alabama Infantry Regiment (Confederacy), 230
First Alabama Cavalry (Union), 8, 19–20
First Bull Run (First Manassas), 73
First Corps of the Trans-Mississippi Army, 194
Fischer, David Hackett, x

Fitzhugh, George, 45, 64–65, 67, 68, 76–77
Flagel, Thomas A., 226
Fletcher, William A., 199
Florida Military and Collegiate Institute, 282
Floyd, John Buchanan, 186
food scarcity, scapegoating and, 212–217
Forrest, Nathan Bedford, 27, 28, 69, 94–96, 101, 129, 190, 203–204, 265, 274–275, 280
Fort Donelson, 243
Fort Henry, 243
Fort Sumter, 154–155, 240
Frederick Douglass' Paper (newspaper), 163
Freeman, Joanne, 277–278
Free-State Party, 179
French leave, 198
Fugitive Slave Act (1793), 166
Fugitive Slave Law (1850), 158, 164–169, 172

G

Gabe, Christopher, 256
gallant, use of term, 87
galvanized Confederates, 7–8
galvanized Yankees, 7, 8
Gamble, Thomas Jr., 270
gambling, love of by cavaliers, 114–116
Garrison, William Lloyd, 162, 163
Gasparin, Agénor de (Count), 147, 164
General Order 28 (Butler), 138
generals, political generals, 236–239
gentleman
    cultural identification of, 25–26
    "false" gentleman, 26–27
    use of term, 88
Georgia Military Institute, 281
Gildersleeve, Basil, 91
Girard, Charles, 73, 113
Glatthaar, Joseph T., 55, 155, 157, 193, 250
God, blaming of for national failures, 217–221
Goodbread, Martha, 101
Gorgias, Josiah, 220
Gould, Andrew, 95–96
Grant, Ulysses S.
    on cooperation strategy among Union armies, 246, 247
    education of, 131
    Lee's surrender to, 291
    on luck, 115–116
    monthly pay of, xi
    as offering parole to captured Confederates, 200
    and Petersburg, 196
    as recognizing allure of desertion among Confederates, 201
    retreat of in Vicksburg, 101
    on surrender terms, 87
    victories of, 243
    visualization of campaigns by, 17, 18
Greenberg, Kenneth S., 114, 272

H

Hale, Stephen F., 61
Hammond, James Henry, 31, 70–71, 208, 234
Hampton, Wade, 27

Hampton, Wade, III, 28, 148, 234, 238–239, 288
Hansen, Harry, 106
Hardesty, Steven, 4, 102
Harpers Ferry, 178, 180, 234–235
Harper's Weekly
  article on planters' debts, 51–52
  on cotton sales, 83–84
  Letcher letter, 164–165
Harris, William L., 60
Helper, Hinton Rowan, 158, 175–178
Herald (Muscogee, Georgia), editorial on social class antagonism, 68
heroism, fatal heroism, 155–156
Heth, Henry, 188
hierarchy, rejection of, individualism and, 190–191
Higher Law concept, 162, 168, 169, 171–172, 182–183
Hill, A. P., 276
Hill, Daniel H., 189, 191
Hindman, Thomas Carmichael, "Lion of the west," 194–195, 263–264
Holcombe, James P., 35
Homestead Act (1862), 53
homicide
  as generally excused or lightly punished in the South when act was based on defense of honor, 267
  Liddell's defense of justifiable homicide, 270
  rates of, 22, 23–24
honor
  as conformity, 141–143
  as courage, 139–140
  defense of, 143–146
  effects of on war, 153–155
  five blows to Southern honor, 158–183
  as good manners, 127–130
  lack of, and social death, 151–153
  and masculinity, 147–150
  and owners of enslaved persons, 156–157
  and pride of rank, 150–151
  as reputation, 140–141
  as theatrical patriotism, 136–139
Hood, John Bell, 70, 116, 152, 194, 242, 248, 287–288
Hood's Texas Brigade, 257. *See also* Texas Brigade
Horry, Elias, 28–29
horses
  Confederate policy of not providing horses for its cavalry, xi, 104, 203–204
  more horses per capita in the North than in the South, 104
Horton, R.C., 110–111
Hundley, Daniel R., 26–27, 128–129

I

The Impending Crisis of the South: How to Meet It (Helper), 158, 175–178
individualism
  and citizen-soldier tradition, 201–202
  Confederate cavalry of individualists, 202–204

and desertion, 196–201
and disobedience, 187–190
and lack of organization, 193–196
and lack of organizational skills, 204–206
overview, 184–187
and refusal to accept military discipline, 191–193
and rejection of hierarchy, 190–191
scapegoating others by individualists' faults, 206–208
inflation, scapegoating and, 212–217
inner-directedness, 142
intellectualism, white Southerners as intellectually isolated, 90
Italian cavalier, 93, 99–106, 116–126
Ivanhoe (Scott), 266

J

Jackson, Patrick Tracy, 29
Jackson, Thomas "Stonewall"
on asking for cadets to volunteer as drill teachers, 261
on desertion, 198
education of, 131
favorite steed of, 103
as filing court-martial against Loring, 186
Forrest's military style as similar to that of, 95
as military educator, 281
as professor, 237
Sam Davis as serving under, 139–140
as Spanish cavalier, 94
on surprising enemy using fast-paced marches, 249
use of aggression by, 283
western Virginian area of, 18
as willing to carry out Lee's orders, 135–136
Jamieson, Perry D., 272
Japan
attack on Pearl Harbor by, 17
claims of superiority by, 72
Jefferson, Thomas
on cultural importance of slavery in the South, 39
and Declaration of Independence, 56
on North-South cultural differences, 9–10
as Spanish cavalier, 94
on value of enslaved women, 39
Johnston, Albert Sidney, 97, 139, 150
Johnston, Joseph E., 17, 141, 150, 194, 227, 244, 288
Jones, Charles, 270
Jones, David Robert, 276–277
Jones, John Beauchamp, 48, 212–213

K

Kawabe, Torashiro, 72
Kean, Robert Garlick, 208
Keegan, John, 73–74
Keith, Laurence, 145
Kentucky fiasco, 288–290
kill rate, 72
knight, use of term, 87

Ku Klux Klan, 28, 47

L

Ladies Clubs, 237
Ladies Home Guard, 149
Lamar, Lucius Quintus Cincinnatus, 15–16, 266
land mines, first use of, 20
Lee, Fitzhugh, 195
Lee, Harry "Lighthorse," 116, 264
Lee, Mary, 226–227
Lee, Robert E.
- anger of toward Cooper, 208
- appointment of by Davis, 150
- and Battle of Gaines' Mill, Virginia, 288
- and Battle of Gettysburg, 286–287
- on battles of Antietam and Gettysburg, 17
- beliefs of, 221–223
- brevet promotions of, 235
- as combination of both cavalier types, 115
- as complaining about shortage of troops, 265
- as considering staff and army as family members, 189
- as courteous, 133–136
- decision to join Confederacy, 226
- on desertion, 196–197, 198–199
- as against dueling, 275–276
- education of, 131, 281
- on failure of Pickett's Charge, 207
- family-based nicknames, 251–252
- father of, 116, 264
- father-in-law of, 38
- and gentleman culture, 25–26, 27
- at Harpers Ferry, 181, 235
- on individualism, 192
- and Loring, 186–187
- monthly pay of, xi
- as most respected cavalier in the Confederacy, 86–88
- nephew of, 195
- order to Stuart, 122
- as pardoning Cooper, 253
- as praising Davis, 97
- prewar career of, 282
- reason for resigning position in US military, 226
- as refusing to be sent by Davis to western theater, 194
- religiosity of, 220–221, 260
- as seldom personally blamed for his mistakes by Southern authors, 112
- as short of ammunition, 111
- as slaveholder, 281
- soldiers as refusing to follow during Antietam and Gettysburg campaigns, 202
- son of, 10
- on the South's anti-intellectualism, 11
- as Spanish cavalier, 94
- surrender of, 196, 291
- use of aggression by, 283
- weaknesses of, 187–189

Lee, William Henry "Rooney" Fitzhugh, 10–11
Letcher, John, 164–165

Letcher letter, 186
"Letter to an English Abolitionist" (Hammond), 70
Lewis, John, 268–269
The Liberator (newspaper), 162
Liddell, St. John Richardson, 270
Lincoln, Abraham
- annual salary of, xi
- establishment of Medal of Honor by, 235–236
- family's migration from Kentucky to Illinois, 52
- and gentleman culture, 25
- on importance of Kentucky, 240
- as not realizing how disliked Northerners were, 228
- position on slavery, 169
- as respecting Kentucky's neutrality, 289
- ridicule of Shields, 275
- and slavery, 43–44

localism
- complex case of, 257–259
- consequences of, 233–235
- and cordon defense, 239–244
- defined, 225
- and desertion, 248–249
- and lack of unified command, 246–247
- and loyalty to family, 230–231
- overview, 225–228
- of Southern railroad lines, 254–257
- states' rights and, 228–229
- strength of, 235–236

Longstreet, James, 115, 190, 191, 255, 276
"Longstreet's Charge." *See* Pickett's Charge (Pickett-Pettigrew-Trimble Charge)
Lonn, Ella, 252–253
Loring, William Wing, 186
Lost Cause, tradition of, 74–75
Lovell, Mansfield, 154

M

Magoffin, Beriah, 289
Mallory, Charles, 167
Mallory, Stephen R., 117
Manet, Edouard, 120
masculinity
- aggression and, 266–268
- honor and, 147–150
- toxic masculinity, 147–148

Massachusetts Anti-Slavery Society, 158
McClellan, George B., 244
McCormick, Cyrus Hall, 50–51
McCullum, Daniel, 256
McElroy, Wendy, 184
McKim, James Miller, 170
McPherson, James, x, 127
McQueen, John, 60–61
McWhiney, Grady, 4, 272
Meade, George C., 287
Medal of Honor (Union), 235
Meigs, Montgomery C., 123
Mexican-American War (1846–1848), 193–194, 283, 284
migration, of poor farmers to Northern states, 53
militancy, and military titles, 280
military discipline, refusal to accept, individualism and, 191–193

military education, the South and, 281–283
military titles, militancy and, 280
Mississippi Declaration of Secession, 58–59
monetary values, x–xi
mono-cultivation, disadvantages of, 49
Montgomery Convention, 229
Morgan, John Hunt "Thunderbolt," 105–106
mortality rates, 149, 155
Mosby, John S. "The Gray Ghost," 155, 227
Murrah, Pendleton, 246

N

Narrative of the Life of Frederick Douglass, An American Slave (Douglass), 158–159
Nashville Whig, Stowe's advertisements of owners of fugitives, 174
The National Review (magazine), serialization of *Uncle Tom's Cabin*, 171
New Orleans Picayune, Stowe's advertisements of owners of fugitives, 174
New York City, as "the capital of the South," 50
norms
  changes in, 2–3
  defined, 2
North Carolina Military Academy, 281
North Star (newspaper), 163
Northern Baltimore and Ohio Railroad, 254
the North/Northeners. *See also* Union; Yankees
  culture of as more realistic, flexible, and able to modernize, 292
  North-South cultural differences, 9–15
  as promoting "Promethean impulse," 89
  religion in, 184
  response of Northerners to Brown's raid, 182–183
  stereotypes of, 65, 88

O

Oates, John, 230
Oates, William C., 230
officers, conflicts between professional and political officers, 233–235
Olmsted, Frederick, 176–177
organization, lack of, individualism and, 193–196
organizational skills, lack of, individualism and, 204–206
other-directedness, 142
Ownby, Ted, 23
Owsley, Frank L., 228

P

Pate, Henry Clay, 179
patriotism
  Confederate patriotism and slavery, 55–56
  theater of, 136–139
Pearl Harbor, Japanese attack of, 17

Pease, Jane H., 178
Pease, William H., 178
Pegram, William R. J., 14
Pemberton, John C., 21, 110, 187, 200
Perry, Benjamin F., 272
personal liberty laws, 166
Philips, Pleasant J., 285–286
Phillips, Jason, 75
Phillips, Wendell, 183
Pickett, George Edward, 76–77, 106, 195, 196
Pickett, John T., 81–82
Pickett's Charge (Pickett-Pettigrew-Trimble Charge), 106–113, 115, 268
Pierce, Franklin, 165
Pierson, David, 94
Pierson, Reuben, 75–76
Pleasanton, Alfred, 124
Polk, Leonidas, 191, 289–290
Pollard, Edward Alfred, 53–54, 92, 100, 106–110
Potter, David M., 33–34
Potter, Robert, 267–268
Potter's Act, 267
prostitutes, 22, 138
"The Provisional Constitution" (Brown), 180

R

railroads, 254–257. *See also specific railroads*
Raleigh Register, on woman engaged to soldier as rejecting him when he left the army, 149
Randolph, George, 247
rank
    Davis as considering rank more important than talent, 233
    differentiation of, as central characteristic of Southern mindset, 66
    honor and pride of rank, 150–151
real culture, 25–27
Rebels. *See also* Confederacy
    as carrying half the weight of equipment than did Union rank-and-files, 277
    knives as more popular among, 277
    officer perks, 6
    officers' show of bravery, 203
    whitewashed Rebels, 7
    as worth five or more Yankees, 142
Red River Campaign, 246
Red Shirts, 28
Redfield, Horace V., 23–24
Regulator-Moderator War, 267
Republican Banner, Stowe's advertisements of owners of fugitives, 174
Republican Party, 49, 143, 159, 163, 166, 270, 278
Rice, Dorsey, 263–264
Richmond Enquirer, editorial deserters stealing from farms, 199
Riesman, David, 142
rifles, 103, 241, 257, 284, 285
Roll of Honor (Confederacy), 236
Rosser, Thomas, 195

Ruffin, Edmund, III, 13–14, 69, 181, 208, 209–210
Russell, William Howard, 11, 66, 71, 78–79, 260, 262

S

Sandbar Fight, 276
Sanitary Commission (Union), 22
scapegoating
  and inflation and food scarcity, 212–217
  of others by individualists' faults, 206–208
  and protection of slavery, 208–211
Scheibert, Justus, 103
Schlesinger, Arthur M., 33
Scott, Walter, 12, 90, 266
secession
  commissioners for, 59–61
  declarations of, 56–59
  slavery and, 54
Second North Carolina Volunteers, USA, 76–77
Seminole Wars (1816–1858), 194
Semmes, Raphael, 117–122
Seven Days Battle (1862), 276
sexual activities, of soldiers, 21–22
Shakespeare, William, 90, 127
Shenandoah Valley Campaign (Jackson), 135–136
Sherman, William T.
  as abandoning Atlanta and beginning Savannah campaign, 242
  as appointing First Alabama Cavalry as his personal guard, 8
  on changing roles (rituals) of war, 3–4
  education of, 131
  as forcing two largest Confederate armies on the defensive, 247
  Forrest's military style as similar to that of, 95
  March to the Sea, 20
  as military educator, 281
  Savannah Campaign, 30
  treatment of Confederate deserters by, 231
  visualization of campaigns by, 17–18
  on white population of Georgia, 30
Shields, James, 275
Sigel, Franz, 261
sinners, blaming of for national failures, 217–221
situational factors
  defined, 5
  and status change, 5–7
slave breeding, 39
slave owners, examples of, 27
slave patrols, 46–47
slavery
  Confederate patriotism and, 55–56
  defense of, 34–35, 40–43, 64
  economics of, 37–38

and enlistment and secession, 54

John Brown's attack on, 178–183

protection of, scapegoating and, 208–211

renting enslaved persons, 48

as root of increasing cultural, economic, and ideological differences between the South and the North, 33–34

southern critics of, 53–54

the South's reliance on, ix

Smith, Edmund Kirby, 244–246
Smith, Gustavus Woodson, 150–151
Smith, Samuel "Red Boot," 169–170
Snyder, Ann, 34–35
social classes, 18, 28, 63, 65, 68, 69, 71, 85, 128, 141, 157, 175, 176, 220, 238, 267, 270, 271
social death, 151–153, 176, 196, 271
social mobility, in the South, 130–132
Sorrel, Gilbert Moxley, 112–113
South Carolina Canal and Railroad, 28–29
South Carolina Military Academy (later the Citadel), 281
Southern West Maryland Railroad, 254
the South/Southerners. *See also* Confederacy; Rebels
  anti-intellectualism of, 11
  aristocrats of, 35–36, 63–64, 65–66, 67, 69–70, 91
  athleticism as more important than learning for, 90–92
  belief in superiority of, 15–16
  cultural diversity of farming population in, 30–32
  culture of as based on mythical, medieval cavalier-related foundation, 292
  culture of as not adaptable to diverse soldier enrollment, 292
  culture of violence in, 22–24
  division and ranking of groups/divisions by, 76
  dysfunctional nature of values of, 4, 12
  fondness of war by, 262
  lack of industrial capacity, ix
  lack of skilled craftsmen in, ix–x
  and military education, 281–283
  New York City as "capital of," 50
  North-South cultural differences, 9–15
  nostalgia of for superior past, 89–90

rank differentiation as central characteristic of mindset of, 66
rejection of criticism by, 147
reliance of on slavery, ix
religion in, 184–185
response of Southerners to Brown's raid, 181–182
response of Southerners to *Uncle Tom's Cabin*, 173–174
social mobility in, 130–132
stereotypes of, 30, 90
Spanish cavalier, 93–98, 115
Spencer repeating rifles, 285
Sprigg, James C., 273
Stampp, Kenneth Milton, 9
Stanley, Henry Morton, 6, 8–9
Starobin, Paul, x
states' rights
and localism, 228–229
negative elements of ideology of, 231–232
positive elements of ideology of, 229–230
status
changes in, 5
defined, 2
stay laws, 51
Stephens, Alexander, 40–42, 153
Steuart, George H. "Maryland Steuart," 193, 195
Stewart, W. H., 248
Stone, Kate, 38–39, 148, 158
Stowe, Harriet Beecher, 144, 171–174
Stowe's advertisements of owners of fugitives, Valley Campaign (1862), 244
Stuart, James Ewell Brown, "Jeb," 45–46, 122–126, 136, 152, 181, 234, 235, 287
subcultures
Appalachian subculture, 19–20
examples of, 18–19
subcultural values of Boston as compared to Charleston, 28–30
Sumner, Charles, 143–146, 266
superiority
claims of, 71–72
the South's nostalgia for superior past, 89–90

T

Tate, Allan, 42–43
tax-in-kind impressment law, 250
Texas Brigade, 248, 250, 257–259
Texas Declaration of Secession (1861), 57–58
theater of patriotism, 136–139
Thomas, George H., 151–152
Thoreau, Henry David, 183
Ticknor, Francis Orray, 85
Tocqueville, Alexis de, 143, 176
Toombs, Robert, 81, 82, 214
toxic masculinity, 147–148
Trans-Mississippi Department, 194, 195, 244, 246, 247
Tredegar Iron Works, 205–206, 265
Trotsky, Leon, 16
Truth, Sojourner, 166
Tubman, Harriet, 48, 166
Turner, Cyrus, 279
Turner, J.A., 42

Twain, Mark, 12, 90
Twenty-First Ohio (Union), 285
Twenty-Sixth North Carolina Infantry (Confederacy), 284
Twiggs, David Emmanuel, 154

U

Uncle Tom's Cabin & The Key to Uncle Tom's Cabin (Stowe), 174
Uncle Tom's Cabin: or Life Among the Lowly (Stowe), 144, 158, 171–174
unified command, lack of, localism and, 246–247
Union. *See also specific individuals; specific units*
  Black Southerners as serving in, 153
  casualties of, 261
  white Southerners as serving in, 153
Union First Alabama. *See* First Alabama Cavalry (Union)
United States Military Academy (West Point), 11, 17, 100, 131, 233, 247, 262, 281, 282, 283–284
US Congress, District of Columbia Emancipation Act, 44
US Military Railroads (USMRR), 256
USS *Kearsarge*, 118, 119, 120, 121

V

Valley Campaign (1862), 244
Van Dorn, Earl, 100–102, 203, 234, 274
Vance, Zebulon, 232
Vandiver, Frank E., 16, 100, 103, 239
venereal disease, rates of, 20–21
violence, culture of, 22–24, 260–290
Virginia Military Institute (VMI), 261–262, 281, 282–283
Virginia's Brigade, 258
Virginia's First Families (VFF), 155
Von Borcke, Heros, 104
Von Clausewitz, Karl, 16, 239

W

Walcutt, Charles C., 285
Walker, Henry M., 149
war. *See also specific battles*
  culture and, 16–18
  effects of honor on, 153–155
  romance of, 265–266
Warfield, Mary Jane, 279
Washington, George, 94, 201
Watson, Ritchie Devon, 90
West Point. *See* United States Military Academy (West Point)
Western & Atlantic Railroad, 255
Wharton, John A., 140–141
Wheeler, Joseph, 190
whitewashed Rebels, 7
Wigfall, Louis T., 78–80
Williams, David, 215
Williams, T. Harry, 16, 239
Winslow, John, 117, 119
Wise, Henry A., 186
Wright, Norris, 276
Wyatt-Brown, Bertram, 141, 183, 266

Y

Yancey, William Lowndes, 82, 140, 275
"Yankee hog," 248
"Yankee Southerner," 213
Yankees. *See also* the North/ Northeners
  galvanized Yankees, 7, 8
  stereotypes of, 88
York, Zebulon, 205
Young, Fanny, 215
Young, James C., 111–112